Resource Mobilization in Poor Countries

Resource Mobilization in Poor Countries

Implementing Tax Policies

Alex Radian

Transaction Books
New Brunswick (U.S.A.) and London (U.K.)

Library of Congress Catalog Number: 79-66440
ISBN: 0-87855-304-5
Printed in the United States of America

Library of Congress Cataloging in Publication Data

Radian, Alex.
Resource mobilization in poor countries.

Bibliography: p.
Includes index.
1. Underdeveloped areas — Taxation. 2. Underdeveloped areas — Tax administration and procedure.
I. Title.
HJ2351.R3 336.2'009172'4 79-66440
ISBN 0-87855-304-5

TO RACHEL, MY MOTHER

Knowing that she would have appreciated this
made the effort worthwhile

Contents

List of Tables and Charts

CHART

Acknowledgments

In preparing for, and carrying out, this work I was fortunate in that I benefited from the professional guidance of truly remarkable persons. I am sure that each knows his worth and none needs confirmation by me.

I wish to acknowledge the contributions of the members of my dissertation committee, Professors Robert Price and George Break. Each in his own field patiently guided me during my research and smoothed the difficult process of learning sufficiently about the many-sided problems of resource mobilization to be able to begin to ask the right questions.

Aaron Wildavsky, the Chairman of my dissertation committee, is a living example of everything he tries to teach. He taught me not only how to think and how to write, how to judge other peoples' work and how to evaluate mine, but also to love and enjoy my work. Writing and research became something that is done over and over again until the result truly pleases the author or he reaches the conclusion that his potential has been exhausted.

The short daily walks with Aaron were a source of inspiration. The questions asked and answers given provided me with intellectual fuel for days. Aaron's professional guidance was made even greater by his true and deep humanity. He never treated his students as mere subjects working for their degrees. He takes great interest in the person, in what he thinks and feels, in the problems he encounters and possible ways for overcoming them. He is always part of your happiness and never allows you to sink too deep into despair. Everyone who knows Aaron well will know that he has done his utmost to prevent me from making errors and to help me improve the quality of my analysis.

Finally, I wish to thank Professor Guy Benveniste of the School of Education, Program in International Education Finance, at the University of California, Berkeley for making it possible for me, through a 211D AID grant, to travel to Washington, D.C. in order to interview officials at the International Monetary Fund and the International Bank for Reconstruction and Development. He also provided part of the funds for the trip to the Caribbean Islands.

My very dedicated and meticulous typist, Mrs. Hilda Sopher, never once interrupted the work for me, even though other pressing demands were made upon her time. She complained only when I failed to bring over a chapter on the day I promised it.

I have made many friends during my travels but S.M. Supersad from Trinidad, Mrs. Velma Wallin from Jamaica, and Messrs. Viroj and Precha from Thailand deserve special mention. They made every conceivable effort to make me feel at home in their countries. They spent hours in their heavily crowded schedules to answer my questions and discuss and illuminate issues they thought I did not understand well enough. Only those who have been in a foreign land, confronting the difficult task of getting by the daily problems of adaptation, and at the same time conducting research under tight time constraints can appreciate the meaning of an open-door policy and a sincere and warm offer to help you out with any problem you might encounter.

The weaknesses of analysis and errors of interpretation are so glaringly my own that I need not absolve anybody of the blame.

Introduction

Money is the essence of contemporary government in both rich and poor nations. Almost everything of importance that a government does, or is expected to do, costs a great deal. To the traditional functions of preserving law and order and providing security against external attacks have been added, in the last two centuries, a host of services ranging from education and health to transportation and recreation. Year in and year out financial resources must be mobilized in ever increasing quantities from various sources to satisfy the rapidly growing demands for spending. In the poorer nations this is especially pressing because they must deal with problems of poverty and development in addition to the normal functions of government. It is not the luxuries that their governments have yet to provide, but the basics. Their immediate problem is to provide elementary education to a rapidly growing population rather than install sophisticated teaching gadgets in existing schools. The daily struggle is in getting rudimentary medical aid to everyone rather than in improving the ability to perform complex surgeries. The problems are urgent and the price of not fulfilling them can be heavy to the politician.

Though the needs are great and pressing, the revenues at hand to meet them are meager. The poverty of the nation is transferred to its government; while the governments in rich countries directly control more than thirty percent of their Gross National Product, those of the poor nations rarely control more than sixteen percent. A poor nation, more than any other, heavily relies, for its economic betterment, on its government which is less capable of fulfilling these expectations. Needs, wants and demands for spending swamp the government from all directions while the revenue to fulfill them does not show encouraging signs of equally rapid growth.

Why are some countries more and others less successful in mobilizing resources for public needs? How does the taxing process work and what are the forces that shape its outcomes? Why does it work as it does? What are the conditions that force participants to behave in one way instead of another which would be more effective in terms of the ultimate goal of producing revenue? What can be done to make the process work slightly better? If we understood well how the process works and what the constraints and opportunities within which it operates are, it should be possible to suggest ways of strengthening it.

Unless one is content with the present situation — and few of the leaders of poor countries, let alone their citizens seem to be, as is evidenced by a Gallup poll showing that the notion of the happy poor man is a myth, since not one of the poor countries surveyed reported that its citizens are content with their lot — it is important to find out how more revenue might be raised. Money alone, even when it comes in large quantities, is not enough to bring about economic betterment, but money is certainly a necessary condition. No amount of willpower or talent can substitute for the lack of resources.

Let us suppose that a new leader comes to power and wants to increase public spending and adopt liberal social policies, as well as make a stronger effort to speed up the process of economic development. What would he need to consider in order to make up his mind as to what will go? What factors can be manipulated, at what cost and in what ways; what constraints must be taken into account and what opportunities can be exploited? Answering these questions, telling which idea, program, or policy has a better chance of being successfully enacted and implemented and thereby improving the policy formulation process, depends on knowing what the determinants of tax revenues are, and understanding how they interact in the taxing process.

Chapter one prepares the setting in which the taxing process takes place in poor countries. It describes the problems budgeters have with the revenue — the meagerness of the resources available, the inability to make the revenue respond to demands for spending and the uncertainty which surrounds them. A comparison between revenues in rich and poor countries emphasizes the acuteness of the shortage of revenues in the latter.

Chapter two examines the determinants of revenue as they are presented in relevant literature in economics, political science and sociology. The literature answers one question definitively: in the majority of poor countries the constraints and opportunities for mobilizing financial resources are not economic.

In chapter three an attempt is made to develop a theory of the taxing process that incorporates, in addition to the economic factors, elements of politics and implementation. Politics determine goals on the basis of values and power. It resolves such questions as: How much should be mobilized for public purposes? What proportion of the national product should be under direct government control? What types of taxes and tax policies can be enacted, given the balance of political power? Implementation determines the extent to which policy goals will be reached. The extent of policy implementation is a function of administrative capability compared to the complexity of the task to be performed and the constraints which participants are likely to encounter. Partial implementation is the rule rather than the exception. In poor countries the extent of this partiality seems to be extensive as evidenced by the tremendous scale of evasion.

Studying the courses of partial implementation is not, as it may perhaps seem, an exercise in enumerating all the accidents that could, but most likely will not, happen to you if you step into the street one busy morning. It is an attempt to find, and then explain, the causes for common patterns of behavior.

How then, and why, do policies flounder at the stage of implementation? It is not enough to announce a tax policy in order for revenues to start flowing into the Treasury coffers the next day. Taxation is a compulsory transfer of resources from the citizen to the government for which he receives no direct quid pro quo benefits in return. There is no mechanism that prevents the tax evader from using and receiving all the services that the government offers. Therefore, unless taxes are made unavoidable there are strong chances that many will evade them.

There is a process that must be followed to ensure the payment of taxes according to the goals set in the tax policies. The extent to which the government will be able to reach its policy goals depends on how complex they are, and on the way in which the various stages of implementation are carried out. The taxing process consists of three stages: identifying and locating taxpayers; assessing their taxable income; collecting tax dues and otherwise enforcing the various requirements of the law. The principal characteristic is that there are never enough resources or personnel to deal with all the taxpayers directly. Since the number of revenue officials is always much smaller than the number of taxpayers, the tasks of audit, collection, and enforcement cannot be effectively fulfilled unless the majority of the taxpayers comply voluntarily.

What kind of conditions, resources and modes of participants' behavior are required to enable an organization to institute such a system? What happens when the conditions in the environment differ, when resources are not what they ought to be? How would participants behave under these circumstances? Why do they behave as they do? And, what effect does their behavior have on the outcome of the process?

Chapter four, the first of four chapters which describe how the taxing process works in poor countries, discusses the limitations of three of the central resources of implementation — information, expertise, and personnel. It describes the immediate environment in which participants work and the obstacles it throws in their way.

Personnel problems are not unique to Revenue Departments, they affect every branch of the government. What makes the problem particularly interesting is that in the case of the Revenue Department, money makes money. With more and better staff, more revenue could be collected. Collection and audit officials are one of the best investments that can be made since the ratio of their salary to the amounts they collect is tremendous. If the revenue shortage is acute and if small investments in personnel could lead to not so small improvements in the amount collected, why do most revenue departments suffer from problems of personnel? Why don't they get first turn at national resources the way central banks do?

The weaknesses of personnel are compounded by difficulties in obtaining relevant and reliable information.

How do participants adapt to this situation? How do they go about obtaining information to enable them to make decisions? Direct observation replaces data scanning. This strategy requires a significant amount of decentralization. But, decentralization will only magnify existing problems if there is lack of trust between the Head Office and its branches.

Next the taxing process itself is examined. In the next three chapters each of the three instruments of implementation is presented and examined with regard to how participants have adapted themselves to the conditions in their environment and how they overcome, or avoid, the obstacles they encounter.

Chapter five discusses audit and assessment — the process by which the accuracy of the information used to calculate taxable income is verified. The task is broken down to its components — classification, examination and obtaining the taxpayer's consent to the auditor's conclusions. At each stage the requirements of the task are juxtaposed with what practitioners are actually doing. Following the description of the participant's behavior, the calculations employed to make the task manageable and the strategies used to accomplish the goals, analysis is geared to provide explanations for the gap between what ought to be and what is done in practice.

What do the auditors do when they must perform a demanding job with limited skills, poor information and resources, and threatening time constraints? They will prefer to compromise with the taxpayer so that they can show some immediate tangible results. Their guiding motto thus becomes: "look deep enough, but not too far, to convince the taxpayer that it is better to agree to pay a bit more now than risk a more thorough investigation later."

The collectors' problems, as chapter six demonstrates, are not substantially different; they are, however, more glaring and even more difficult to avoid. Huge amounts of unpaid tax bills, and unknown, but certainly large, numbers of taxpayers who are not filing returns make their task formidable. There are too many taxpayers to enable the department to collect from each individually.

Chapter seven illustrates the single most powerful instrument — enforcement — and its equally potent problem of gaining compliance. Of all the tasks that the Revenue Department must fulfill, this one seems, at first glance, to be the easiest. The constraints limiting the effectiveness of audit and collection are not quite as overwhelming with regard to enforcement.

Lax enforcement, indeed, is one of the most glaring characteristics of the taxing process in poor nations and one of the most serious causes of the gaps between policy and outcome. Chapter seven describes the task of enforcement as it is seen through the eyes of those who are responsible for carrying it out.

The problem of compliance and enforcement is a classical example of the chicken and egg riddle. Which comes first — compliance or enforcement? Does enforcement breed compliance, or is compliance necessary to develop enforcement? We need to know the answer before we can make suggestions as to how enforcement should be strengthened. The answer is probably both, and at the same time. The development is parallel and mutually enforcing — a little bit of this and a little bit of that gets you more of both.

Understanding does not equal agreeing with. Behavior that is completely rational to the individual may nevertheless be quite irrational when the interests of the collective are considered. What is perfectly all right for the individual auditor, may be ruinous for the broader goals of audit. This leads to questions about reform. What are the factors that can be manipulated to create a situation where what is rational for the individual participant will also be rational for the organization as a whole? This is the logical sequence that must be followed in designing reforms. The other alternative, deciding what would be desirable for the organization and then imposing it on the participants, has created reformers with some very peculiar ideas which have not carried them far in the world of action.

Talk about reform, and about the urgent need to do something that will increase revenues, abounds. Actual improvements are scarce, short-lived and very limited in breadth and depth, usually leaving the portion of taxes in the Gross National Product almost unchanged. If additional evidence is needed to strengthen the assertion that implementation is not automatically guaranteed, this is it. Knowledge about the taxing process used to design reforms does not seem to be complete since its products do not work sufficiently well.

Chapter eight starts with normative theories for reform, followed by a survey of the experience of implementing reforms in policy and administration. Attempts to increase the revenue:GNP ratio by strengthening policy are smashed against the wall of implementation. The self-evident notion that good policy is preferable to bad policy is true only when effective implementation is assured. When the ability to implement is very limited, good policy and bad policy may both end up giving the same results. Improvement must start with implementation since it is there that the fate of any policy is determined, for better or for worse.

Attempts to institute administrative reforms have had some successes, but they have encountered all the difficulties found in the existing taxing process — limited information and personnel, insufficient expertise — plus those that usually accompany attempts to break up routine. These include a reluctance to admit that things have not been going well and must therefore be changed, the lack of redundancy in financial resources, and the shortage in facilities and personnel to run two processes, the reform as well as the routine work, simultaneously.

The results normally attained were changes in structure and formal procedures. But, behind the new facade, the old processes kept on flowing almost as if nothing has happened. Participants' behavior, their modes of selecting, approaching and solving problems had not been changed significantly.

If the theories that helped frame reform proposals were valid what went wrong? It would be a mistake to reprimand failures, and hope for better luck next time when participants will be more "rational" and resources more adequate. If circumstances would change by themselves there would no longer be such a compelling need for reform nor would it be so difficult to put it into effect. The question of reform is what can be done to reach some improvement today within the existing limitations, and what can, rather than simply should, be done to ameliorate these constraints to make room for additional improvements in the future.

Chapter nine starts with a discussion of reform and poverty aimed at clarifying the phenomena of cycles of ineffective reforms. Then, a number of approaches for cutting into the vicious circle of poverty and weakness will be reviewed. In the third part of the chapter principles for designing reforms that will survive implementation and produce their desired outcomes are suggested. Finally, specific proposals to strengthen audit, collection and enforcement, are developed from the knowledge accumulated on the taxing process.

Methodology and Field Research

I realized, soon after I started my research, that studying a single country would not do. I would never know whether the findings had general validity or whether they were unique to one particular country. How would I ever know if there was a pattern of behavior, and what that pattern was? Data from a number of countries were definitely required, but how could they be obtained? The first source examined was cross-country studies of aggregate data. What these studies achieve in terms of wide coverage they lose in superficiality. The weaknesses of statistical analysis, based on partial and incomplete data, have been combined with those of aggregate economic analysis. Only those questions and factors which quantitative measures and data are available for can, and are, studied; others, regardless of how important they are deemed to be, are left out. Chapter two, which discusses these studies, shows that they help understand only part of the puzzle; there are more questions raised than answered, and it is mostly those questions which interest policy-makers — what can be done to make things work better, what variables should be manipulated (among those that can be) in order to increase the capability to mobilize resources — that are left unanswered.

The literature in political science, organizational theory, sociology and public policy is even less helpful. It contains very few analytically descriptive studies of the taxing process. There is no pool of raw data to show the taxing process in a variety of countries, rich or poor. The material available describes tax laws and tax structure[1] but, there is no way of knowing what shape they have in practice. For all anyone knows, they may not even be implemented. There is at least one study which shows that tax laws are completely disregarded in practice and decisions are made to suit the interests of the moment.[2]

The basic problem was that there was no complete information on all the aspects of the taxing process, or even on how it works in one individual country. There were bits and pieces that could be fitted together to obtain an overall picture, but there was not enough information to understand why it looks as it does. It was not difficult, for example, to find out the role that enforcement plays in the taxing process and to learn that in poor countries it is very lax. But, the question as to how enforcement works and why it is not stricter could not be adequately answered. Many of these countries are not known for their great respect for personal freedom. So, why is the government tough with its citizens on, say, freedom of speech and so lax when it comes to the collection of taxes?

The question faced was not whether comparative field research had to be done, for that was quite obvious, but what specific kind of research should be undertaken. One alternative was the traditional method used by area study specialists — a comprehensive study of one country embracing important aspects of the political, social and economic structure of the country, in addition to its history and culture. The advantages of such an approach are evident and need not be repeated. It is its limitations which convinced me that I should consider a different approach.

An area study approach is time consuming. It would have taken years before enough material could be obtained to even begin thinking beyond the peculiarities of a particular country and theorizing about the process which is the same wherever conditions of poverty and low compliance exist. It was the process of resource mobilization that I was interested in and not in the specific ways in which, say, Thailand or Jamaica are collecting their taxes. I was looking for the typical forms of behavior that emerge under certain conditions — poverty, lack of information, and lack of voluntary compliance — regardless of the particular nation, or even period in history. Granted, each nation has its uniquenesses and peculiarities, and they are difficult to grasp and fathom unless one acquaints himself thoroughly with the many aspects of its life and history. But if these peculiarities are the only, or even the principal, factors that matter in social, political and economic behavior, then either social science is not possible or we are simply not capable of seeing beyond what merely appear to be differences.

Once the decision was made to study a number of countries, additional questions came up: how many, and which ones? What specific information was desired, and, what methods would be used to obtain this information? The first question had a simple solution. If the choice was between knowing a little bit and knowing a little bit more, the latter would always be preferred. So, the decision was made to try to stretch research funds to cover as many countries as possible. That meant limiting the period of stay in each country to the minimum necessary and organizing an intensive schedule of interviews.

The second question: what countries should be studied, was answered by the nature of the relations between Israel and the poor countries after the Yom Kippur War. A social scientist, unlike his colleagues in the life sciences, needs a visa before he can proceed to study a case that interests him. That condition eliminated almost all African and Muslim countries. As an Israeli citizen I had no hope of gaining entry to, say, Indonesia, Pakistan, Afghanistan, Mali, Ceylon or Ethiopia. Another group of countries had to be excluded because it was neither possible, nor advisable to interview in English. So, the list of potential nations was reduced to those which would grant a visa and research permit to an Israeli student, and had English as its spoken language. Since a common pattern of behavior was being looked for, studying crazy, unusually deviant cases, whose experience would be so unique as to make it irrelevant for generalizations, would have been futile. Variations in structure of government and economy, culture and history as well as the relative size of the public revenues were desired. As a result of all these factors Jamaica and Trinidad in the Carribean Sea, and Thailand and the Philippines in the Far East were chosen as subjects of study.

The real questions remained: what, specifically, should be studied and how can this be accomplished? There were little more than clues to the elements that compose the taxing process and how that process works. So, the first task was to find how each function in the process is carried out, what kinds of problems are encountered, what kinds of constraints there are, how problems are overcome or why they are evaded. The second task was to find out why things are done as they are, why participants behave as they do, and what the rationale behind behavior is.

In trying to understand behavior, the assumption was made that officials are rational; they know, better than outsiders, what is best for them and they have chosen a course of action which allows them to both pursue and attain their goals. The task was seen to be not in terms of moralizing about how corrupt or irrational behavior is, but in finding out what reasons they have for behaving the way they do. Behavior is always apparent; it does not take too much effort to discover how someone goes about performing his job. Goals, however, are much less evident and harder to get at, particularly when what is being done in practice differs from what should have been done according to official policies. Goals must be identified since it is only when they are known that behavior ceases to appear erratic; actions that seemed irrational no longer look that way; and recommendations for reform which ignored participants' goals and the constraints and opportunities which shaped them lose much of their original luster.

The best method for getting an accurate description of behavior as well as explanations as to why it is so, is the open ended questionnaire. Open ended questions allow the respondent to reveal as much of his experience as possible by not limiting him to predetermined issues or forcing him to relate within the conceptual boundaries set by an outsider. The method also permits one to probe for better answers and to pursue interesting issues as they come up. Many interviewees indicated later that they felt more at ease when answering open than closed questions; more importantly they hinted that in the course of the discussion, which developed during the interview, things were said that would never have been learned in a more formal encounter. What was lost through lack of rigor was gained through flexibility. Flexibility was especially vital when so very little was known about the taxing process so that it was hard to even pinpoint in advance all the questions that needed to be asked and the possible answers. Many important questions were generated during the interviews themselves as understanding of the subject improved.

The questionnaire (see the appendix) was pretested during the summer of 1974 in a series of interviews with revenue officials from Liberia, India, Jamaica and Trinidad who attended a Tax Administration Seminar at the University of Southern California.

In choosing informants it was tried not to limit subjects to the handful of officials at the top of the hierarchy. That would create a picture that was removed from reality. The procedure was to start from the bottom of the hierarchy with the collection agents and auditors and gradually work up to the top. By the time the "knowledgeable people" were reached, quite a few things were known about what was going on in the department and that allowed a discussion to be navigated toward real, rather than imaginary issues.

Interviews lasted from half an hour to several hours; most lasted between an hour and a half and two hours. Some informants were interviewed more than once; these were well-informed people who, for one reason or another, showed willingness and interest in helping beyond the minimum required by the norms of cordiality. Luckily there was at least one such person in each country, which provided an opportunity to obtain a broad perspective on the department under study, as well as to verify tricky or sensitive pieces of information.

On two occasions — once in Thailand and the other in the Philippines — I was invited to participate in trips to rural areas. This provided an excellent opportunity to study, from close range, the differences between the capital city and the poorer, more tradition-bound parts of the society. The trip in Thailand deserves special mention; it included a small group of senior officials who went on their annual inspection tour of the Chieng Mai province in the northern part of the country. The journey, which lasted two weeks, included some of the most isolated communities in the country. Three days were spent in the village of Mae Hong Song, close to the Burmese border. Here was an opportunity to observe how taxes are assessed and collected from, amongst others, the importers of water buffalos and the small traders in the village. Business records are unheard of. Information is obtained through bargaining in which the past serves as the best indicator for the present and future. Mutual trust is essential in order to make any progress. The official from Bangkok commands a great deal of respect but carries very little power of enforcement. Central government is a truly remote force. The secret of the taxing process is not to expect too much, nor to settle for too little. What would be considered reasonable is determined through a process of bargaining in which all parties concerned — the local revenue officer, the village headman, the regional revenue officer and a representative of the head office — participate. Nowhere is the weakness of government more vividly apparent than it is here. There appeared to be no blatant refusals to comply, but going part of the way depended on the mutual understanding that full compliance would not be insisted upon. The rural revenue offices are also a striking demonstration of the poverty of the nation and the government. Only the most rudimentary facilities are available; even such a simple device as a filing cabinet does not exist and papers are simply stacked in piles on shelves, desks and in cupboards. Even the most highly motivated and ambitious official will find it quite difficult in this environment to work long hours and to reach a high rate of productivity.

All told, sixty-three interviews were carried out. With only one exception, there were no difficulties in penetrating the organization, finding enough people prepared to be interviewed and getting them to talk sincerely about their work and difficulties. Though it was initially planned to interview customs and excise, in addition to income tax, officials, the experience of the first week in the field was convincing that covering both direct and indirect taxes was not going to be a feasible task. Two totally separate and independent organizations were responsible for these two types of taxes; this meant that in each country two organizations would have to be penetrated instead of only one and two sets of officials would have to be interviewed instead of just one set. This could not have been done without substantially prolonging the period of time spent in each country, which would have meant reducing the number of countries studied. Furthermore, the few studies which have been carried out on the implementation of indirect taxes indicated that there are more similarities than differences between the two processes (beyond the level of technical details). So research was limited to the organization responsible for direct taxes, particularly, though not solely, income tax.

An effort was made to write down word for word everything that the informants said in the course of the interviews so that as many direct quotes as possible would be available to rely upon later. Frequently, when a sensitive issue was discussed, I was asked not to take notes. In such cases the answers were memorized and the interview typed up immediately after it was over. It was understood that though the information could be used freely, it could not be used by directly quoting something that was said or even referring to the person who said it. As a rule, names of informants are not mentioned and quotes refer to "senior official" or simply "informant." The promise to follow this procedure strictly helped in convincing participants to discuss sensitive issues of their work which they would have otherwise avoided had they suspected that their identity would be disclosed.

Under these conditions how can the reader be certain that the picture reported was not totally invented? Firstly, my findings fit in well with the general pattern of behavior described by numerous other scholars. Secondly, the study can be repeated, in either the same countries or in other countries. Thirdly, the opinion of senior officials in the countries studied may be sought.

Once the information was obtained, the next problem was what to do with it, how to organize and use it to draw useful conclusions and generalizations with wide applicability.

The method used to solve this problem was to take all the information, my own interviews, previous scholarly studies, administrative reports and statistical information, and begin piecing the puzzle together. Unlike the children's toy, the picture was not there, or at least was not immediately apparent. It had to be visualized before the pieces could be placed together. Since the quality of the information was not even and some parts of the process were missing for some countries, the composite method developed by Caiden and Wildavsky[3] — throwing every relevant bit of data in regardless of where it comes from as long as it fits the pattern — was the only feasible way that allowed the construction of a complete picture of the taxing process.

> . . . we took steps in the process of planning and budgeting and applied to each whatever data were at hand even though it came from the same country in different periods or from different nations altogether. If our work is seen as an attempt to create theory, then the proper test is not how it was derived but how well it stands up to the tests of experience.[4]

The results obtained fit most, if not all, poor countries regardless of differences in culture and politics. Socialist-centralized economies are perhaps an exception; their process of resource mobilization is different, but this is outside the scope of the present study. It would not be surprising to find exceptions both to the pattern as a whole and to certain specific parts of it. There is too much variation in the world of practice and there is not enough knowledge and information to design explanations with proper answers for all of it. The question ought to be put in relative terms: Compared with the universe which is being dealt with, is the pattern described dominant or does it apply only to the four cases studied? It appears conclusively dominant not only because there is almost nothing in the available literature that would indicate otherwise, but also because there is no reason to assume that Jamaica, Trinidad, Thailand the the Philippines have something in common which makes them a unique phenomenon among the rest of the poor countries.

Notes

1. The International Tax Program of the Harvard Law School has a series of country studies titled *World Tax Series.* There are volumes on Colombia, the Federal Republic of Germany, France, Italy, Switzerland, and the United States.
2. Harley H. Hinrichs, "Certainty as Criterion: Taxation of Foreign Investments in Afghanistan," *National Tax Journal* XV, 2 (1962).
3. Naomi Caiden and Aaron Wildavsky, *Planning and Budgeting in Poor Countries* (New York: John Wiley, 1974), see introduction.
4. Ibid., p. xv.

Theories and Policy

Chapter One

Aspirations and Reality: Mobilizing Financial Resources in Poor Countries

Aspirations

> Fiscal Policy . . . derives its meaning and direction from the aspirations and goals of the society within which it operates, of the people whom it serves. The aspirations of the peoples of the underdeveloped countries are clear: economic betterment and stability to provide the material soil within which human dignity and political freedom can grow.
>
> Walter E. Heller, "Fiscal Policies for Underdeveloped Countries," *Taxes and Fiscal Policy in Underdeveloped Countries. p. 1.*[1]

Reality

> . . . the proportion of governmental revenue to gross national product in poor countries is considerably less than in rich countries. The poor need the help of government more but get it less. Their governments mirror their own poverty.
>
> Naomi Caiden and Aaron Wildavsky, *Planning and Budgeting in Poor Countries,* p. 52.

The purpose of tax policies, and the organizations responsible for implementing them, is to produce revenues to meet government spending commitments. Spending grows incrementally every year, even when no major policy changes are made, because of the desire to do more in a greater number of areas and because as the population grows there are more people consuming government services and benefits.[2] Life would be relatively comfortable for finance officials if all they worried about was finding the additional resources which this incremental annual increase in spending demands. In poor countries, as Prest informs us, the pressure for higher spending is greater than elsewhere: "It is, of course, true that all governments at all times have to face demands for additional spending but . . . the pressure in underdeveloped countries tends to be particularly intense."[3] The reason is that the governments of poor nations, in addition to running existing public services, have undertaken to make their countries richer. "The primary economic goal of the underdeveloped countries" writes Due, ". . . is a substantial increase in the rate of economic growth, which is hoped will bring the countries in a relatively short period to the levels of per capita real income comparable to those of the more developed economies."[4] Caiden and Wildavsky brush aside any doubts about the desire of the poor to become richer. According to them: "poor nations undoubtedly wish to grow richer." Being poor is no great pleasure and "there is no reason to suppose that poverty and nobility go together."[5]

To attain the desired rate of economic development and to alleviate poverty the government must provide a large number of basic public services, particularly in fields such as education, public health, and transportation, which must be maintained in order to ensure the growth of the remainder of the economy.[6] In addition to the provision of services, the government must encourage a higher rate of capital formation. It is a paradox that one of the main reasons that poor countries stay poor is that they spend too much of their limited resources trying to alleviate today's problems instead of investing in the future. Due reflects standard economic thinking when he writes that "the key to economic growth . . . is the transfer and better utilization of resources from current private consumption to government and capital investment."[7] Nicholas Kaldor adds that all poor countries, irrespective of the prevailing ideology and particular form of government, must, if they wish to improve their lot, increase, expand and improve "a whole host of revenue-yielding services — education, health, communications systems . . . which require to be financed out of government revenue."[8]

It has come to be accepted as fact that once we decide what we want and how we want to get it, revenue organizations will indeed produce the resources year in and year out. As Karl de Schweinitz stated, "The tax problem in a democracy is to determine which taxes to raise or lower and by how much and typically the percentage changes proposed are not great."[9] Rich countries have reached a level of economic development and political consensus on principal social values which permit the government to function within the scope of limited decisions on resource mobilization. Poor countries on the other hand, are yet to develop broad agreements on political values and solving principal economic problems. They have more far-reaching decisions to make and are confronted with a much more difficult task in carrying them out.

Grand aspirations to increase the population's standard of living, speed up the rate of economic development, alleviate poverty and improve health and education have not been matched by equally grand accomplishments in mobilizing. Although aspirations are often spectacular, achievements are generally meager. Soberano's description of the Philippines fits most poor countries:

> There is the unmistakable substantial divergence between ambition and

> accomplishment with respect to economic development . . . Actual expenditures, which may be taken as the measure of fulfillment, were exceeded by the Programmed, Estimated and Projected expenditures . . . by very large substantial amounts which were expressive of the high hopes and intentions of the fiscal planners.[10]

Following a comparative study of fourteen poor countries and an extensive survey of the literature, Caiden and Wildavsky wrote that lack of revenues is the main reason most poor countries fail to reach their desired levels of economic growth. They describe the sources of this failure in these words:

> The poor country finds it hard to increase its wealth rapidly because its population lacks skills, its information base is poor or nonexistent, and its government unable to mobilize resources. The whole life of the society is affected by scarcity.[11]

In an evaluation of economic performance in the Philippines, government experts concluded that: ". . . government efforts to speed up development were hamstrung by the limited funds that the tax system could generate."[12] The director of the Philippine National Economic Council admitted recently that "to some extent, the underperformance in terms of the rate of economic growth is related to the failure to impose a higher tax burden."[13]

When the tax system does not produce and the revenues obtained are meager, there is barely enough to run existing services and little or no surplus to invest in the future, or to be put aside for unexpected events. Skimpiness is compounded by a lack of built-in flexibility which would ensure an automatic increase in revenues from one year to another, at a rate faster than that of economic growth and public spending. Since revenue does not grow quite as fast as the economy, it fails to catch up with inflation and other economic changes. There are no automatic bonuses for the government at the end of each year. Each time additional funds are needed rates must be increased or new taxes added, actions that every finance minister who cares about his job dreads. Last, though certainly not least, the revenue lacks the element of stability which is the first requirement of budgeting. There are sharp and unpredictable fluctuations in the flow of revenues that prevent firm commitments for spending and hinder the establishment and maintenance of priorities. A rise or fall in expected revenues in the course of the financial year completely changes the perspective towards both indispensable and luxury programs. What was indispensable yesterday becomes dispensable tomorrow, when actual revenues fall short of projections. It is not possible to maintain priorities when the fiscal foundation on which they were set suddenly changes.

Thus, in poor countries accomplishments fall short of aspirations because of specific revenue problems: skimpiness, lack of flexibility and instability. In the following sections of this chapter, each of these revenue problems will be examined separately in an attempt to see how it is created and how it affects the ability of a government to carry out plans, programs and services. The most acute problem is that of insufficient revenues.

The Problem of Skimpiness

How much is enough? When are revenues sufficient, adequate or insufficient? What makes a government poor? What makes it rich? Budgetary decisions are constrained everywhere by the scarcity of resources. If resources were unlimited, there would be no need to budget, nor would there be conflicts on priorities because everyone would be able to obtain just as much as he desired.[14]

Not all governments operate with similar conditions of scarcity. For example, it is known, that the scarcity of resources in the USA is not of the same order and magnitude as the scarcity in India or the Philippines. How much is enough and what is insufficient depends on the level of demands that must be satisfied, but demands are unlimited and priorities are set by the availability of resources. It would be nice if an objective measurement of spending demands could be obtained and then compared with existing revenues. Unfortunately, there are no known methodologies for doing that.

Actual spending does not reflect the amounts that Ministers of Finance have been asked to authorize.[15] And, as Prest explains, "an excellent case can be made without the slightest trouble for each line of expenditure considered by itself — social security is a 'must' for a self-respecting society, road improvements are indispensable, modern sanitation is urgent."[16] Urgent needs abound in the poor countries. There is no need for systematic research to unveil what must be done. One need only look around to find scores of problems that require prompt attention. Yet, even if it were feasible to go about adding up what it will take to tend to all of these problems, the amount of resources needed would exceed any country's financial capability. What is needed is a way of arriving at a level of spending that is reasonable.

Virtually every study of budgeting and taxation in poor countries ends with the conclusion that revenues are insufficient. A sample of the characteristic statements made is contained in Chart 1.

How are conclusions about the adequacy or inadequacy of revenues reached? When no objective measures are available, comparisons do just as well. Revenue ratios can be compared in poor and rich countries and

CHART 1-1
Fiscal Experts Agree that Revenues in Poor Countries Are Insufficient

The fact is that in relation to gross national product the tax revenue of the underdeveloped countries is typically much smaller than in the advanced countries . . . Is this an ineluctable consequence of their poverty? (a)

A major characteristic of the tax system in underdeveloped countries is that it does not provide governments with much revenue . . . (b)

Mexico's fiscal performance has been far from adequate to support even the most modest revenue requirements as revealed by . . . international comparisons . . . tax policy has been inadequate to cope with even the normal requirements for increased public expenditures in growth. (c)

Despite increased tax revenues, the funding requirements of the development programs are still far from being met. Considering the growing budgetary requirements, whatever surplus is left would hardly be sufficient to meet even slightly the investment requirements on a year to year basis. (d)

The Philippine tax structure is replete with flaws. Revenues generated have been far from adequate . . . From 1960 to 1969, total tax revenues consistently lagged behind total expenditures. (e)

Source:

(a) Nicholas Kaldor, "Will Underdeveloped Countries Learn to Tax?," *Foreign Affairs,* (January 1963), p. 410.
(b) U. Tun Wai, "Taxation Problems and Policies of Underdeveloped Countries," *International Monetary Fund Staff Papers,* (November 1966), p. 429.
(c) Clark W. Reynolds, "Public Finance in Postrevolutionary Mexico," in *Government and Economic Development,* Gustav Ranis (ed.), (New Haven: Yale University Press, 1971), pp. 351-352.
(d) Cesar B. Abrencia, "The Budget and Development Policy from 1955 to 1966," *Economic Research Journal,* XIV, 2 (September 1967), pp. 111-112.
(e) Avelino B. Lim, "Reshaping Tax Policy for Economic Development," *Congressional Economic Bulletin,* (September 1970), p. 8.

observations made as to what governments do with the money that they have or try to find out what they fail to accomplish because they could not raise the needed resources. Finally, budgetary decision making processes are examined — are governments able to allocate efficiently the resources that they have?

Governments of rich nations are substantially larger than governments of poor nations and control a far greater proportion of national resources. Most rich countries collect taxes in excess of thirty percent of gross national product (excluding social security) while most poor countries raise less than seventeen percent.[17] The desirable size of the government is a normative question. Some people would prefer their government large, while others would struggle to keep it small. Though the desirability of having a rich, strong and big government can be questioned, there seems to be no doubt that a poor, weak and small government would not be able to provide decent public services, nor would it be able to push ahead with economic development. Lewis points out that:

> These differences in the share of national income used by government are, of course, associated with considerable differences in the quality of government . . . good public services cannot be provided for five percent of the national income.[18]

The effects of a limited supply of public revenues on government services cannot be missed by even the most casual observer. Chart 2 exemplifies the problems governments encounter when their revenues fall short of their rudimentary spending needs.

Budgeters everywhere waste no time in pointing at hosts of projects and programs that had to be given up for lack of funds, as well as many others that progressed only halfway because funds originally authorized ran out or had to be transferred elsewhere. Ministers of Finance, while praising their achievement last year, emphasize that much as they would like to do more next year their hands are tied by the skimpiness of the revenue. After salaries are paid and last year's commitments fulfilled, very little remains for new ideas. The amount of revenue raised each year is too low to allow for much thinking about how it should be spread around, there is enough room for only the bare bones of government. Here is how the President of the Philippines described the problem in his budget message to the Congress:

> Fiscal year 1969: Despite increases in revenue collections, our financial resources cannot fully fund existing appropriations. General fund appropriations total P7.5 billion as against an estimated income of only P2.4 billion for the fiscal year 1969 . . . Unless we find new sources of revenues, we cannot undertake many meritorious projects. I, therefore, appeal to Congress to provide the additional funds that we need.

CHART 1-2
Insufficient Revenues Are the Main Cause of Poor Public Services and Slow Social and Economic Development

There is little difficulty in recognizing a poor one, whose poverty is blatantly and painfully obvious. The effects of hunger and malnutrition are a common sight. Overcrowding and slums characterize cities as soon as prestige business centers and elite suburbs are left behind. A safe water supply and medical services . . . may be beyond the reach of a large part of the population . . . The whole infrastructure of public services, accepted as normal in affluent countries, tends to be more or less absent. (a)

Budget deficits in the Philippines do not arise from excessive government spending for luxury welfare services. The government is not spending enough for essential public services . . . Government is not big enough to play its proper role in the economy. (b)

Over the years, the demand for greater and more efficient volume of social and development services had not kept pace with the level of development. In fact, it has created a bigger wedge of new demands.

All these demands have been witnessed in the straining of all facilities like school houses, hospitals and clinical services, to mention only the obvious social needs. In the area of development, the requirements for sea and airports, highways, irrigation, sewerage and water systems, electrical power generation and distribution . . . of course are growing . . . this has necessitated the expenditure of more than what the government can afford from tax money and has led to long term borrowings based on the future capability of the economy to repay. (c)

Source:

(a) Naomi Caiden and Aaron Wildavsky, *Planning and Budgeting in Poor Countries,* (New York: John Wiley), 1974, p. 46.

(b) Louis Shere, "A Tax Program for the Philippines," *National Tax Journal,* IV, 2, (June 1951), pp. 97-115.

(c) Gerardo P. Sicat, "Spending Public Resources for Development," *The Philippine Review of Business and Economics,* (December 1973), X, 2, p. 33.

Two years later, the situation did not seem to have changed and a similar complaint was lodged:

> Fiscal year 1971: We will curtail our general fund expenditures because of limited tax revenues. The yearly increase in our general fund resources has not kept pace with the appropriations which have been authorized by Congress.

With too little to spend and too much to spend it on, recurrent expenditures use up most of what is available. New investments are pushed aside because the ongoing spending overwhelms revenues. Here is how the Jamaican Minister of Finance described the problem to the Parliament:

> Notwithstanding this large increase [in spending], it is true to say that the structure of the increase has not been satisfactory, and I say this because the increase in Recurrent expenditure last year was twenty-four percent over that of the previous year; whereas increase in capital expenditure was only nine percent. This increase in Recurrent expenditure was to some extent accounted for by the fifteen percent regrading of salaries in the civil service and Local Government.[19]

Caiden and Wildavsky found this problem to be typical and conclude that "poor countries are continually up against a situation in which they can just about pay for the cost of past decisions."[20]

W. Arthur Lewis made a useful attempt at estimating the proportion of GNP that should be mobilized to provide the quantity and quality of government services and investments which poor countries demand for themselves. He breaks down the budget into categories representing major government services — health, education, public works, general administration and so on — and then estimates what it would cost to satisfy the minimum spending requirements in that particular area. Crude as it is, this is the only quantitative method available, short of purely normative models, and it has been widely used by practitioners. Here is how Lewis describes his conclusions:

> The quantity and quality of Government activity which underdeveloped countries now demand for themselves cannot be provided for less than twenty percent of gross domestic product, even when defense and debt charges are excluded. Recurrent expenditure on general and economic administration takes, say, six percent, education three percent, health two percent, welfare services two percent, capital expenditure on public works (including roads, schools and hospitals) three percent, and at least four percent is required for capital expenditure . . . by enterprises in the public sector.[21]

Lewis' results reinforce the conclusions drawn from the studies of planning and budgeting. If twenty percent is the minimum, then most poor countries are very far from having an adequate revenue according to Chelliah's study.[22] Since the average tax ratio (in a group of forty-seven poor countries) in 1969-71 was 15.1 (excluding social security contributions). Only two countries — Zaire and Zambia — have revenue ratios that exceed Lewis' minimum (in fact they come near the lowest ratios in rich countries — 29.4 and 31.3 respectively). Ten countries have a tax ratio of twenty percent, give or take one percent. The other thirty-five barely reach fifteen percent, while eight have less than ten percent (these are: Rwanda, 7.9; Nepal, 4.4; Pakistan, 8.8; Philippines, 9.1; Bolivia, 8.2; Guatemala, 7.9; Mexico, 7.1; Ethiopia, 8.6).

Never judge anything or anyone by how he looks in the present before assessing his potential for future development. The problems of revenue inadequacy would vanish if the revenue could be made to grow quickly. This is the question of flexibility.

The Problem of Flexibility

It is certain that next year's spending will be greater than this year's. The pressure on revenues never eases off, but gets worse. Most governments are constantly faced with demands to do things next year that they have not managed to accomplish this year. A substantial part of the budget is uncontrollable so that there is very little room to accommodate new needs among old resources. Just as spending grows each year, so will the revenue have to grow. Annual increments in revenues are even more important in poor countries than in rich ones because their starting base is so low initially. A bad situation becomes worse unless revenues grow slightly faster than expenditures.

In rich countries most of the increase in revenues is obtained automatically by a system of rates that ensures the government of getting a substantial proportion of additions to wealth brought about by economic development. The government not only preserves what it has in relation to national income, it constantly improves its conditions. Thus, according to W. Arthur Lewis:

> Every year, in the absence of increases in military expenditures, the Minister of Finance finds revenue tending to increase faster than current commitments, and can if he wishes announce a tax cut. Underdeveloped countries are in an opposite situation.[23]

Revenue flexibility is important because the alternatives to automatic growth in revenues are the frequent increase in rates or the addition of new taxes, both of which are politically undesirable. When the revenue grows faster than the annual increase in GNP, it enables the government to meet its expanding needs without having to go through the painful and prolonged process of levying new taxes.

It is easier to tax increments to wealth as they evolve, rather than taxing existing wealth itself, because giving up part of a future increase is much less painful than foregoing something one already has. Blough explains that taxpayers are more concerned with the possibility that their standard of living will be lowered, than with having to be satisfied with slower improvements.

> The intensity of tax conflicts is likely to be less when incomes are rising than when they are falling, because people are more aggressive in trying to prevent a decline in their living standards than in trying to raise them. Tax conflicts tend to subside during periods when it is not necessary to change the tax system for a considerable length of time.[24]

W. Arthur Lewis adds that taxing increments to wealth is the main hope poor countries have for improving their low revenue base.

> While it is difficult to increase the government's share of a given national income, it is not so difficult politically to ensure that a greater share of increases in the national income should accrue to the government. This is the main hope of increasing the share of government in the national income. In less developed economies the marginal rate of taxation should always be greater than the average rate.[25]

A comparison of income elasticities (change in revenue resulting from a change in GNP) and marginal tax rates (percentage of the increase in GNP taken up by the tax system) shows that the rich get richer while the poor remain poor.[26] Table 1-1 shows average elasticities and marginal rates computed for a randomly selected group of twelve rich and twelve poor countries.

TABLE 1-1
Fraction of the Increase in GNP Mobilized for Public Purpose in Rich and Poor Countries*

	Rich	Poor
Income Elasticity	1.33	1.34
Marginal Tax Rate	36	13.4

*SOURCE: Adapted from Raja J. Chelliah, "Trends in Taxation in Developing Countries," International Monetary Fund Staff Papers XVIII (1971): 254-331.

An income elasticity higher than unity means that revenues grow faster than GNP. The marginal tax rate shows the percentage of the increase in GNP taken up by taxes to be nearly three times larger in rich countries compared to the poor. On the whole, most poor countries have been able to keep their revenue slightly ahead of their rate of economic growth. But, they have managed to obtain only fourteen percent of the increase in wealth compared to the thirty-six percent average in rich countries. This means that despite absolute increases, the ratio of tax revenues to GNP has changed but little. Thus, the poor remain poor.

The average increase in tax ratio in poor countries, between 1953-55 and 1966-68 was only 2.5 percent (from 11.3 percent to 13.8 percent). A similar rate of growth was maintained in later years. The average ratio in 1969-71 was 15.1, up two points from the previous period.[27] There are quite a few countries where the ratio has hardly changed and in at least one case (Ghana) it has even fallen back. The average increase in a group of six rich countries has been 6.9 percent. Table 1-2 presents these trends in detail. What do these figures mean to finance officials? What effects do they have on the ability to meet demands for spending and on the way in which available resources are allocated among competing proposals?

Here is how a group of Filipino government tax experts describe the problem:

> While there has been some degree of economic growth during the past few years, the tax system has remained ineffective in directing real resources to productive investments. As the economy grows, the ideal situation is that tax potentials necessarily broaden. All that is called for is a systematic and sustained effort to tap these potentials . . . but this is not the situation in this country.[28]

If revenues do not grow as fast as expenditures, sooner or later spending will have to be curtailed. According to Caiden and Wildavsky, "Unless the [poor] nation has a rare period of affluence, it is faced either with the need to cut some expenditures to make room for others, or to make drastic reductions."[29] The usual procedure of determining priorities by discussing and comparing the desirability of different projects is replaced by one where priorities are determined by the availability of money.

Current spending must be put under tight control, capital investments curtailed and programs that will require substantial maintenance costs in the future postponed. All this and more must be done to ensure that next year's expenditure will not be substantially greater than this year's, since there is little or no hope that the revenue will be increased accordingly. Therefore, the unique role of the Ministry of Finance in a poor country is to say "no" to anyone who asks for money. "If the nation is not to go bankrupt, nor to sink into inflation, nor to run out of foreign exchange,

TABLE 1-2
Poor Governments Remain Poor While Rich Governments Are Generally Growing Richer — Rates of Change in Tax-GNP Ratios*

Degree of Change	Country	Mid-Fifties (1953-1955)	Late Sixties (1966-1968)	1971	Total
Practically No Change (0-2%)	Kenya	13	14	14	1
	Guatemala	8	8	8	0
	Lebanon	10	10	11	1
	Columbia	10	11	12	2
	Ecuador	13	13	13	0
	Costa Rica	12	11	13	1
	Thailand	11	12	12	1
	Philippines	7	9	9	2
	Ceylon	16	16	18	2
	Peru	12	14	14	2
	Trinidad & Tobago	16	15	18	2
Negative Change (Decline)	Ghana	18	13	16	-2
Small Change (3-4%)	Pakistan	6	8	9	3
	France	33	36	36	3
	United States	25	28	29	4
	West Germany	32	34	35	3
	Indonesia	6	8	10	4
	Turkey	12	14	16	4
	Honduras	7	11	11	4
Large Increase	Paraquay	5	10	11	6
	Brazil	15	21	23	8
	Jamaica	13	17	19	6
	Tunisia	16	21	22	6
	Korea	6	12	15	9
	India	6	12	14	8
	Great Britain	28	35	36	8
Very Large Growth	Chile	10	19	20	10
	Sweden	29	37	42	13
	Netherlands	29	39	42	13

*Rounded Figures

SOURCE: Chelliah, "Tax Ratios and Tax Effort".

the finance ministry must limit expenditures *in relation to available revenues.*"[30]

Chart 1-3 contains examples of the prevailing view among tax experts, that in the poor countries, the key to spending decisions is the revenue. Since the revenue is not flexible, the sequence of decision-making must run from taxing to spending, and not the other way round.

CHART 1-3
Revenue Inflexibility Limits the Ability to Formulate Spending Priorities According to their Political Desirability (Comments Made by Fiscal Experts)

In a highly developed economy, tax policy tends to accept the level of expenditures as its revenue goal . . . The sequence of decision tends to run from expenditures to taxes. But in underdeveloped countries the level of expenditures depends much more heavily on the ability of the tax system to place the required revenues at the disposal of government. . . . the sequence of decisions tends to run from taxation to expenditure.(a)

In developed countries political decisions governing public expenditure are relatively independent, for although they are not free from obstacles, they ordinarily find themselves with an economic structure and administrative mechanism capable of obtaining the larger receipts needed. On the other hand, no forecast of public expenditure in developing countries can seriously be made before formulating a carefully planned policy of public receipts which assures, in a realistic way, the appropriate financing. For this reason, the revenue policy acts in such cases . . . as a conditioning factor of public expenditure . . . (b)

In developing countries taxation policies, and tax revenues, are geared to cover the amount of socially desired expenditures . . . the underdeveloped countries find it difficult to increase the level of taxation and amount of revenue collected. Therefore, governments desiring to promote economic growth and simultaneously to maintain financial stability have been forced to limit much-needed development expenditures.(c)

Source:

(a) Walter W. Heller, "Fiscal Policies for Underdeveloped Countries," *Taxes and Fiscal Policy in Underdeveloped Countries*, (New York: United Nations Technical Assistance Administration, 1954), p. 4.

(b) Antonio Barrera de Irima, "Administrative and Political Problems in Raising Tax Yields," in Alan T. Peacock and Gerald Houser, eds., *Government Finance and Economic Development*, (Paris: O.E.C.D.) p. 214.

(c) U. T. Wai, "Taxation Problems and Policies of Underdeveloped Countries," *International Monetary Fund Staff Papers*, (November 1966), p. 428.

The Problem of Instability

"Adequate revenue does not necessarily mean stable revenue. An efficient tax system is expected to be responsive to changes in prices and in economic conditions."[31] The problems of skimpiness and lack of flexibility are compounded by instability. When the meager resources flow into the treasury coffers irregularly, at unpredictable times and in uncertain quantities, it is hard to predict exactly how much will be available in the near future and, precisely, when the monies will be at hand. Revenue estimates are frequently way off the mark. An amount expected to be obtained through a certain tax may show up months after it was due or may turn out to be smaller than what original estimates anticipated.

Here is an extreme example as described by the Jamaican Minister of Finance to Parliament:

> The actual collection of revenue by the 31st of March [1973] totalled $291.8 million . . . That is the position in reality, but I must call attention to the fact that this position is not fully reflected in the Financial Statement and this is due to a somewhat unusual situation. Of this $291.8 million some 6.1 million came in on the very last day of the financial year and it came in such volume that it was not possible for the Income Tax and Revenue Departments to reflect that before the 31st of March.[32]

Since the money came in so late, it could not be spent during the current fiscal year and had to be carried over to the next. The Treasury, unnecessarily, had clamped down on the spending departments throughout the year, and was now left with a substantial amount without being able to spend it. It is nice to begin a new year with a surplus carried over from last year but the damage done to programs that did not receive enough funds in the previous year may be irreversible.

The lack of budgetary surplus makes it hard to cope with uncertainty.[33] Every unexpected change in revenues leads to a major shifting of funds to prevent any one part of the system from falling under. Suppose money reserved for a certain project fails to materialize. In order to save it, funds will have to be brought from elsewhere and since there is no surplus this means that some other project, perhaps less important at that moment, will lose its funds and so on down the line. Financial uncertainty wreaks havoc in budgeting. It sharpens the effects of scarcity because at no point in time is the Treasury in a position to allocate all the funds that are available. When a surplus does not exist, finance officials work hard to create one artifically. The Treasury must make it hard for everyone both to get new proposals approved and to receive the money later on, for unless this is done, the Treasury takes the risk of running out of resources before the year is over. This, according to Caiden and Wildavsky, leads to repetitive budgeting — making and remaking the budget in the course of the year, changing priorities to meet the new revenue conditions — and to the paradox of underspending. On one hand, resources are insufficient and, on the other, not everything that is available is spent. By the time everyone concerned is assured that there is going to be enough money, it is too late to start something new. Here is how Caiden and Wildavsky describe the consequences of uncertainty:

> Never knowing what will come next, fearful of depleting their meager reserves, concerned that the merely urgent will take precedence over the absolutely critical, finance ministries continuously revise their expenditure priorities.[34]

The causes of uncertainty are numerous. They include lack of proper records and statistical data and the vulnerability of the tax structure to economic changes.[35] Who can tell at the beginning of the year what the rate of inflation will be at its end? Who can predict, with reasonable accuracy, what fluctuations there will be in world prices of rice, coffee, cocoa, sugar, bauxite, or copper? When taxes are imposed on these export goods, fluctuations in their prices are reverberated through the revenues that they produce and when these taxes are the mainstay of the revenue structure, the fluctuations can be disastrous.

The way to protect revenues against these uncontrollable and largely unpredictable changes is to rely on direct taxes levied on personal and company income and property. Then, if inflation strikes, revenues will increase with it. U Tun Wai explains:

> The direct tax system has a built-in structure for giving governments larger revenues from growth without changing the level of taxation.
>
> The progressive direct tax system also provides governments with built-in protection against inflation. When prices rise, money incomes increase, and the tax system causes government revenues to increase at least *pari passu* with national income. On the other hand, if indirect taxes are a large component of revenue, government revenues will lag behind the increases in money incomes and prices.[36]

Only a handful of poor countries have been able to institute a tax structure that would ensure revenue stability. In the majority of poor countries the bulk of the revenue is produced by indirect taxes (primarily custom, export and excise duties)[37] and to make things worse many are levied at fixed rather than *ad valorem* rates. Table 3 exemplifies the problem.

Countries like Ghana, Brazil and Thailand, which depend heavily on revenues drawn from taxes imposed on their few export goods (cocoa, coffee and rice respectively in this example), must live with a great amount of uncertainty. The revenue situation may change virtually over-

TABLE 1-3
The Element of Instability in the Revenue Structure of Poor Countries — Composition of Tax Revenues (in Percent of Total) 1969-1971

	Country	Total Direct Taxes	Total Indirect Taxes
INDIRECT TAXES ARE DOMINANT IN THIS GROUP OF COUNTRIES	Bolivia	21.24	78.74
	Brazil	13.61	74.55
	Burundi	42.34	64.80
	Chile	37.60	61.67
	China, Republic of	24.07	74.81
	Colombia	43.46	46.44
	Costa Rica	22.52	74.82
	Ecuador	21.97	77.52
	Egypt	26.36	66.19
	Ethiopia	28.70	71.30
	Ghana	23.16	76.84
	Guatemala	18.17	81.83
	Guyana	44.43	52.19
	Honduras	30.19	69.81
	India	26.46	73.54
	Indonesia	40.63	59.37
	Ivory Coast	19.05	77.07
	Kenya	42.30	52.59
	Korea	37.53	62.04
	Lebanon	25.36	74.62
	Malaysia	29.03	55.80
	Mali	27.10	59.78
	Morocco	27.17	70.52
	Nepal	28.76	70.35
	Pakistan	19.03	80.95
	Paraguay	15.98	83.37
	Peru	34.01	62.67
	Philippines	33.04	65.64
	Rwanda	34.48	64.46
	Senegal	30.36	69.16
	Sri Lanka	23.01	76.99
	Sudan	10.80	89.19
	Tanzania	33.25	62.69
	Thailand	18.11	81.77
	Togo	17.34	74.77
	Tunisia	35.20	62.01
	Turkey	45.57	54.43
	Upper Volta	28.73	70.99
	Zaire	26.42	73.29
HERE THE ELEMENT OF STABILITY SHOULD BE STRONGER	Iran	73.61	25.48
	Jamaica	51.73	48.24
	Mexico	54.14	44.38
	Singapore	61.72	35.89
	Trinidad & Tobago	63.08	36.91
	Venezuela	83.85	16.14
	Zambia	61.10	38.84

SOURCE: Raja I. Chelliah, "Tax Ratios and Tax Effort in Developing Countries".

night as it did recently when Brazil lost more than half of its annual coffee crop or a few years ago in Ghana when the price of cocoa plummeted in the world market.

Even when such dramatic events do not occur and the changes in total revenues from one year to another are relatively mild, there still remains the problem of midyear fluctuations. The inflow of revenues must be stable, predictable and continuous to allow the government to maintain stability and continuity in its spending. Since there is very little or no surplus, the money is spent just as quickly as it is earned. So, even if the revenue fluctuates mildly from one month to another it forces the Treasury to postpone payments, or to resort to expensive short term loans.

Conclusion

The financial problems of poor countries are three: there isn't enough money, revenues are unstable and they do not grow fast enough from one year to another. Each of these limitations has pervasive effects on the government's ability to pursue its goals in providing social services and instituting development projects. Skimpy revenues result in poor government services. The money available barely covers the expenses of current activities; there is no surplus to spend on improvements or new projects.

No matter how hard the government tries to curtail, cut, stop, and otherwise limit spending, it always grows. The problem with revenue adequacy becomes worse and not better, unless the revenue can be made to grow faster than spending.

Most poor countries do not have a highly flexible tax structure. Though revenues grow from one year to the next, the ratio of revenues to GNP remains rather fixed. The resource situation does not improve. The annual increases in revenues are taken up by similar increases in the costs of running the government and, again, investments in future betterment, and economic development are pushed aside. It is not possible to maintain a continuous effort to support economic development unless each year there is more to invest than was available last year.

Financial uncertainty exacerbates the problems of poverty. Since the revenue sources are exposed to frequent, unpredictable and sometimes wild changes, it is not possible to maintain the same list of spending priorities formulated at the beginning of the year until the end. Priorities must be changed when revenues change. What seemed to be sufficiently important to be included in yesterday's budget is no longer considered because revenues have fallen short of expectations. With less to spend, something must be excluded from the budget to permit other more vital activities to continue. Financial uncertainty thus leads to repetitive budgeting — the constant making and remaking of priorities — and to the paradox of underspending. By the time it becomes known how much money is available, how much has been spent and how much will be spent until the end of the year, it is usually too late to put the artificially acquired surplus to good use.

The next chapter takes a critical look at attempts to identify the determinants of government revenue. It examines the validity of theories suggesting that these determinants are the key factors in explaining the differences in revenues among nations.

Notes

1. Walter E. Heller, "Fiscal Policies for Underdeveloped Countries," *Taxes and Fiscal Policy in Underdeveloped Countries*, (New York: United Nations Technical Assistance Administration, 1954).
2. W. Arthur Lewis stated the issue simply: "The needs of government for finance grow all the time, because the public sector grows faster than the economy as a whole," *The Theory of Economic Growth* (London: George Allen and Unwin, 1956).
3. A.R. Prest, *Public Finance in Under-developed Countries* (New York: Praeger, 1963), p. 14.
   Walter E. Heller adds that:
   > In underdeveloped agrarian economies, strong pressures for economic development are typically accompanied by heavy demands on governments for capital forming and capital-supporting activities. This confronts them with the task of drawing off, via taxation, a larger proportion of the national income, both initially and as that income expands with economic growth.

   "A Survey of Agricultural Taxation," in *Papers and Proceedings of the Conference on Agricultural Taxation and Economic Development*, eds. Haskell P. Wald and Joseph N. Froomkin (Cambridge, Mass.: Harvard Law School International Program in Taxation, 1954).
   A similar view is expressed by M.H. Gopal, "Towards a Realistic Tax Policy for India," *The Indian Economic Journal*, VII, 3 (1959): 291. He writes:
   > The problem of resources as an objective of tax policy claims top priority because, apart from the need to meet normal public expenditures, the State, in a backward and mixed economy, undertakes developmental functions also . . . Resources are also needed since the redistributive side of fiscal policy cannot altogether be neglected or deferred, and funds would be required for slowly expanding welfare projects.

   See also John F. Due, *Taxation and Economic Development in Tropical Africa* (Cambridge: MIT Press, 1963), p. 144.
4. Ibid, p. 144.
5. Naomi Caiden and Aaron Wildavsky, *Planning and Budgeting in Poor Countries* (New York: Wiley, 1974), p. v.
6. Due, p. 145.
7. Ibid.
8. Nicholas Kaldor, "Will Underdeveloped Countries Learn to Tax?" *Foreign Affairs* 4, 12 (1963): 410-419

9. Karl de Schweinitz, Jr., *Industrialization and Democracy* (London: Free Press, 1964), p. 22.
10. Jose D. Soberano, "Philippine Fiscal Planning: A Quest for Economic Fulfillment," *Philippine Public Fiscal Administration,* eds. Jose D. Soberano and H. Odell Walby (Manila: Graduate School of Public Administration, University of the Philippines, 1965), p. 780.
11. Caiden and Wildavsky, p. 47.
12. National Tax Research Center, *Assessment of Tax Reforms in the Philippines (1972-73),* Manila (mimeo), January 1974, p. 2.
13. Gerardo P. Sicat, *Taxation and Progress* (Manila: National Economic Council, Republic of the Philippines, 1972).
14. Aaron Wildavsky, *Budgeting: A Comparative Theory of Budgetary Processes* (Boston: Little, Brown, 1975).
15. Prest, *Public Finance in Under-developed Countries.*
16. Ibid., p. 16.
17. Raja J. Chelliah, "Trends in Taxation in Developing Countries," *International Monetary Staff Papers* XVIII (1971): 254-331.
18. Lewis, *The Theory . . .*, p. 397.
19. Budget speech by David Coore, Deputy Prime Minister and Minister of Finance, Kingston, Jamaica, April 18, 1973, p. 20.
20. Caiden and Wildavsky; *see also* Cesar B. Abrencia, "The Budget and Development Policy from 1955 to 1966," *Economic Research Journal* XIV (1967).
21. W. Arthur Lewis, *Development Planning* (London: George Allen and Unwin, 1966), pp. 115-16.
22. Chelliah, pp. 261-65.
23. Lewis, *Development Planning,* pp. 116-17.
24. Roy Blough, *The Federal Taxing Process* (New York: Prentice Hall, 1952), p. 47.
25. Lewis, *The Theory . . .*, p. 402.
26. Chelliah, pp. 261-65.
27. Raja J. Chelliah, Hessel J. Baas, and Margaret R. Kelley, "Tax Ratios and Tax Effort in Developing Countries, 1969-71," *International Monetary Fund Staff Papers* XXII (1975): 189ff.
28. Report on Revenue System and Administration, Prepared for the Commission on Reorganization by the Reorganization Panel on the Revenue System and Administration, Manila, October 1970 (mimeo).
29. Caiden and Wildavsky, p. 112.
30. Wildavsky, *Budgeting,* p. 102.
31. A.M. Abdel Rahman, "Tax Policy Issues in African Countries," in *Notes for Discussion,* United Nations Economic Commission for Africa (Addis Ababa, Ethiopia, October 1973), p. 9.
32. David Coore, Deputy Prime Minister and Minister of Finance, Budget Speech, Kingston, Jamaica, April 18, 1973.
33. The best analytical use of the information available about problems of uncertainty is in Wildavsky's *Budgeting* (p. 140). This is how Wildavsky describes the uncertainties that budgeters confront in making allocation decisions:

    In assessing revenues and spending . . . they [budgeters] face not merely the uncertainties of the future but also those of the past. Often they don't know where they stand with respect to the basic features of national financial life . . . They have no firm base from which to predict changes in the amounts available for public purposes. Fluctuations in external trade, foreign aid and foreign currency reserves make it hazardous to predict revenues even over a short period.

34. Caiden and Wildavsky, p. 162.
35. The relation between surplus and financial uncertainty is described by Wildavsky in *Budgeting*.
36. U Tun Wai, "Taxation Problems and Policies of Underdeveloped Countries," *International Monetary Fund Staff Papers* (1966): 433-34.
37. The best study of indirect taxation in poor countries is John F. Due, *Indirect Taxation in Developing Economies* (Baltimore: The John Hopkins Press, 1970).

Chapter Two

Theories of Tax Level Determinants

> The economic structure of low income countries imposes severe limitations on the structure of the tax system. The predominance of agriculture and the difficulty of reaching it through income taxation make land taxes vitally important . . . Outside agriculture, the organization of early manufacturing in small-scale establishments limits the effective base for manufacturing excises . . . The fluid and atomistic structure of retail outlets bars effective retail sales taxation . . . Personal income tax, to the extent that it can be applied at all, has to proceed on a highly schedular non-global basis . . . effective taxation is typically limited to the wage income of civil servants and employees of large firms.
>
> Richard A. Musgrave,
> *Fiscal Systems*, pp. 126-27.

Introduction

Why do governments of poor nations have lower tax revenues than the governments of rich nations? Is it only because the poor countries are poor, or is it that, because of weaker demands for government services, there is no need to raise more money? Perhaps, it is because the bureaucracy is incapable of absorbing and spending more than its present budget, or that the government finds it politically dangerous to increase the tax burden. If it is willing to take this risk but unable to find an acceptable formula, then it could be a problem of implementation rather than of policy. Perhaps, extracting the tax dues is the rock against which great policies are wrecked. Yet another possibility is that the level of taxation is determined primarily by economic factors — national wealth and economic structures.

The process by which governments raise their revenues has not been systematically studied by any of the social sciences, except economics, where the thrust is normative: if you want to reach certain goals — controlling inflation, providing jobs, redistributing income, maintaining a certain level of public services and economic growth — you ought to impose various taxes at specified rates with particular allowances and deductions, on occupations, income groups or goods.[1] While these theories are helpful in designing fiscal policies, they provide little insight into the factors determining the ability to carry them out. There is always a difference between what should be done and what can be done. Experience shows that the compromises that must be made to accomodate, within the same policy, the conflicting interests of various groups whose support is a necessity for enacting the policy, as well as the various problems encountered later on (at the stage of implementation), are sufficiently strong to turn the most elegantly designed policy into meaningless action.

A number of economists have recently begun to ask questions about the factors that determine what kind of tax structure and what amount of revenue different types of economies are able to sustain. The basis of their approach is the assumption that though revenues are raised by acts of government, what can be done politically is dependent mainly on economic factors. Thus, according to Raja C. Chelliah:

> Tax ratios and changes in them over time are subject to control by governments. Nevertheless, it may be hypothesized that the changes in tax ratios brought about in different developing countries are partly dependent on major characteristics of the economy.[2]

What are the characteristics of the economy that determine the level of taxation in poor countries, and are these the only important determinants? Under what conditions are they likely to overwhelm other noneconomic factors and when will their influence be weaker? The tax means for mobilizing resources are limited to a fairly narrow range of alternatives. Each tax can be imposed on a certain source of wealth, on wealth transfers, or various forms of economic production. Hence, what determines the particular combination is the range and size of available tax bases. The broader the range and the size of the bases, the larger the number of taxes that produce a greater quantity of revenues will be found.

Economic development is the most important factor affecting the range and size of tax bases.[3] Musgrave distinguishes between two types of economic structures. The first is found in the early stages of economic development and is characterized by the predominance of agricultural production by small farmers. Manufacturing is a simple activity concentrated in a large number of small establishments, and the retail outlets are fluid and atomistic, rather than fixed and formally organized. The bases that can support income, sales, and corporation taxes are therefore weak. There are more constraints than opportunities for taxing agricultural income,[4] profits from small manufacturing — cottage industry style outfits — and the purchase and sale of life's basic necessities.

More developed countries will be able to mobilize more resources than less developed ones because they have a greater number of accessible tax bases and each one is larger than what is found in a country at a lower level of development. The assumption on which this analysis is built and the conclusions drawn is that the participants in the taxing process — fiscal policy makers and taxpayers — act as rational decision makers. The taxpayer pays taxes only when he is convinced that the costs of avoiding payment are likely to be greater.

Similarly governments do not levy a tax if its implementation is based solely on the willingness of taxpayers to comply. A broadly based income tax, for example, levied on ten million Thai or Filipino farmers, would not go far because it is impossible to assess, collect or otherwise enforce it. The taxpayers recognizing this would not pay. Paul A. Baran describes this mechanism well:

> Although an income tax might seem to be a simple solution of this problem [mobilizing economic surplus], this device is all but useless in the framework of a dwarf peasant economy. Neither the assessment of income . . . nor the collection of the tax from the now multiplied number of subsistence farmers is a manageable task . . . the very nature of a subsistence farm's outputs renders the payment of the tax well-neigh impossible. Consisting of a wide variety of agricultural products and marketed to a minimal extent, it leaves the subsistence peasant with insignificant money receipts. The gathering of taxes in kind, however, is an administratively hopeless undertaking.[5]

Indirect taxes by comparison require much less effort to assess and collect. Their relative administrative simplicity makes them the mainstay of the revenue structure in poor countries. Hence, a nation that has larger bases on which indirect taxes can be levied can also be expected to have a higher revenue ratio than another at a similar level of economic development, but with a less favorable economic structure. Arthur W. Lewis summarizes this point better than others:

> The biggest yielders of revenue in under-developed countries are the taxes on commodities — import, export and excise duties. These are easiest to collect, administratively, when commodities pass through the hands of a few wholesalers in a small number of places. This is why the countries that raise most in taxes are those which depend most on foreign trade.[6]

Economic development affects revenues by reducing constraints and opening opportunities for taxation. It makes available a greater number of taxable bases and places concentrations of wealth within reach of the means for their mobilization. Musgrave describes this process thus: "As the structure of the economy changes with economic development, the nature of the tax base changes as well, and with it the 'handles' to which the revenue system may be attached."[7] The economy moves away from simple forms of agricultural production and manufacturing to more complex and large scale industries. A greater number of people are employed in a small number of large establishments. In this economy, money, products and services move through formally organized markets where they can be diverted into the treasury coffers, at almost any point.[8] Thus, Hinrichs concludes that "conventional wisdom holds that government revenue shares of gross national product increase with economic development."[9]

To test this theory we must compare tax revenue ratios of countries at different stages of development. The question, as Chelliah phrased it, is: "Do the less poor among the developing countries tend to have a higher tax ratio than the poorer ones?"[10] If economic development increases the ability to raise resources, then more developed nations should have higher tax:GNP ratios than the less developed. To see whether this is really so the empirical studies of revenue determinants are examined.

Extractive Capability — Taxable Capacity-Tax Effort Approach

The first studies of aggregate cross-country data were simple comparisons of ratios between tax revenues and GNP.[11] The main finding, of Williamson and others, was that he who has more collects more. Rich countries collect more revenue than poor. Therefore wealth, usually represented by per capita income, is the major determinant of the ability to mobilize resources. There was nothing surprising in this finding. Wealth explains itself — the more a nation has the more it can give up for public use. The only problem is that wealth remains related to revenues only as long as the separation between very rich and very poor countries is retained.

When countries in similar economic circumstances are compared among themselves — the poorest against the poor — the effect of wealth on revenues, as Hinrichs found, disappears.[12] According to Hinrichs it is only after a certain level of income (at the time of his study $750 per capita per year) is attained does wealth begin to make a difference.

To demonstrate that high tax:GNP ratios are not highly correlated with high per capita income, a twofold matrix is used in which the horizontal scale measures per capita income and the perpendicular scale measures tax:GNP ratio. The matrix shows sixteen countries in the upper right box (low per capita income — high tax:GNP) and one country in the bottom left box (high per capita income — low tax:GNP).

The matrix indicates that though high per capita income is often associated with high tax:GNP ratio, low per capita income is not always associated with low tax:GNP ratios. The explanatory weakness of this variable is further emphasized when the spatial location of the various countries is considered. Tunisia, for example, is situated at the upper middle of the top right box, while Singapore is placed at the bottom middle of the upper left box. In other words, Singapore has a per capita income three times that of Tanzania's, yet its tax:GNP ratio is lower by nine points (23-14).

Wealth, as a single explanatory variable, is at its best when very rich countries — USA, Sweden, Britain — are compared with very poor ones — Nepal, Ethiopia, Pakistan, India. But, because these countries differ greatly in virtually every relevant aspect — political institutions, education, size and efficiency of government bureaucracy — any variable will work equally well and, therefore, it will be impossible to tell which is the independent one.

Why doesn't wealth work well within the same income group? Why does revenue differ between countries that are equally poor? To answer this question a new framework that goes beyond wealth and its components had to be developed. Drawing on historical studies of economic development, Musgrave suggests that the government's ability to tap available wealth may be limited by noneconomic constraints. As he describes it:

> Lack of availability of tax handles may be an important limiting factor . . . at low levels of income. But as the economy develops, these restrictions become less severe, and the size of the public sector can respond more freely to rising levels of GNP.[13]

It is not only sheer wealth, but also the way in which it is distributed in a society that determines how much money can be extracted from an economy. The taxable capacity of a country — the total amount that can be mobilized through taxation — is a function of both wealth and the constraints on and opportunities for tapping it.

Taxable capacity refers to a potential that may or may not be utilized. It means that wealth is not the only determining factor, and doesn't work consistently because there are "other" variables that may have a stronger effect under certain circumstances. As such the concept is useless if we wish to understand why one country mobilizes more revenue than another from a similar quantity of wealth. The importance of the concept comes from the claim that economic factors are the main determinants of revenues in poor countries. According to this theory, revenues would equal capacity, and would not exceed it, nor would they be likely to fall far below the potential.

Taxable capacity is actually a better measure of the stage of economic development than simple GNP figures. According to Roy W. Bahl, "The conventional wisdom of tax ratio and tax effort analysis holds that the tax revenue share of the GNP in developing countries is a function of the stage of development."[14] Similarly, Richard Thorn claimed that taxable

TABLE 2-1
Ability to Sacrifice Is Not the Only Determinant of Revenue

TAX/GNP RATIO		PER-CAPITA INCOME: HIGH				
		$800	$700	$600	$500	$400
HIGH	26			Chile		
	25					
	24					
	23	Venezuela				
	22					
	21					
	20					
	19					
	18					
	17					
	16					Jamaica
	15			Argentina Trinidad-Tobago		
	14			Singapore		Costa Rica
LOW	13					
	12					
	11					Mexico
	10					
	9					
	8					
	7					
	6					
	5					
	4					
	3					

SOURCE: Data is taken from Raja J. Chelliah, "Trends in Taxation in Developing Countries," *International Monetary Fund Staff Papers,* XVIII, 1971.

Table 2-1 (Continued)

PER-CAPITA INCOME

LOW			
$300	$200	$100	$50
Brazil			
	Tunisia	Congo (Rep. of)	
		U.A.R.	
Guyana			
	Senegal		
Malaysia	Ceylon		
Peru	Turkey		Tanzania Mali
	Ecuador, China		
	Ghana	Kenya	Chad
		Somalia	Upper Volta
		Sudan	
	Thailand		
Columbia	Paraguay	Korea	India
	Honduras	Bolivia	Togo
			Burundi
		Ethiopia	
Guatemala		Pakistan	Rwanda
		Indonesia	
		Nepal	

capacity determines revenues because economic development influences potential and the willingness to use it in the same way. Increments in capacity brought by economic development will be matched by increments in the desire to spend.

Thorn describes this mechanism in these words:

> The growth in national product resulting from economic growth increases the relative taxable capacity of a country and permits the government to obtain a larger share of national product . . . The growth in demand for public services . . . compels governments to tap this increase in taxable capacity.[15]

The government will use up any additional capacity because of rising pressures to spend. There will be a short period of adaptation in which spending may either exceed or lag behind taxable capacity, but over the long run the two will equalize. Lotz and Morss based their studies on the same assumption:

> The capability of collecting more taxes should be looked upon as a necessary but not sufficient condition for a high tax level. However, in developing countries, tax collection capabilities are especially likely to be fully utilized because public expenditure aspirations are usually high.[16]

So, unless important variables affecting taxable capacity have been left out, the actual tax ratio in a given country should equal or closely approximate its taxable capacity. It would serve no purpose to go through the results obtained from all formulas built around these hypotheses. Instead, the one study that came closest to the expectations laid out at the theoretical stage will be concentrated on. In this study Lotz and Morss calculated taxable capacity for fifty-two countries with a formula based on three factors: first, the size of the foreign trade sector — degree of "openness" in the economy; second, the degree of monetization — percentage of the population that handles money, or percentage of the GNP that passes through the market; and third, the size of the mineral and oil sector.

In Table 2-2 the Lotz and Morss' findings have been rearranged to emphasize the percentage difference between actual collection and projected taxable capacity. The number assigned to each country shows the degree of fit between capacity and actual revenue ratio; thus, unity stands for perfect fit and every figure higher than one stands for either over or under extraction. For example, according to Lotz and Morss' model, Afghanistan uses only twenty-one percent of its taxable capacity while Turkey exceeds its capacity by nearly twenty percent.

A reasonable fit between capacity and actual collections is obtained in only thirty-five percent of the countries while in the rest the deviations —

TABLE 2-2
Some Are Too Big, Others Too Small, Only a Few Are Just Right — Differences Between Actual Collection and Taxable Capacity Projections

Country	Just About Right	Not Doing Enough	Doing More than Expected
Iran	6.7		
Cameroon	4.7		
India	2.8		
Sudan	2.4		
Thailand	2.2		
China	1.9		
Portugal	1.5		
Chad	0.8		
Argentina	0.1		
Malaysia	0.9		
Panama	2.4		
Nigeria	2.7		
Tanzania	4.5		
Jamaica	4.5		
Brazil	7.7		
Liberia	8.4		
Niger	9.7		
Korea		10.9	
Haiti		11.6	
Trinidad & Tobago		12.5	
Malawi		12.7	
Costa Rica		13.6	
Philippines		13.8	
Paraguay		15.5	
Iraq		16.0	
Nicaragua		19.0	
Ghana		22.5	
Mexico		28.2	
Ethiopia		31.5	
Spain		32.0	
El Salvador		32.8	
Honduras		40.2	
Columbia		40.7	
Guatemala		50.8	
Afghanistan		79.0	
Congo			35.7
Burundi			27.5
Chile			24.5
South Africa			21.3
Turkey			19.7
Venezuela			18.5
U.A.R.			18.3
Malagasy			18.2
Dominican Republic			16.7
Ceylon			15.7
Uganda			14.4
Peru			14.2
Uruguay			13.8
Ecuador			13.8
Mali			13.5
Algeria			13.5
Greece	10.4		

over and under extraction — are substantial. The differences between projections and outcomes are too big to be blamed on the inaccuracy of the data or the lack of finesse of the formulas. The possibility that an important independent variable has been omitted has been casually mentioned but not seriously explored, and no such variable is in sight.

What then explains the existence of such substantial differences between what a country supposedly can mobilize (according to the taxable capacity theory) and what it actually collects. Once the models have failed to measure up to expectations we are sent back to square one and reminded that there is much more to revenue mobilization than what is determined by economic factors. The taxable resources may be there but the political willingness to tap them or the administrative capability to implement may lag behind. Similarly when the will is strong and ability high, economic constraints that otherwise seem overwhelming are mitigated and out of a narrow taxable base more is mobilized than what appears to be possible.

What then, is the value of a theory if it works only occasionally and doesn't specify the conditions under which it won't work? Since the economic factors — per capita GNP and degree of "openness" — did not work satisfactorily by themselves, attempts have been made to save the theory by adding an entirely new set of determinants. This new starting point is the assumption that taxable capacity is only a rough indicator of a country's revenue potential, and does not determine the extent to which the potential will be utilized. That depends on the "tax effort."

What precisely is "tax effort" and what causes it to vary? We know that the taxable capacity theory is based on rational choice assumptions, with economic growth as the major factor responsible for variations in capacity. What are the comparable components of effort? Is it possible to calculate effort independently of taxable capacity just as capacity is calculated independently of effort? Under what conditions will effort be high rather than low?

Lotz and Morss start at the end by telling us, not what tax effort is, but how it is measured: "Tax effort is measured by relating actual tax collections to some indicator of taxable capacity."[17] This allows everything which we do not understand to be called "tax effort." If with taxable capacity factors it was possible to understand only a small percentage of the variations in revenue ratios, with the aid of "tax effort" every conceivable deviation can be explained. When actual collections exceed taxable capacity by thirty percent it is because the government of that particular country made a tremendous "effort"; if, on the other hand, revenues lag far behind capacity, it is because the government is not trying hard enough. When tax effort is measured and explained by relying exclusively on taxable capacity it cannot say much more than what is already known.

Chelliah, by separating "volitional" from objective determinants, tries to clarify the distinction between capacity and effort. This is how he describes the components of the ability to mobilize resources:

> The ability of the government to collect taxes is determined partly by objective, structural factors, and partly by such "volitional" factors as efficiency in administration and the nature of political leadership. The former taken together with the ability of the population to pay taxes may be said to constitute the total "capacity" factors affecting the tax ratio.[18]

Tax effort, then, refers to the degree of intensity of the government's willingness to tap available resources. Effort is a nonobjective determinant because it can be manipulated by the government. A similar distinction is made by Musgrave who calls attention to the fact that revenues are determined not only by what could be extracted from the economy, but also by the ability of the government to implement its fiscal policies:

> It would be thoroughly unrealistic . . . to determine the optimal tax revenue to GNP ratio by normative considerations only. Allowance must also be made for a country's ability to collect taxes, and hence to meet a desired revenue target . . . A second aspect of performance, therefore, related to the country's ability to overcome the more or less objective difficulties of securing a certain revenue to GNP ratio.[19]

Finally, in a later study, Lotz and Morss proposed a more detailed explanation of the differences between their estimates of taxable capacity and actual revenue ratios; it is essential to quote it in full:

> Political, cultural, and sociological factors and differences in the method of financing important services . . . may help to account for the variations of tax ratios which are not explained by our equations. No doubt, unmeasured — and probably statistically unmeasurable — factors such as the quality of political leadership, government personnel, and administrative organization and procedures are important in accounting for countries' success or failure in overcoming restraints on their taxing capabilities.[20]

Who can say that they are wrong? The problem with these explanations is that they can never be disproved. As they stand they merely suggest certain broad factors that may influence taxation, but they do not tell us when these factors will overpower or succumb to the economic determinants. We still do not know whether effort will increase or decrease with economic development (as capacity does). Will richer countries use a greater or smaller portion of their taxable capacity than poorer nations? Is effort dependent on the structure of political institutions? What kind of structure will produce higher effort? What specific factors in what Lotz and Morss call "administrative organization and procedures" affect effort and in what ways? Are there systematic variations in political aspirations? Is political willingness to tax higher in rich countries and lower in poor nations or vice versa? What are the components of culture that make a difference? Is culture always an important variable, or are there occasions on which its effect is negligible because more powerful factors are present? These are only a few of the questions raised by the use of tax effort as a determinant of government revenue.

Only a few components of effort — quality of political leadership, and administrative efficiency — have been identified and examined. More is left for speculation than has been clarified. According to Chelliah the "quality of the political leadership" affects both the revenue goals that will be set and the likelihood that they will be realized. The willingness to mobilize economic surplus will supposedly be higher when a modernizing liberal elite is in power, than if the government is under the control of a conservative traditional aristocracy.

But, Chelliah quickly points out that we should not expect to observe large increases or decreases in revenue:GNP ratios when a country's ruling elite is changed and replaced by a more or less competent one. In fact, as his own studies exemplify, revenue ratios around the world are fairly stable. Either they do not change at all, or when they do, they hardly ever decrease but usually go up at a very slow rate.[21] These findings are presented in Table 2-3.

TABLE 2-3
Increases in Revenues Are Incremental — Percent Increase in Revenue Ratios in 47 Countries Between 1966-1968 and 1969-1971

per cent increase	No Change	2 points & less	2 to 5 points	5 to 10 points
Number of countries	6	32	8	1

Revenue ratios do not respond immediately to new opportunities because taxation like so many other social processes is complex and hence incremental. To enact a new policy is a lengthy process, and implementation takes even longer.

The leadership's ability to influence revenue aggregates is severely limited by the magnitude of the task. This is especially true in poor countries where the resources needed to launch a new policy or program may not be at hand. Chelliah describes it well:

> Strictly speaking, tax effort is a process; it takes several forms, including reform of existing taxes, improvement in administration, and introduction of new taxes. All these steps . . . require time to plan, legislate, and implement. Countries that for historical or other reasons started out with a low tax ratio a decade ago might have undertaken considerable effort to raise their respective tax rations but may not yet have reached even the average level of taxes in developing countries.[22]

This is how grand political aspirations may end up producing small incremental changes. The quality of the political leadership may be an important factor in understanding why one country is trying a bit harder than another but it is of little help when the scope of the problems it seeks to overcome overwhelms the meager resources available for completing the task.

Perhaps more could be learned about the components and inner workings of the effort factor by looking at the patterns and deviations from common forms of effort behavior. Yet, the problem with cross-country studies based on aggregate data is that they are limited to providing general answers to very general questions. Ask, "does administrative efficiency matter?" and the answer will likely be "yes" or "no" and more frequently a certain combination of the two. To know more it is necessary to study how the taxing process is actually carried out in practice.

An examination of the variations in tax effort reveals two trends: effort varies according to geographic location and wealth. Bahl's data seem to indicate that there is an association between the degree of effort made and the geographic location of the country.[23] As Table 2-4 shows, effort appears to be a more salient determinant in some regions than in others. Countries with low capacity and high effort are usually found in Africa, while countries making a low effort compared to their capacity are usually to be found in South and Central America. There are also regional effects on tax structure and the overall revenue:GNP ratio. In some regions there is a heavier reliance on direct taxes that is usually accompanied by higher revenue rations than those obtained by countries in regions where indirect taxes predominate.

According to Hinrichs, these variations are a consequence of exposure to different tax traditions. Once a tax structure and the means for implementing it have been institutionalized, for better or for worse, they tend to stay. Complex economic and administrative structures and processes can only be changed slowly, because changes are hard to enact and implement. Hinrichs describes this well:

> A tax system style is not some arbitrary set of laws that can be shifted about by legislative fiat . . . Such tax systems are products of the historical interplay of social, political, and economic forces within each country. Tax sys-

> tems not only help to allocate political and economic power, but . . . are themselves a reflection of that allocation.[24]

Since some of these structures are more revenue productive than others, two countries with similar economic conditions will have different revenue ratios. One country may be doing better than another in terms of utilizing its tax potential simply because it inherited, from its colonial government, a more powerful tax structure. Just as the past can explain favorable performance in the present it can also explain why in some areas the effort made to mobilize resources has been consistently low. Institutionalizing a weak structure is a much easier task than replacing it with a stronger one.

Culture, according to Hinrichs, has a stronger effect on revenues at higher levels of income and economic development. At the lower levels of wealth and development the economic constraints are so pervasive that little room is left for cultural preferences. Richer nations can maintain different life styles while the poorer must succumb to the dictates of their meager means. Hinrichs concludes that, "The level of economic development of a low-income country seems to wipe out most differences that one might expect to emanate from a certain tax style."[25]

Another important trend, discovered by Roy Bahl, is that tax effort is

TABLE 2-4
Culture and Historical Experience May Have an Effect on Tax Effort

	High Tax Effort = Actual Revenues > Taxable Capacity	Low Tax Effort = Actual Revenue < Taxable Capacity
Tropical Africa	Ivory Coast; Chad; Senegal; Mali Tanzania; Sudan; Upper Volta	
Asia & the Far East	Ceylon	Singapore
South America	Brazil	Peru, Bolivia, Venezuela
Central America		Trinidad and Tobago; Jamaica Guyana
North Africa and Middle East	Egypt	Iran

SOURCE: Data is taken from Roy W. Bahl, "A Regression Approach to Tax Effort and Tax Ratio Analysis," International Monetary Fund Staff Papers, XVIII, 1971 pp. 570-607.

higher in poorer countries — those with low incomes and low shares of foreign trade and manufacturing in national income. The countries that are making the strongest effort are countries with low or mediocre taxable capacity. This pattern is shown in Table 2-5.

This is a striking finding since it is generally assumed that the political and administrative capability to tax goes hand in hand with the level of economic development. This is why there is no need to study these factors separately. If you know in what stage of development a country is you can predict what its political and administrative capabilities are. A poorer country will make a lower effort because its effort ability is lower — it is weaker, politically and administratively. Recall that effort does not stand simply for aspirations, but is used to account for actual differences in revenue ratios. When a country does not use up its entire taxable capacity it is because it did not try hard enough. According to the tax effort studies, the unlikely happened and the weaker runner has overtaken the stronger one. The turtle's dream has come true, he did win the race with the rabbit. We know that this can happen only in the cartoons, so what can explain the fact that weaker countries have succeeded in making a higher tax effort than stronger ones?

Bahl admits that this was unexpected, but offers no convincing explanation. We may hypothesize, he says, that the poor are trying harder, because they must. According to Bahl:

> Countries in which taxable capacity is relatively low a much greater effort is required to provide a minimal package of public goods. A second explanation is that, in estimating taxable capacity, some important component of the base is not accounted for . . . with the result that taxable capacity is underestimated and therefore tax effort is overstated.[26]

The first explanation does not really answer the question since it takes for granted that the ability to make the effort indeed exists. Bahl addresses the wrong question; the problem is not so much why the poorer countries aspire to have more revenue but how they succeed in overcoming economic constraints of their taxable capacity to obtain it.

The second alternative suggested strikes at one of the principal conceptual flaws of the entire approach. One of the reasons why effort seems to count so heavily, particularly in those instances when it shouldn't, is because too much has been placed on its side of the formula. It has been assumed that the ability to implement is a volitional factor and, therefore, part of the effort. The ability of the administration to implement tax policies is conceived to be a function of how hard the political leadership is trying to make the administration efficient. Musgrave states this clearly: "The quality of the tax service (including administration and enforcement) is of major importance, but it is part of the effort and hence should

TABLE 2-5
Some Who Have Less Try Harder than Those Who Have More

CAPACITY RANKINGS

EFFORT RANKINGS	Low		High	
Low	Nepal	47/49	Bolivia	7/48
	Philippines	26/39	Trinidad & Tobago	3/44
	Thailand	25/27	Jamaica	9/25
	Korea	37/31	Guyana	5/16
	Burundi	48/30	Venezuela	2/26
	Honduras	32/34	Iran	4/28
	Ethiopia	46/35	Peru	11/32
	Paraguay	33/38	Singapore	12/33
	Rwanda	45/40	Mexico	16/45
	Pakistan	40/43		
	Indonesia	37/46		
	Guatemala	28/47		
High	Ivory Coast	36/1	Zaire	8/4
	Brazil	20/2	Tunisia	10/9
	Chad	49/3	Zambia	1/13
	Senegal	23/5	Malaysia	14/14
	Egypt	21/6	Morocco	13/15
	Mali	42/7		
	Ceylon	38/8		
	Tanzania	39/10		
	Sudan	44/11		
	Upper Volta	43/12		

SOURCE: Data is taken from Roy W. Bahl, "A Regression Approach to Tax Effort and Tax Ratio Analysis," International Monetary Fund Staff Papers, Volume XVIII, 1971, p. 596. Figures are comparative ranking scores.

be treated as a dependent variable."[27] Nothing could be more misleading than to assume that it is completely up to the government to determine how efficient its administration will be. The structure and behavior of organizations is heavily influenced by the environment in which they function. No matter how strong the government will is, such constraints as a shortage of trained personnel, reliable statistical data, facilities and budgets, to say nothing of public attitudes that regard taxation as a theft practised by the Treasury and avoiding payment as the right thing to do, will continue to determine the scope of implementation.

Just as the components of taxable capacity are defined and measured for each individual country, we must assess its ability to formulate and implement tax policies. Then, the difference between taxable capability and actual revenue will reflect political preferences concerning the size of the government. Furthermore once this is done, the Lotz and Morss' hypothesis will prove to be valid — taxable capacity will, more or less, equal the actual revenue ratio because demands for spending will drive the government to use up all of its resource potential.

What can be said in conclusion about tax effort? Perhaps the most important finding is the confirmation that such a thing exists. The process of resource mobilization is not governed solely by economic forces. A second important finding is that tax effort is an important, if not the most important, determinant of revenue differences among poor countries. The majority, sixty-five percent to be specific, of poor countries that have been studied are either doing too well or not well enough in terms of their taxable capacity.

The cross-country aggregate studies yield few general indications concerning the components of tax effort. To learn more about it, it is necessary to study how the taxing process works in individual countries. This is the point where we turn to the political and administrative aspects of the taxing process.

If economics provides a clue to how tax policies should be designed and on the economic constraints and opportunities for reaching their goals, political science, sociology, and public administration offer only a handful of scattered ideas about the factors that determine policy formulation and implementation. Research in this area has remained pretty much in the days of "no taxation without representation." A list of the principal scholarly works in the field barely covers a single page.[28] There are no scholars identified with the field and no full blown studies of any specific issue of political or administrative importance. The first study on fiscal sociology, according to Musgrave, has also been the last.[29] Political scientists have shunned taxation completely despite the fact that the leading economists in the field of public finance have repeatedly pointed out that political, social and administrative factors play an important, if not the most important, role in the taxing process. Musgrave describes this conclusion better than most others:

> History testifies to a close interaction between changes in political settings and in tax structure; and standards of tax equity, closely linked with the social philosophy of the time, have always been a major factor in the choice of appropriate tax instruments. The rise of egalitarian philosophy . . . has been the driving force behind the rise of progressive taxation.[30]

In their influential study, *Comparative Politics,* Almond and Powell proposed that we should study what political systems actually do by looking at their capabilities. The "extractive capability" is the most important of government capabilities because it determines the level of performance in all other fields of public activity. "Extractive capability" is defined as

> the range of system performance in drawing material and human resources from the domestic and international environments. The capability to obtain such resources underlies the other capabilities, and limits or expands the possibilities of attaining various goals for the system.[31]

Almond and Powell identify four factors as affecting the extractive capability. They are: the goals and actions of the political elite and the extent to which the elite responds to societal demands and supports; the nature of the economic resources upon which the tax structure is based; the organizational means for implementing policies — well developed bureaucracy based on specialization and secular cultural patterns; and finally, popular support for government activities expressed in the level of voluntary compliance with tax laws.[32]

Cyril Black in his comparative history of modernization identifies essentially similar factors. He begins by saying that the state cannot accomplish its mobilization goals unless its actions are acceptable to the citizenry. As he puts it, "The state cannot fulfill its functions in regard to taxation . . . and a myriad of other matters unless the citizenry understands and in a considerable measure accepts its role."[33] This acceptance of the need to pay taxes in order to finance government activities is dependent, according to Schumpeter,[34] on the existence of a sense of "national exigency" — separation between the ruler's private affairs and his public function and the existence of a public sphere of action where common interests are expressed. When people see themselves as members of a community and not a state they will not willingly support the state financially. The concepts of general tax liability and a legally controlled distribution based on some form of majority decision are strongly dependent on the acceptance of the principle of common public interests. When a "common exigency" does not exist, only those who directly undertake to pay taxes are committed "while he who had mounted his horse before the concession and had ridden off did not have to pay."[35] Schumpeter's historical analysis is corroborated by Hirschman's study of Latin American countries. Hirschman found that tax measures did not receive public support when people were not convinced that the money was being used for the public good: "The tax can hardly be expected to muster political support unless the public is aware of and sympathetic to the uses to which the money is going to be put."

Greater mobilization of resources, continues Black, is dependent on the increased authority of the state. The reason why traditional societies mobilize only a small portion of their national resources is the weakness of their political institutions. The government is limited to a small number of functions that affect only a very small percentage of the entire population. According to Black:

> The authority of the state has in the past not normally reached down to every citizen. It has tended to be limited to defense against foreign attacks, the preservation of law and order at home, the maintenance of essential public works, and collection of sufficient taxes to perform these functions.[36]

Government laws and regulations enacted in the capital city do not elicit the behavior at which they are directed because they carry little or no authority among people living in the countryside.

In his study of Indonesian economic development Douglas Paauw found that central government authority does not reach far beyond the capital city, as he writes: "Central government administration in Indonesia tends to be primarily an urban phenomenon, radiating out from the capital, Djakarta, with ever decreasing scope and effectiveness."[37]

The problems of authority and legitimacy are compounded by problems in implementation. The main conclusion emerging from the large literature on development administration is that policies are not effectively implemented because public organizations are insufficiently rational or bureaucratic in Weber's terms.[38] They are insufficiently rational because the society in which they operate is not organized around the values of rationality, and it is not possible to maintain a rational bureaucracy in a traditional environment.[39] There is no need to add yet another review of this literature to the many that already exist.[40] This literature has been chewed dry. The relevant finding to note is that there are problems in carrying out policies that are caused by the structure of public organizations and that this structure is a result of the traditional values. In other words, the economy may develop while the level of organizational performance will lag behind. A Liberian senior Treasury official gave an example taken from personal experience:

> My friends will be insulted if I will uncompromisingly enforce the tax laws on them . . . You see, we are a small country. Everyone knows everyone else. Everyone is related to everyone else either by blood or by friendship ties. So there is a strong reluctance on the part of tax officials to impose hardships on the people they know . . . If I were to go too far in collecting tax from, say, a cousin of mine, I will probably get a phone call from my father who will say something like this: "There is a misunderstanding, you may not have known that X is family, but now that you known, you will not impose this hardship on him."

Riggs is among the few authors who tried to link the abstract hypotheses about the interrelations between bureaucracy and social structure to actual government processes such as budgeting and taxation. Riggs believes[41] that the economy in poor countries could sustain a higher level of taxation; the reason why public revenues are frequently insufficient is the administration's inability to enforce the tax laws on taxpayers who do not feel that they should pay to run the government. Those with the largest pockets buy or threaten their way out of the tax net. What makes this possible is the weakness of the tax collector compared to the power of the traditional elites. The rational values of bureaucracy are still inferior to the traditional basis of the society where a person's social status endows him with certain privileges, one of which is not paying taxes.[42] Hirschman[43] and Hansen[44] reached similar conclusions. The problem of taxation in the poor countries as described in their studies grows out of the conflict between those who press for increased spending and those called upon to pick up the bill. The lines between the majority which is very poor and a small minority which is very rich are too sharply drawn to permit a simple workable solution of the conflict. Comparative empirical studies of how the taxing process works in a certain nation are not available.

We are, however, saved by the historians. There are few major studies of any period of human history that do not discuss the problems of taxation. Historical studies are valuable not only because they are just about the only descriptions we have of how the taxing process actually works; but perhaps even more importantly, they provide us with insights on the conditions that facilitate or make it hard for governments to rely on taxes as means for resource mobilization. The advantages that rich countries have over the poor in every field of public activity are so overwhelming that it is difficult to isolate those that are critical for taxation. History permits us to look at today's rich countries, when they were poor, when their governments were weak and small. It enables us to watch how they struggled with rapidly rising public expenditures at a time when the means for mobilizing resources were barely functioning.

Since a systematically organized history of world taxation does not exist, it has not been possible to draw conclusions as to how different governments behaved under a large variety of circumstances. Instead, a short period in modern history when the main issues of taxation resembled the problems of resource mobilization in today's poor countries has been concentrated upon. This period extends from the end of the sixteenth century to the beginning of the eighteenth. The most interesting and best documented (in the English language) developments occurred in England and France. The main issue was how to meet increasing needs for spending out of a small, fixed and rapidly dwindling purse. Imperialism and international commerce created new tasks that only governments could shoulder. These tasks had one thing in common. They were vastly more expensive than anything that governments did before, and they necessitated long range and stable financing. This was a century when there was much that could be done, many new opportunities that could be exploited and political leaders with desires to make the best of everything. But, ambitions, dreams and good intentions were not enough. To make things work, money in great quantities that would flow into the government coffers in a regular and certain way was needed. The operations that had to be financed were not in the style of hit and run, short range projects that characterized government activities in the past and could be provided for out of the king's private purse. Building and sending a large fleet to sea, just like building roads and instituting national social programs, requires assurance, at the beginning of the project, that funds to run it will be available in the required quantities at the appropriate times right down till the end.

This is the difference between modern and traditional finance. Traditional finance was operated on an ad hoc basis out of a small and highly rigid source of revenue. When unusual expenses were anticipated special measures were designed to meet them. The nobility was asked to make contributions, the very poor were conscripted into forced labor and others were simply forced to surrender a certain portion of their income or property. Neither of these methods became institutionalized, neither became a routine that outlived a specific purpose for which it was initiated.[45]

These methods had to be used very economically. It is easy to raid people's pockets once in a while but it is dangerous to do it frequently and systematically unless they give their consent. Force can be met by force; when the government relies on force alone to obtain its revenues the citizenry is likely to use force to protect itself against such actions. Modern finance is based on routinization, the amounts that were collected yesterday will be collected today and tomorrow. The only difference is that more will have to be raised next year.

Poor countries today are confronted by problems resembling those which preoccupied seventeenth century Europe. Government operations during the colonial period were limited to a few basic tasks, such as maintaining law and order and preserving existing forms of social organization. Though most of the required revenues were raised through taxation, coverage was limited and amounts meager.[46] When local revenues fell short of spending, the colonial government was called upon to fill in the gap. This is equally true, even for those countries that were not colonized, such as Thailand, Nepal and Ethiopia. These were ruled, and some still are, by traditional elites that kept government as small as they possibly could so as not to disturb the old way of life from which their power was drawn.

The period of decolonization was followed by a great surge of developmental efforts. Few of the new leaders that assumed control were prepared to limit government as not to disturb the old way of life from which their power was drawn.

The period of decolonization was followed by a great surge of developmental efforts. Few of the new leaders that assumed control were prepared to limit government ken. In spite of this, most of these countries are still a long distance away from the basic aspirations of the early independence period.

These great aspirations were faced with a revenue structure that couldn't fulfill all the needs of the old regime and now there was no one to call upon to bridge the gap. Foreign aid and loans are handy but they have never been given in sufficiently large quantities under favorable conditions to solve national revenue problems. Quite a few countries have learned that nothing comes free and that the strings attached to foreign aid may, in the long run, prove to be politically unbearable. There are few convenient alternatives to the mobilization of resources from the domestic economy. In fact, international aid organizations require evidence showing that the country is trying as hard as it possibly can to rely on its own resources, prior to granting loans.[47] The experience accumulated during the last two decades shows that no country can expect to be saved by foreign aid if its revenue system collapses.

What are the problems confronting a government that needs to substantially increase its revenue to meet rising expenses? What may hamper or facilitate its progress? Today's rich nations devote more than thirty percent of their gross national product to public spending. Why is it that the governments of poor nations must make do with less than half of that amount?

The Extractive Capability — A Historical Perspective

"He who knows how to listen to its [fiscal history] message . . . discerns the thunder of world history more clearly than anywhere else."[48]

Though taxes in various forms and shapes have been with us from the early beginnings of social life, they were not imposed or collected regularly. The ruler was expected to live off his own, i.e., from the revenues he derived from his own property or from his feudal dues. Only in cases of dire emergency such as war was he entitled to demand that his subject contribute to his finances by paying taxes, and even then only on an *ad hoc* basis.[49]

Government was a personal affair of the monarch as were his finances. The idea that the government must provide services in the public interest and that the citizenry should finance these services by paying taxes did not exist in Europe prior to the sixteenth century. As Martin Wolfe put it: "The belief that the state should, and must contrive to make its subjects wealthier, and that in part this can be done through its taxing powers, certainly is one of the most powerful concepts in modern times."[50]

As long as the state engaged in a limited number of activities, the traditional system of finance operated in a rather satisfactory way; however, problems arose the moment these activities began to expand in scope and variety.

> The increasing activities of the modern state demand additional expenditures and at the same time the rise of prices was reducing the effectiveness of the fixed income for defraying the necessary disbursements.[51]

Instantly the king's revenues became inadequate since they were fixed and had no built-in flexibility. The royal domains and their feudal dues produced a revenue which could not be increased to adjust to changing needs. The process of inflation caused by the expansion of world trade and the constant influx of gold from the Americas further reduced the value of these fixed revenues.

Schumpeter describes the monarch's dilemma:

> The Prince did what he could: he got into debt. When he could borrow no more, he turned begging to the estates. He acknowledged that he had no right to demand, declared that accession to his plea was not to prejudice the rights of the estates, promised never again to beg.[52]

All this was to no avail. In England the King did not succeed in imposing new taxes for well over a century. The bureaucracy failed to collect effectively and the citizenry strongly refused to pay. The result is described by Mariott:

> Money came in very slowly, the city refused to lend money even on the security of the crown's jewels, some counties excused themselves on the plea of poverty, others refused to contribute except through the constitutional channel of parliament.[53]

The situation was made worse by the fact that almost no one was willing to lend money to the crown, thus closing off the last resort by which the state could have been financed. Loaning money to the government was considered a very risky investment, because there was no real assurance that the principal would be refunded or that interest would be paid. The only security that creditors had was the king's word and this was something which, at that time, no one took very seriously.

England, at least up to the eighteenth century, "was a land of local government, local armaments, local feeling . . . bureaucrats and soldiers were almost unknown."[54] The King ruled in London but his word did not reach beyond fifty miles of the city. The roads connecting London with the various parts of the country were in poor condition and during the winter they were virtually impassable by anything but pack horses. Even during the short dry season, travel was very slow and hazardous. Feelings of identity with the polity, with the central government were very low and local interests almost always took precedence over national interests. The local units viewed the affairs of the government as the private affairs of the king. Hence, they thought it proper that he should finance them with his own monies. The royal tax collectors sent from London to the countryside were regarded as foreigners and trespassers and were often driven away by force. Even when taxes were legally imposed, numerous counties refused to pay them.

The seventeenth century was an era of conflict. There was hardly an issue — political, social, or religious — on which agreement could be reached. Most notable was the conflict between parliament and the royal house which reached a climax in the beheading of Charles I and the civil wars. The legitimacy of Cromwell's protectorate established after the civil wars was never fully accepted. Upon his death the Stuarts were recalled only to be thrown out again at the Glorious Revolution.

Taxation became a major battle ground in the fight over political supremacy. Parliament recognized that the only hope for expanding its power rested in preventing the king from acquiring the revenues he needed. By keeping him short of supply parliament ensured that it would not be ignored when spending decisions were made. Power concessions were demanded in exchange for authorization to impose taxes. The Stuarts, as well as Cromwell, refused to make such concessions and hence their requests for higher taxes were repeatedly turned down. They retaliated by dismissing parliament and tried to rule without it. They found out, to their dismay, that the people refused to pay, arguing that the taxes imposed were illegal.

Extraction by force was the only alternative left, yet, despite much talk about the power of power, no one was quick to adopt coercion as a systematic means for revenue mobilization. At the end of the civil wars

Oliver Cromwell had at his command the largest standing army that England had known until that time. Though his budgetary problems were so grave that at times he could not pay or feed the army, whose support he needed to stay in power, he never used it to enforce his tax laws. Cromwell was not averse to using force, but in the case of taxation he was convinced that such action would not be accepted as legitimate and would lead to his overthrow. The local communities had enough power to fight back and just as they fought for the Puritans they would rise against Cromwell if he gave them sufficient cause.

Since the army could not be used and a central bureaucracy that would implement policies simply did not exist, the King was forced to rely on the administrative apparatus of the local communities. The local administrations, however, did not jump to the task. They valued their own interests more than the King's, and anything done for the central government was subjected to this constraint. Policies were carried out only to the degree that they did not conflict with local interests. The assessment and collection of taxes was performed with minimal effort and intensity — administrators thought it more important to spare their neighbors than to enrich the King who sat in London and hollered, but was not heard.

Throughout the seventeenth century, despite intensive efforts, revenues from taxation hardly increased at all. When Cromwell died there was not enough money in the Exchequer to pay the costs of his funeral and his son had to ask for a loan from the French government.

The situation changed after the Glorious Revolution which settled the conflict between parliament and the royal house. The new system of government, in which parliamentary supremacy was firmly established, enjoyed broad consensus. Feelings of trust in the central government were regained. Government was no longer a private affair of the King, and neither were its finances. The personal expenses of the royal house were separated from the general expenditures of the government. The King was allowed to maintain full control over his own finances but he was no longer the master of the public expenditures. On these terms parliament was prepared to assume responsibility for providing the resources for government activities.

Resolving the political conflicts did not close the issue, policies that could now be legally enacted had still to be implemented before the desired revenues would show up in the Treasury accounts. Tax policies do not implement themselves. They must be implemented by a bureaucracy with proper tools to assemble and assess information, pursue taxpayers and force them to pay. Until a central bureaucracy was developed, the king was dependent on the local communities who were either unwilling or incapable of changing centuries old traditions of noncompliance.

Revenues remained as low and inflexible as they were before. To keep the government running and to finance the development of new institutions the King started borrowing. This could now be done since it was possible to offer taxes already authorized by Parliament as security for loans. Although the King could not immediately obtain the revenue from his taxes he could mortgage them, thus creating a powerful source of long-term credit upon which the government could draw. The public accumulated capital as a result of the industrial revolution and the expansion of trade and was prepared to invest it in government bonds for profit.

The end result of these changes was that "the King of England was able to mobilize a greater proportion of his resources for war than could any of those great monarchs (the French, Spanish and American)."[55] A glimpse into the level of revenues and the public debt during the seventeenth to eighteenth centuries would give us an idea of the magnitude of these changes.[56]

	Revenues	Public Debts
Charles II	1,517,247	increase to 664,263
William III	2,001,855	increase to 15,730,439
George I	5,691,803	increase to 52,092,235
George III	15,572,971	increase to 246,222,392 (at the end of the American War)

Having overcome the problem of resource mobilization, the British could now concentrate on improving and expanding their central bureaucracy.

The old regime in France enjoyed an abundance of taxes and mobilized twice as much revenue as the English monarchs prior to the Glorious Revolution. Still, the old regime was perpetually in financial distress. This raises two questions. First, how was it possible that while the British monarch had almost no tax revenues at his disposal his French counterpart enjoyed such a largesse? Second, given this abundance of taxes why was it that the regime could not make ends meet?

The first question first. Bendix summarizes Tocqueville's analysis of the *ancien regime* in a manner germane to the present discussion: "The *ancien regime* has destroyed the century old pattern of political life by concentrating power in the hands of the king and his officials and by depriving the various autonomous jurisdictions of their judicial and administrative functions."[57] The old regime eliminated the problem of local autonomy by plucking the aristocracy from the countryside and placing it at court. The aristocrats had neither the power nor incentive to obstruct efforts to levy and collect taxes because they were removed from their estates, made financially dependent on the king, and exempt from taxation themselves.

The king was free to increase the burden of taxation since his authority was unchallenged. Taxes were collected by tax farmers who performed this task with great efficiency since they worked for their own profit. Since local units had no real power of their own and could not prevent the tax farmers from extracting every penny that was owed, taxpayers did not enjoy the relative safety which was the lot of their British counterparts, although tax avoidance was not unknown.

Though the revenue raised was large, it never seemed to suffice. The king, in buying the support of the aristocracy mortgaged most of his revenue. The lavish court and the need to pay for the maintenance of a nonproductive aristocracy consumed most of the tax revenues. In addition, the king had no budget, no central record of revenues and expenditures and no bureaucracy to perform these functions. Whenever he needed money he either drew on one of the innumerable tax funds or borrowed from the tax farmers by mortgaging future tax revenues. Bosher's description is well worth quoting:

> The Controller General of Finance . . . managed no money . . . but endeavored to meet all the Crown's commitments by assigning payments to the various *caisses* of the accountants tax farms and other agencies. He could exercise no budgetary control over the whole revenue and expenditure because there was no central consolidated revenue fund. The Minister never knew on any particular day, or even in any particular year, exactly how much revenue there was to spend. Much less did he follow the budgetary procedure of planning expenditures for each year, and then finding the ways and means to carry out the plan. Finally, the debt did not in fact accumulate in the form of annual deficits . . . The debt merely trickled into the system as did the revenues, half-known, eternal like poverty itself, posing only such problems as governments and nations choose to see in it.[58]

According to Bosher, the public revenues and expenditures were managed by a curious combination of private business and political power. Personal profit, rather than public interest, was the major driving force. The result was that a substantial part of tax revenues was siphoned into private pockets. The fact that the king could extract a large revenue from his subjects was not very meaningful, since not all of this revenue was his to spend. Though this situation was resented by virtually everyone except those who profited by it, there was nothing that the king or his ministers could do about it. The class of rentiers and tax farmers became so embedded in the country's social structure that the crown lost much of its power over the nation's finances.[59]

The French Revolution swept away the social structure wrought by the absolutist monarchy, but it was too dramatic and occurred at a time when the cleavages in the society were deep and complex, to succeed in establishing a new social order with political institutions society could agree upon.

As consensus on the political modes of conflict resolution could not be found, the energy created by the revolution was directed at developing a rational and efficient bureaucracy.[60] More than anything, the revolutionaries aspired to put an end to the rule of private interest in the nation's finances. Thus, in lieu of the aristocratic system of the *ancien regime,* which was based on a personal position in a social hierarchy, the revolution instituted "a bureaucracy with an administrative hierarchy in which the organization of public functions took precedence over the claims of individual officials."[61]

The revolution, by doing away with the aristocracy, eliminated one source of drain on the revenue, and the establishment of the bureaucracy eliminated the other. The already large revenues could now be better utilized by the central government. The force of the French system of finance may be seen in the fact that France fought single-handed against most of the nations of Europe for more than twenty years.

Conclusion

Attempts to identify the determinants of government revenue through statistical analysis of aggregate economic variables yielded few definite results. Economic factors, such as national wealth and the internal structure of the economy, have been found to set the broad limits and opportunities for resource mobilization; however, there are substantial variations that are unexplainable within the framework of the economic theories. The findings indicate that the factors responsible for these variations are in the area of politics — the ability to formulate, administer, and effectively implement tax policies.

Studies on the taxable capacity of poor countries show that the main constraints imposed by the economy on the revenue raising capability are low incomes, the large size of the agricultural and the nonmonetized sector of the economy. The opportunities for taxation are in the area of foreign trade and the large trading and manufacturing companies. Economic development is the main mechanism leading to increases in the revenue ratio. Economic growth not only increases personal wealth, it also changes the internal structure of the economy from forms of production that are hard to tax — agriculture and cottage industries — to ones that can be more easily reached — trade and manufacturing carried out by large companies. It was found, nevertheless, that there are significant deviations. Practice does not completely support the capacity theory predicted on the assumption that economic factors set both ceiling and floor to revenues. Even the most powerful formulas produced results showing that there is a substantial number of countries where revenues are far in excess of capacity. What was assumed to be an effective limit did not prove to be such. The second important assumption stated that though capacity refers merely to a potential, actual revenues will either equal or come very near it. The potential will be completely used up as a result of the strong pressures for spending exerted from all sides on the governments of poor nations. Here again, as before, we find a substantial number of countries that do not go along. Revenue ratios below taxable capacity are not a rare phenomenon.

The attempt to rescue the theory by adding "tax effort" as a noneconomic determinant traveled little distance. Tax effort has been turned into a surrogate for "everything else" outside the economy that may affect revenues. It stands for the extent to which the government is willing, and able, to tap its potential. But, though the difference between taxable capacity and actual revenues attributed to tax effort is elaborately measured for a large number of poor countries, no more is told about it other than the fact that it exists. One can only guess what tax effort is composed of and why it is so high in one country and low in another.

The experts in the field would agree with Chelliah that:

> All evidence points to the conclusion that limits to the government's ability to mobilize a larger share of national income for the public sector, are set by administrative and political barriers rather than by the economy's taxable capacity.[62]

A recent study by M. M. Best confirms this proposition. Best's hypothesis was that the tax structure and the size of the revenue are both a reflection of political choice which in turn is primarily affected by power considerations. He estimated the preference ordering of different groups in the society regarding types of taxes and compared them with the actual tax structures in Latin American countries. He found that "the actual composition of taxes is in fact nearly the same as the hypothetical preference ordering for only one group — the large landowners."[63] According to Best the reason for this similarity is the ability of economic elites, in Latin American countries, to overwhelm the influence of other groups and to obtain the tax policies which suit them best. He concludes that "the major obstacle to expanded tax efforts in Central America is the distribution of power."[64]

What are the political and administrative components of the ability to mobilize resources? Historical experience indicates that it is necessary to distinguish between policy and implementation factors. The ability to design good policies does not necessarily go hand in hand with the ability to implement them. The conditions and requirements for success in each of these two fields are different. The making of policies requires strong political institutions whose authority is widely accepted as legitimate. The task of these institutions is to resolve the conflicts between those who consume most of the government's services, and those who must shoulder the bulk of the cost of providing them. The ability to find workable compromises depends on the structure of the society. The less differentiated in terms of economic and political power a society is, the more acute the conflicts become (because the distinction between those who get more than they pay and those who pay for much more than what they get back from the state is drawn sharper), the harder it will be to reach agreement on policies that would lead to large revenues.

Reaching agreement on policy does not safeguard its effective implementation. Implementation is not a simple extension of policy; it is an entirely independent task with completely different requirements. The components of effective implementation which emerge from the analysis of historical experience are compliance and central bureaucracy. No policy stands much chance when evasion goes beyond a certain minimal scale. When the majority is not prepared to obey government laws there isn't much that can be done to extract resources except using force. But force can be met by force. A government that relies systematically on force to collect its taxes against the will of its citizens is likely to encounter sooner or later an effective opposition.

The second requirement is a central bureaucracy with the means to enforce policies and the know-how to use them. When the means of enforcement are under the control of local authorities they are likely to be sparsely used. Local interests claim first priority and no one will rush to squeeze local pockets in order to fill central government's coffers.

Too little is known about how the organizational means for implementing policies work. What are the required resources and conditions for effective implementation? What are the administrative constraints and opportunities, apart from those created by the organizational environment? External constraints may be mitigated or reinforced by internal administrative ones. The fact that few report their true income is likely to be made worse if the bureaucracy is unable to design and carry out a program that would help to identify evaders and unveil evasion. To understand how the mobilization of resources is affected by the characteristics of the organizations implementing tax policies, it is necessary to go beyond the literature. The chapters that follow describe the process of implementation — how the various tasks leading to the collection of taxes are carried out — and how it affects the attainment of policy goals.

Notes

1. Examples of this normative literature are: Ursula K. Hicks, *Development Finance Planning and Control* (Oxford: Clarendon Press, 1965); Nicholas Kaldor, *Essays on Economic Policy* (London: Duckworth, 1964); see also his *An Expenditure Tax* (London: Allen and Unwin, 1955). See the collec-

tion of articles in David Krivine (ed.), *Fiscal and Monetary Problems in Developing States: Proceedings of the Third Rehovoth Conference* (New York: Praeger, 1967). John F. Due, "Policy for Financing Economic Development," *United Nations Planning Domestic and External Resources for Investment* (New York: , 1967), pp. 33-40.

2. Raja J. Chelliah, "Trends in Taxation in Developing Countries," *International Monetary Fund Staff Papers* XVIII, (1971), p. 266.
3. Other factors include mineral resources and oil.
4. On the administrative difficulties involved in taxing agricultural income see: Walter W. Heller, "Survey of Agricultural Taxation and Economic Development" in Haskel Wald (ed.), *Conference on Agricultural Taxation.*
5. Paul A. Baran, *The Political Economy of Growth* (New York: Modern Reader, 1968), p. 267.
6. W. Arthur Lewis, *Development Planning* (London: George Allen and Unwin, 1966), p. 21. An empirical study confirming this argument is Harley Hinrichs' "Determinants of Government Revenue Shares among Less Developed Countries," *Economic Journal* 75, (September 1965).
7. Richard A. Musgrave, *Fiscal Systems* (New Haven: Yale University Press, 1969), pp. 126-27.
8. Ibid., p. 131.
9. Harley Hinrichs, *A General Theory of Tax Structure Change during Economic Development* (Cambridge: Harvard University Press, 1966), p. 7.
10. Chelliah, p. 280.
11. The seminal work was written by Jeffrey G. Williamson, "Public Expenditure and Revenue: An International Comparison," *The Manchester School of Economic and Social Studies* XXIX, (1961), pp. 43-56.
12. Harley H. Hinrichs, "Determinants of Government Revenue Shares among Less Developed Countries," *Economic Journal* 75 (September 1965). Hinrichs' findings were later confirmed in Chelliah's and Musgrave's studies.
13. Musgrave, *Fiscal Systems,* p. 119.
14. Roy W. Bahl, "A Regression Approach to Tax Effort and Tax Ratio Analysis," *International Monetary Fund Staff Papers* VXIII, (1971), p. 605.
15. Richard Thorn, "The Development of Public Finance during Economic Development," *Manchester School of Economic and Social Studies* 35, (January 1967).
16. J. R. Lotz and E. R. Morss, "A Theory of Tax Level Determinants for Developing Countries," *Economic Development and Cultural Change* 18, (April 1970), p. 229.
17. Jorgen R. Lotz and Elliot R. Morss, "Measuring 'Tax Effort' in Developing Countries," *International Monetary Fund Staff Papers* XIV, (1967), p. 478. A similar approach is taken by Roy Bahl in his "A Regression Approach to Tax Effort and Tax Ratio Analysis," pp. 571-75.
18. Chelliah, "Trends in Taxation . . .", p. 293.
19. Musgrave, *Fiscal Systems,* p. 101.
20. Lotz and Morss, "A Theory of Tax Level Determinants for Developing Countries," p. 338.
21. Raja J. Chelliah et al., "Tax Ratios and Tax Effort in Developing Countries, 1969-71," *International Monetary Fund Staff Papers* XXII, 1, (March 1975), pp. 187-205.
22. Chelliah, "Trends in Taxation . . .", p. 301.
23. Bahl, "A Regression Approach . . .", pp. 600-04.

24. Hinrichs, *A General Theory of Tax Structure Change during Economic Development*, p. 63.
25. Ibid, p. 64.
26. Bahl, "A Regression Approach . . .", p. 597.
27. Musgrave, *Fiscal Systems*, p. 162.
28. Arnold J. Melstner, *The Politics of City Revenue* (Berkeley: University of California Press, 1971); Oliver Oldman, "Controlling Income Tax Evasion," in *Problems of Tax Administration in Latin America* (Baltimore: The Johns Hopkins Press, 1965); Stanley S. Surrey, "Tax Administration in Underdeveloped Countries," University of Miami *Law Review* 12, (Winter 1958), pp. 158-88.
29. Musgrave, *Fiscal Systems*, p. 134. The reference is to Goldscheid's "A Sociological Approach to Problems of Public Finance," in Musgrave and Peacock, *Classics in the Theory of Public Finance.*
30. Musgrave, *Fiscal Systems*, p. 132.
31. Gabriel Almond and Bingham Powell, *Comparative Politics: A Developmental Approach* (Boston: Little, Brown, 1965), p. 195.
32. Ibid., pp. 205-07.
33. Cyril E. Black, *The Dynamics of Modernization: A Study in Comparative History* (New York: Harper and Row, 1966), p. 15.
34. Joseph A. Schumpeter, "The Crisis of the Tax State," *International Economic Papers*, (New York: MacMillan, 1954), p. 7.
35. Ibid., p. 15.
36. Black, p. 13.
37. Douglas S. Paauw, *Financing Economic Development — The Indonesian Case* (Boston: Free Press MIT, 1960), p. 197.
38. Joseph La Palombara, "An Overview of Bureaucracy and Political Development," in *Bureaucracy and Political Development*, Joseph La Palombara (ed.), (Princeton: Princeton University Press, 1967).
39. Martin Landau, "Linkage, Coding and Intermediacy: A Strategy for Institution Building," *Journal of Comparative Administration* II, 4, (February 1971).
40. The most recent addition is: William J. Siffin, "Two Decades of Public Administration in Developing Countries," *Public Administration Review* XXXVI, 1, (Jan.-Feb. 1976).
41. Fred W. Riggs, *Administration in Developing Countries* (Boston: Houghton Mifflin, 1964).
42. Fred W. Riggs, "Bureaucrats and Political Development: A Paradoxical View," in *Bureaucracy and Political Development*, Joseph La Palombara (ed.), (Princeton: Princeton University Press, 1969), pp. 147-51.
43. Albert O. Hirschman, *Journeys toward Progress: Studies of Economic Policy-Making in Latin America* (New York: Twentieth Century Fund, 1963), p. 137; see also, F. J. Herschel in Joint Tax Program, *Fiscal Policy for Economic Growth in Latin America*, (Baltimore: The Johns Hopkins Press, 1965), p. 91.
44. A. H. Hansen, *Public Enterprise and Economic Development* (London: Routledge & Kegan Paul, 1959), p. 8.
45. This is the main thesis of William Kennedy's original study, *English Taxation 1640-1877* (London: G. Bell, 1913).
46. See Milton Esman, "The Politics of Development Administration," *Approaches to Development: Politics, Administration and Change*, J. D.

Montgomery and William J. Siffin (eds.) (New York: McGraw-Hill, 1966), pp. 59-112.
47. See Roy Bahl, "A Regression Approach. . . ", pp. 573-75.
48. Joseph A. Schumpeter, "The Crisis of the Tax State," *International Economic Papers* (New York: MacMillan, 1954), p. 7.
49. Robert T. Holt and John E. Turner, *The Political Basis of Economic Development* (Princeton: Van Norstrand, 1966), p. 148ff.
50. Martin Wolfe, "French Views on Wealth and Taxes from the Middle Ages to the Old Regime," *Journal of Economic History* XXVI, (1966), p. 466.
51. W. D. Scroggs, "English Finance under the Long Parliament," *Quarterly Journal of Economics* XXI, (1907), p. 463.
52. Schumpeter, p. 14.
53. John A. R. Mariott, *The Crisis of English Liberty: A History of the Stuart Monarchy and the Puritan Revolution* (Oxford: Clarendon, 1930), p. 75.
54. George M. Trevelyan, *England under the Stuarts* (New York: Barnes, 1915), p. 67.
55. *The New Cambridge Modern History,* VII, p. 152.
56. John Sinclair, *The History of the Public Revenue of the British Empire* (London: Strahan, 1790), pp. 1-2; 93.
57. Reinhard Bendix, *Nation Building and Citizenship* (New York: Anchor, 1969), p. 57.
58. J. F. Bosher, *French Finances 1770-1795; From Business to Bureaucracy* (Cambridge: University Press, 1970), p. 304.
59. Ibid., p. 305.
60. Hoffman, "Paradoxes of the French Political Community," in Hoffman (ed.), *In Search of France* (Cambridge: University Press, 1963), p. 12.
61. Bosher, p. 311.
62. Chelliah, "Trends in Taxation." This view is supported by overwhelming evidence reported in numerous world bank and UN studies, for example: International Bank for Reconstruction and Development, *A Public Development Program for Thailand* (Baltimore: The Johns Hopkins Press, 1959), p. 245ff; A. M. Abdel Rahman, "Tax Policy Issues in African Countries," Notes for Discussion, Training Course on Tax Policy, Legislation, and Administration, U.N. Economic Commission for Africa, (Addis Ababa, Ethiopia, October, 1973).
63. Michael M. Best, "Political Power and Tax Revenues in Central America," *Journal of Development Economics* 3, (1976), p. 71.
64. Ibid., p. 74.

Chapter Three

How the Elements of the Taxing Process Affect the Size of the Revenue

It is a truism to say that a tax system is no better than its application, however modern and sophisticated it may look on paper.

Raja J. Chelliah, "Tax Potential and Economic Growth in the Countries of the ECAFE Religion," p. 44.[1]

One of the problems constantly faced in these [poor] countries is whether to concentrate on effective administration of relatively crude or primitive tax forms, or run the risk of falling short in trying to administer more refined measures.

Walter W. Heller, "Survey of Agricultural Taxation and Economic Development."

The Taxing Process: Making and Implementing Policies

What part do noneconomic factors play in the taxing process? How do the institutions that participate in the process affect its outputs — the amount of revenue collected? How are tax policies made? What determines how much policy makers will ask for? Is policy the only determinant of outputs? Can we tell by looking at the policies adopted at the beginning of the year what the revenues will be at its end? Can the policy maker be certain that he will get everything or just about all of what he is asking for? The answer is that policy, until it is implemented, is no more than a plan, a statement of intentions.

The amount of revenue obtained through taxation is a function of policy (how much is asked for, in what form, and from whom) and by implementation (ability to ensure that what is being asked for will be handed over). Policy is determined by political values (what portion of national income should be taken by the government, by wealth, how much is available for asking, and by political structure), how much it is feasible to demand. A richer country will usually have more revenue than a poorer one because it can ask more of its citizens and in a greater number of areas. The rich not only can afford to pay higher rates on any given tax, they can also be taxed on a larger number of items.

Rich societies have the ability to formulate tax policies that impose a heavy tax burden on anyone who can afford to pay, because their social and political structure is plural. No one single group controls enough power to effectively prevent the state from taxing it. There may be variations in levels of progressivity and it is not uncommon to find that the incidence of some taxes is biased in favor of richer taxpayers, but the principle that all groups are heavily, as opposed to symbolically, taxed does hold. The big American corporations may not pay as much tax as some people would like them to, but there is no denying that they are making substantial contributions to the treasury. This is something that cannot be said for their counterparts in poor countries.

In a poor nation, the majority of the population is too poor to afford to give up anything. Ten percent taken from a subsistence income may tilt the delicate balance of survival in favor of hunger. In a poor country there are fewer items that can be meaningfully taxed so that a substantial amount of revenue will be produced. Political feasibility is limited by the dominance of a small number of business interests. It is difficult to impose a heavy burden on the poor because they have little to give up; it is even harder to impose it on the rich because they are the most politically influential.

If formulating strong tax policies is a hard task, implementing them is even more demanding. Writing high tax rates into the law is easier than actually collecting them. The best designed policy is not worth much unless it is implemented and the revenue aspired to is realized. Noble aspirations unaccompanied by an equally potent ability to implement can never be more than what they are.

Scope of implementation (the extent to which a policy is carried out) is a function of the relation between the magnitude of the task — level of compliance, simplicity and stability in policy — and the resources available to carry out policy — personnel, expertise and information. There will be less implementation when the task is difficult — policy is complex or unstable — and the resources for administering it meager.

From this general framework of the components of the taxing process that affect performance and outputs a closer look will be taken at the elements that determine policy and implementation in the poor countries.

Elements Affecting the Formation of Tax Policy

At the beginning of every financial year those responsible for the revenue side of the budget face the same dilemma: more money must be raised from an unwieldly environment that has already succeeded in convincing everyone who tried that last year's revenue was the limit. After all efforts have been made to curb and cut next year's expenses they invariably turn out to be greater than last year's revenues. Besides uncontrollable increases brought about by inflation and population growth, there are always new programs and activities that the government wants to undertake. The spending ministers in the cabinet are ever asking for additional funds and it is not possible to reject all of their demands all of the time. The government does want to stay in power, hence it must spend. But, every time an approval is given to a new commitment the cash register rings and the minister of finance loads another burden on his tools for mobilizing revenue.

Elsewhere, in certain rich countries, revenues grow faster than national wealth thereby enabling the government to undertake new activities and improvements in existing programs without much tinkering with the tax policies. In poor countries revenues are not that elastic; they usually catch up with the growth in GNP but their share in the GNP remains almost unchanged. This means that if the government undertakes, as it normally does, to do just a tiny bit more than it did last year, some action will have to be taken to bridge over the gap between expected revenues and planned expenditures.

If demands for spending and government assistance (subsidies, investment loans) are pouring in from all conceivable corners of society, prospective candidates for taxation are not at all obvious. No one offers to pay taxes. Quite the other way around. The politics of taxation is characterized by the attempt of individuals and organizations to shift the burden "from me to someone else." The politics of taxation is the mirrored opposite of the politics of expenditures where each group tries to divert a greater share of the goods and services the government produces to its members. So, when the policy maker brings a new tax proposal to the public he can always expect a hostile reaction.[2] The strategies used to get things done and the content of the policies formed depend on the political structure of the environment and the policy makers' ability to ignore some pressure groups at least some of the time. Strategies and content are the factors that have an impact on implementation.

Strategies — the methods by which policy makers get their policies enacted — might have adverse side effects for implementors. What works well for policy makers may produce difficulties for bureaucrats. For example, policy makers confronting an alien environment would look for strategies that enable them to introduce measures in such a way that would make it difficult for the average taxpayer to know exactly what he would be paying. A very complex policy with numerous rates and differentiation between various sources of income that is frequently changed makes calculations to determine tax burden sufficiently complex to assure that most would not even attempt the task. Yet, what is difficult for the taxpayer is not going to be easy for those who have to implement the law; they are in a worse position. They have no choice; they must make those calculations in order to collect the tax.

Content affects implementation in a similar way. Indirect taxes are a convenient way to overcome conflicts over the question of who should pay, and how much. Their burden is not as obvious as that of income tax, and except for taxes on special items they are not directed at any particular individual or group. The problem with indirect taxes is that their revenue yield is low. Thus as Melstner points out:

> By these tactics, indirect taxes and nominal charges are introduced into the tax structure . . . and result in low yielding taxes and small, attentive tax publics.[3]

What types of strategies and policies are likely to be found in poor countries? Are policies stable, undergoing only small technical changes from one year to another, or are they unstable? Are they capable of meeting spending commitments or is it necessary to strengthen them during the course of the year?

Studies of tax policy formation in poor countries describe the process of decision making as being characterized by a high rate of change and its outputs as being complex, unwieldly policies. Chart 3-1 contains three typical illustrations of the process and its outputs.

What are we to conclude from these descriptions? That policy makers are irrational or perhaps that they are incompetent? What other reasons could they possibly have for acting in a way which clearly does not make the life of the implementor an easy one?

We should at least acknowledge that policy makers know what they are doing. It would be self-defeating to end where we started by recommending, as many taxexperts[4] do — Chart 3-2 contains illustrations of the typical statements — a stabler and simpler tax structure on the grounds that stability and simplicity speed implementation.

Let us look first at one "good" reason for retaining complexity which some will even call rational. Complexity in taxation is not all "evil" in fact it is mostly "good." Complexity is created by the multiplicity of measures, regulations, definitions, rates, specific exclusions, differentiated deductions and exemptions. The more of these there are the more precise is the law, that is the closer to what the politician wants to achieve. Special rules allow the politician to adapt the law to the specific needs and preferences of the various groups to which it applies. One result of this specificity is what economists call equity — that people pay according to a certain agreed upon capability.[5]

There are hardly any countries today that completely and openly disregard equity to facilitate the implementation of their tax laws. Though we hear daily that tax structures in poor countries are regressive — that the

CHART 3-1
Tax Policy Formulation Is Repetitive

India: Policy has been faltering, confused, inconsistent and, latterly, unreal. Since independence there have been half a dozen changes in policy and half a dozen custodians of the country's finances . . . What is amazing is that, although the party in power remains unchanged, the Ministers and their policies should alter so frequently and radically. To quote one instance, in 1954-56 the Finance Minister swore by the Taxation Enquiry Commission's recommendations and began putting them into operation, while in 1956, the succeeding Minister practically forswore the Report. The trouble appears to be that the Government always itches to have too many policies and to aim at too many objectives.(a)

Trinidad: . . . the law is very complex and complicated. Since the last revision . . . in 1950, twenty amendments have been enacted and several regulations and orders passed under the law. Considerable other legislation was enacted to amend the substantive law . . . (b)

Latin America: . . . the imperative need for increased resources has led many of our countries constantly to increase tax rates in force and to introduce others, in order to meet government expenses.(c)

Source:

a. M. H. Gopal, "Towards a Realistic Tax Policy for India," *The Indian Economic Journal,* VII, 3 (January 1959), p. 291.
b. Board of Inland Revenue, "Background Paper on Trinidad and Tobago Tax Administration," submitted to the Conference on the Administration of Income Tax in Commonwealth Caribbean States. (St. Augustine, Trinidad, April 1970), p. 31.
c. Jaime Ross Bravo, "Planning for Efficiency in Tax Administration," *Inter-American Center of Tax Administrators, Documents and Proceedings of the Second General Assembly,* (Buenos Aires, 1968), p. 14.

CHART 3-2
Do What Every Policy Maker Already Knows: Simplify and Stabilize Policy

Taxes should be simple to compute and easy to understand by the average man, assesssed on an obvious base easily arrived at, levied at moderate rates and payable in a convenient manner. [Changes in policy should be avoided and the revenue increased by] . . . better organization, more efficient methods and more thorough training of staff. (a)

I would like to see a simplification of the system. I would like to have a flat rate for all companies regardless of their legal stature. Also a single rate for all individuals and a single rate for deductation. Right now we have multiple rates that complicate our work. (b)

Tax changes are both politically and administratively costly; as stable and certain a tax system as possible should therefore be establised. The administrative machine with its limited capacity is always in danger of strain brought on by too complex or costly special tax gimmicks. (c)

Source:

a. Raja J. Chelliah, "Tax Potential and Economic Growth in the Countries of the ECAFE Region," *Economic Bulletin for Asia and the Far East,* XVII, 2 (September 1966), p. 44.
b. Senior Jamaican official.
c. Richard M. Bird, *Taxation and Development: Lessons from the Colombian Experience* (Cambridge: Harvard University Press, 1970), p. 55.

---

rich pay less than the poor — the rules by which tax dues are calculated are patterned on the principles of equity. A person's taxable income is calculated taking into account various exemptions and deductions and assigning different weights to income derived from different sources.[6] The rates that are applied to the taxable income are lower at the low income levels and higher at the high income levels. The results in economic terms may turn out to be regressive but that does not change the fact that the rules by which they were reached were designed to promote equity.

It is the economists who make calculations of incidence (and even they have difficulties reaching a clear cut solution) and not the taxpayer. If the rules seem to promote equity they promote equity; if the poor are asked to pay lower rates than the rich that means taxes are equitable. If the top rates are as high as sixty percent or even higher that means that the government is taking a proper share from the rich, maybe even soaking them. Anyone who advocates simpler tax structures tells politicians to propose to their publics taxes that in their view are not modern, are not economically rational and are not equitable. What argument could a politician use to convince taxpayers to accept such a form of taxation? Saying that it is administratively expedient would not take him far. The appearance of rationality and equity is vital, particularly since practice is so remote from these principles.

The tax structure is complicated and unstable because it is difficult to find a simple policy on which consensus could be reached that would also be powerful (in terms of its revenue potential). The problem of levying taxes in a poor country is that the majority of the population which is politically weak does not have enough to pay, and the small minority which does, has enough political and economic power to either convince legislators to spare them or to bribe tax officials into not enforcing the law.[7] A Thai informant described his experience bluntly: "The people who control most of the country's resources occupy the top positions among the political elite. It may prove to be a very trying experience for an auditor to get tough with one of these big businessmen." Chart 3-3 contains illustrations of typical analyses of the impact of the political and social structure in poor countries on tax policy making.

A strategy that keeps all parties reasonably content is the illusionary progressive tax structure which imposes a light burden on the poor and a heavy burden on the rich. This, progressivity in rates, is sufficient to secure the assent of the low and middle classes. The support of the economic elites is obtained quite simply by means which ensure that only a handful of taxpayers will pay the high rates and even then only on a fraction of their true income. As Prest shows, one reason why the yield of the income tax in poor countries is low is not because the rates are low but because the tax is not levied on equal income percentiles as in rich countries.[8] The poor are asked to pay very little, the rich are required to pay high rates but allowed to slip out of the tax net through the back door. Everyone is happy except the national treasury which stays empty.

Solutions like this can hold only part of the time. There comes a moment when bills must be paid and money must be raised; what then? A crisis is what the politician needs to enact tax measures that under normal circumstances would be blocked. At the beginning of the year everyone fights for increased spending and against higher taxation. Unable to overcome the pressures, the policy maker proposes what tax measures will go at that stage, being fully aware that the revenues would run out before the year is over. Then, as the budget is carried out and the treasury coffers are rapidly being emptied, new measures to increase the revenue are introduced. Harsh measures that would have encountered severe opposition at the beginning of the year have a better chance of surviving the political battles now that the treasury faces the danger of insolvency. But, it is one thing to overcome a particular crisis and quite another to create a situation that would preclude the recurrence of similar crises. The first problem can be solved by temporary, limited measures while the

CHART 3-3
Political Structure Is an Impediment to Simplicity in Policy

The high income group is the focus, or more accurately the essence, of whatever political and economic stability exists . . . this group tends to dominate the social, political and economic structures of the nation.(a)

Politically, the main factor is the willingness and ability of a government to 'soak the rich,' which partly depends on the extent to which the rich control the government. If it is dominated by the holders of large fortunes . . . it will be limited in the ways it can use taxation . . . Its desire to promote economic growth will conflict with its tenderness towards the financial interests of its backers, almost inevitably to the detriment of the former.(b)

In our country, there is an interlocking relationship among political power, wealth, and social status. Political power can be used to promote economic dominance. People use their riches to gain political power. Naturally, they resist moves that threaten their interests. (c)

Source:

a. David E. Shirley, "Income Taxes for Lesser Developed Nations," *National Tax Journal,* XII, 3, (1959), p. 265.
b. A. H. Hanson, *Public Enterprise and Economic Development,* (London, Routledge and Kegan Paul, 1959), p. 77. Nicholas Kaldor makes a similar argument in his "Will Underdeveloped Countries Learn to Tax?", *Foreign Affairs,* (January 1963).
c. Avelino B. Lim, "Reshaping Tax Policy for Economic Development," *Philippines Congressional Economic Bulletin,* (September 30, 1970). Another prominent Filipino observer expresses a similar view: "In a country such as ours, it is not an easy task to espouse the passage of laws which seek to raise the level of taxation . . ." Gerardo P. Sicat, *Taxation and Progress,* National Economic Council, Republic of the Philippines, (Manila, 1972), p. 1.

---

second requires a more thorough change in structure and procedures. Small crises that recur every now and then are continuously overcome by limited measures which add to the complexity of the tax structure.

The results of this pattern of policy formation are characterized by a high level of complexity and instability. If political structure precludes policy makers from adopting in an orderly way the policies that are required to meet the government's spending commitments, administrative problems ensure that they would not even reach the little that they managed to ask for.

In rich countries, policy makers can normally count on getting what they ask for: policies are implemented. Deviations from expectations, though inevitable, are not too extreme to affect overall outputs.[9] The main problem in the area of taxation is to find a policy that would be economically desirable and politically feasible. Once an acceptable formula is reached, only marginal changes in policy will have to be made from one year to another, primarily to adapt to changing conditions in the environment. Policies need not be made and remade. Tax policy as Blough describes it resembles an island:

> Tax policy is like a large island. The main body of the island stands firmly, but along the shore there is continual shifting. Wind and waves are washing away land here, and building up new land over there . . . What may be new, unfirm land emerging on the water's edge today may be a solid part of the island tomorrow. In time, the form and size of the island may be altered out of recognition.[10]

The reason why the main body of the policy can be left undisturbed and carried over from one year to another is that the expected outputs are reached. The tools need not be replaced because they work satisfactorily. As long as there is no radical change in needs (war, severe economic crisis) or political preferences, no more than continuous small adjustments are necessary.

In poor countries, policy makers rarely enjoy that measure of certainty and stability. Normally they can expect to get only part of what they have asked for; approaching policy goals is quite unusual. Policies are formulated and goals are set with the knowledge that it will not be long before they will have to be changed because implementation is partial. According to a former Filipino Internal Revenue Commissioner:

> During the last ten years the Philippine fiscal planning has failed . . . fiscal policy for the current year is directed towards making up for the shortcomings of the previous year whereby the conditions and standards sought to be attained failed to materialize.[11]

Here is another source of instability, which policy makers amplify when they manipulate policy to bridge the gap between revenue outputs and budget commitments. They keep their heads above water not by trying to remove the source of partial implementation but by adding more weight to it. The alternative is to stabilize policy by strengthening implementation. At first glance this course of action seems to have political appeal as well as policy rationality. Here is an opportunity to increase revenues by relying on existing taxes without having to go through the painful exercise of a tax increase.

When asked why this rationale does not work in practice, informants usually responded saying that ministers of finance take administrative capability as it is. They do not believe that it is possible within their resource and time constraints to meaningfully upgrade the administration's ability to collect taxes.

A policy analyst in the Philippines describes the odds thus:

> There is a prevailing feeling here that the investment in improving the administrative machinery is not going to be as productive in terms of revenues as changes in rates and structure may be. Whenever we consider new revenue sources we mention the implementation factor but we stop at that. Most people feel that what would be achieved in that area would be negligible.

Fiddling with structure and rates is not only simpler and cheaper, but, most importantly, it is a faster way of assuring some increase in revenue. The Minister of Finance, whose task it is to ensure that there will be enough money to defray the government's spending, needs money tomorrow for pay hikes he authorized today and has no time to wait for improvements in collection or enforcement which may never bear fruit; so much so, when such improvements may turn out to be politically costly. A senior official in the Thai Ministry of Finance described the Minister's way of thinking as:

> He is not particularly enthusiastic about programs that would bear their fruits ten years from now. He is also not too interested in the Revenue Department. He can't go out and claim credit and win public support for collecting more taxes, for improving audit, for making life more difficult for thousands of businessmen. He is interested in spending and in reforms that would bear their fruits immediately. If he needs more revenue than he already has, he needs it now, not ten years from today. From his point of view, either the Revenue is going to come up with the sum supposedly by intensifying collections . . . there are so many delinquent accounts that they don't have to look around too much — or rates will have to be increased . . . administrative reforms . . . are a less desirable alternative because time, money and energy must be invested before any benefits are seen and you can't be sure of getting anything either.

Taylor expressed similar doubts concerning the feasibility of increasing revenues substantially in a short time through administrative improvements: "It appears to be unrealistic to assume that 'better' administration will result in an appreciable increase in revenue during a short period of five or ten years."[12] The trouble with administrative reforms is that they take time, quite often a long period of time, before showing results. This is why suggestions for obtaining additional revenues (needed to pay for unexpected expenditure), through better implementation of existing policies, does not elicit much enthusiasm. Adding new taxes, increasing rates on existing ones or lowering exemptions and deductions is a more appealing course of action because results are immediate. Poor implementation will produce less than what has been demanded but, an increase in rates, unlike most administrative reforms, can start producing some results the day after it is enacted.

Policy affects revenues by setting goals — ceilings of revenue to be mobilized. Implementation separates setting goals and reaching them.

The next section discusses the elements — the volatility of policy, lack of voluntary compliance, and the paucity of data and expertise — of partial implementation.

Elements Affecting Scope and Extent of Implementation

> . . . the study of implementation examines those factors that contribute to the realization or non-realization of policy objectives.
>
> Donald S. Van Meter and Carl E. Van Horn, "The Policy Implementation Process — A Conceptual Framework."

> . . . inherent or tacit in the tax system's revenue goal is an assumption about the extent to which the Tax Administrator and taxpayers can and will comply with the responsibilities placed on them by the tax system.
>
> Marius Farioletti, "Tax Administration Funding and Fiscal Policy."

What is needed to get a policy implemented? What conditions will make it possible to come close to planned outputs and which factors are responsible for partial implementation? What happens during the process of implementing policies which leaves results lagging far behind goals? Success or failure in implementation depends on what needs to be implemented and on the organization's ability to do what it is expected to. Gaps in implementation are caused by a task which is too difficult to carry out and (or) by administrative constraints; according to Van Meter and Van Horn, failures in implementation are produced "by such factors as overworked and poorly trained staffs, insufficient information and financial resources, or impossible time constraints."[13] To understand why the results of implementation are what they are, it is necessary to weigh tasks against the skills and resources required to carry them out well. Starting with the task, how does policy affect implementation? We continue to limitations in the resources on which the taxing process is based.

The Volatility of Policy — Complexity and Instability— Increases Difficulties of Implementation

> Company income tax is not fully enforced because the law is too sophisticated for our manpower, the law is too complicated. There are different rates for different types of companies . . . In theory existing tax policies are good but, the problem is that we cannot get the right people to make them work.
>
> Senior Jamaican Official

It is not only what is being asked for that determines what will be received, it is also the way in which the requests are made that influences outputs. The policy's content — types of taxes levied, rate deductions and exemptions, definitions of taxable bases (income, property, goods and services) — defines the outer limits of implementation. Content determines the potential, what could be obtained "if." The "if" is determined by the nature of the task. A policy is a task which can be simple or complex, stable or unstable. A policy is easier to implement when it is simple and stable than when it is sophisticated and flexible. Complexity has been identified by Martha Derthick[14] and Jeffrey Pressman and Aaron Wildavsky[15] as the principal factor responsible for failures in implementation. Task simplicity is particularly important when administrative capability is low. Much may be lost, in terms of economic rationality — equity, excess burden disincentive effects — when a tax policy is simplified, but one thing will definitely be gained: more of the same will be implemented, and that normally means more revenue.

Simplicity refers to the tax structure — types of taxes levied — and the calculations required to determine each individual's share. The greater the number of taxes, rates, deductions and exemptions, the greater the amount of data needed, the more complicated the calculations become and the more difficult to verify the accuracy of the information the taxpayer submits. The principle of equity — levying taxes according to ability to pay — requires differential rates and deductions, detailed information about every individual taxpayer and complex rules of calculation to determine tax so that it is equitable. Complex rules of calculation and the demand for accurate and extensive information make it harder for the revenue official to carry out his job while increasing the opportunities the taxpayer has to evade. Consider, for comparison, the great ease with which a poll or head tax can be implemented: there are no calculations to be made nor is there need to obtain a great deal of information; name and address suffice.[16]

The second policy feature which influences implementation is stability. Stability refers to the volume and scope of changes in policy, introduced from one year to another. Radical and frequent changes make it as hard for the taxpayer to comply as for the administrator to enforce. Frequent changes destroy routines that simplify complex and unpleasant tasks.[17] Every time policy is changed administration must immediately follow suit. Yet, while policies are changed by writing on a piece of paper, administration requires changes in action — rules, procedures and the behavior of participants who apply and comply with them. Changes in policy do not in themselves produce parallel changes in performance as a senior Trinidadian official describes:

> Major tax policy changes have been made in 1958, 1963 and 1966. The administrative machinery was not really geared to effectuate these frequent

and major changes; it did not adequately respond to them by making corresponding changes in programmes, systems and procedures.[18]

When policy is changed, implementation is likely to suffer since the same organization is required to perform additional tasks, some of which may be completely new and hence hard to adapt to. A change in policy forces officials to depart from their daily habits, to start doing something in a different way than that which they were accustomed to. If changes are very rapid, officials are likely to decide to ignore them altogether and follow their own preferences. According to a recent study in the Philippines:

> One of the factors that adversely affect the efficiency of the BIR and the Bureau of Customs, especially in tax administration, is the disruption in the continuity of policies . . . Programs for the improvement of the performance . . . cannot be fully implemented because of the quick turnover of commissioners . . . new policies are not given serious attention by the employees since the commissioner and his policies will not be there tomorrow.[19]

Changes in policy are hard on taxpayers too. Accustomed to a certain form, or to calculating their tax according to certain rates, taxpayers learn that they will have to use a new form and that the present set of rates no longer apply. They will have to be reminded more than once because they will forget and act according to habit. It takes a great deal of time and patience before a new routine replaces an old one. Frequent changes in policy make implementation difficult because routines must be learned and relearned. An Indian observer describes the effects of a rapidly changing policy on tax officials and taxpayers:

> With every dose of amendment or alterations in the Act it became more intricate and obstruse. The taxpayers and the taxgatherers have to learn, unlearn and relearn the Law . . . On account of the instability and incomprehensibility of tax-laws, many assessees are forced to avail the services of the tax advisers who are . . . experts in tax avoidance.[20]

Stability and simplicity are vital because compliance is facilitated by routine and made more difficult when it has to be thought about prior to each action. A routinized process has better chances of eliciting compliance by a greater number of people since it requires a smaller investment in time and effort. A task that is unpleasant to begin with is made less so by the fact that every step of the process is familiar. According to Johnson, the incremental nature of tax policy in America is an important factor in the high level of voluntary compliance in the country:

> Most taxpayers go through a life-cycle in which the nature of their income and tax situation changes slowly, so that once started they need watch out

> only for marginal changes in the tax laws which will be built into the tax forms themselves . . . [21]

Frequent nonincremental changes in policy make compliance harder because the taxpayer must learn a new set of rules each times he files — a fact which makes an unpleasant task even more unpleasant. Frequent changes make the administration poorer than it already is: scarce resources become scarcer. A great deal is spent in introducing changes, printing new tax tables and calculation guides, retraining officials, reprogramming machines, throwing out outdated forms and printing new ones. After all this is paid for — time, energy and money — less is left for routine work. There are never enough time and resources to concentrate on a certain problem area or on a certain procedure. Instead of perfecting existing practices, the administration is constantly struggling to adapt to changes in policy.

Illustrations of the impact that frequent changes in policy have on the ability to implement are contained in Chart 3-4.

By contrast, a policy process that is incremental, where changes are limited in scope and volume and proceed from an established base, produces results that are easier to implement because they require no new procedures, routines or organizational setups. Anything that can be carried out by existing procedures has a greater chance of fulfillment than something that is dependent on innovation.

Changes in policy that do not require extensive parallel changes in administration are usually of technical nature — legal definitions of income and spending, rates, exemptions and deductions. The introduction of a new tax, a new method of calculating deductions (itemized vs. standard), a new method of collection (withholding, pay as you earn, field vs. office collection), or a new method of filing and auditing (self-assessment and selective audit) requires reforms in procedures, training and means of collecting, storing and using information. Each of these changes is difficult to effectuate in its own right; when they are piled one on top of the other, the administration may either ignore them altogether, choose those that are convenient or be crippled trying to implement all.

In poor countries both types of policy changes are found. The technical changes are a result of political pressures and the radical changes are brought about by financial crises. The poor countries are less capable of handling changes in policies and are forced to adapt to more and more difficult changes than the rich (for a description of changes in policy turn to Chapter Eight). If the policy is volatile, the administration responsible for implementing it is not redundant with strength.

At this point, only the general components of implementation are presented; in the following chapters each one will be discussed separately.

CHART 3-4
Repetitive Policy Results in a Complicated Tax Structure that Is Hard to Implement

Indonesia:	The complexity and diversity of Indonesia's present tax structure clearly have much to do with the efficiency of the administration as a whole. Taxes are too numerous and their regulations too complex to make it feasible for the government to effectively reach all of the tax base which is nominally subject to taxation. (a)
Trinidad:	In the last few years we have changed the form so many times that the taxpayer is virtually confronted with a new form each year and he must learn the whole thing from scratch. (b)
Philippines:	The exercise of the taxing power is far from methodic. Because of pressure on tax policy formulation tax laws do not fit into a cohesive frame. Deficiencies attending tax administration thwart even the most soundly conceived tax policies. The net result: revenue to meet developmental requirements remains scanty — a lopsided taxing pattern against which the masses complain . . . (c)
Latin America:	Their taxes, usually petty in scope, ran literally into many hundreds in some countries. They rarely fit into any general pattern of taxation or fiscal policy but constitute a hodge-podge of taxes, enacted, apparently, with scant study, to finance some project, to assist some quasi-public entity, to meet some emergency, or to help fill a deficit. (d)
	Many . . . taxes overlap so that a single commodity or transaction may be subject to a number of taxes, imposed at different or supplementary rates, involving different tax bases with different times of payment, different returns, and separate administrative and judicial procedures . . . (e)

Chart 3-4 (Continued)

Source:

a. Douglas S. Paauw, *Financing Economic Development — The Indonesian Case,* (Boston: MIT, Free Press, 1960), p. 197.
b. Senior Trinidadian Official.
c. Avelino B. Lim, "Reshaping Tax Policy for Economic Development," *Philippine Congressional and Economic Bulletin,* (September 30, 1970), p. 8.
d. Joseph P. Crockett, "Common Obstacles to Effective Tax Administration in Latin America," in Joint Tax Program, *Problems of Tax Administration,* p. 23.
e. Stanley S. Surrey, "Tax Administration in Underdeveloped Countries," *University of Miami Law Review,* XII (Winter 1958).

Chapter Four describes the limitations in two of the most important resources in the taxing process — information and accounting expertise. Chapters Five, Six and Seven analyze how the three main tasks of the process — audit, collection and enforcement — are carried out under conditions of large scale evasion and insufficient resources and skills.

The taxing process is much in the grip of compliance. Most of the constraints and opportunities for making and implementing tax policies are created by the scope and level of compliance. Were it not for compliance, there would be few problems of implementation that could seriously affect policy goals.

The problem of implementation is that a small number of officials must extract a substantial amount of money from a very large number of taxpayers. Therefore, the level of compliance — the degree to which the majority of the population is prepared to do what it is expected without a significant amount of prodding — determines the extent of implementation: how much of what has been asked for will actually be realized. The strongest organization will not be able to achieve its policy goals when the majority of the population waits to be dragged into court before paying. As Nowak observed, enforcement methods are effective only when applied to a small number of people: "None of the techniques of forced compliance . . . can be extended to enough taxpayers to have an important direct effect on the tax intake."[22]

But, noncompliance is a built-in factor in the process. Since taxation is a transfer of resources from citizens to government for which individuals receive no direct and proportional (to the amount paid) material benefits, rational taxpayers will have a strong incentive not to pay. As Mancur Olson aptly reminds us, governments were never, nor is it likely that they ever will be, financed through philanthropic contributions

> . . . despite the force of patriotism, the appeal of natural ideology, the bond of common culture, and the indispensability of the system of law and order, no major state in modern history has been able to support itself through

voluntary dues or contributions. Taxes, *compulsory* payments by definition, are needed.[23]

There is more to compliance than rational choice calculations, or else no country would have had a high level of compliance. The reason is that it is not possible to obtain high compliance through the implementation of tax laws alone. No country, no matter how rich, has sufficient resources to seek out and penalize more than a very limited number of deviants. Thus if there is a significant amount of noncompliance it is more likely that it will limit the effectiveness of implementation than the other way around, that effective implementation will reduce evasion and increase voluntary compliance. This seems to be the prevailing view according to Heidenheimer, Heclo and Adams:

> It would be a mistake to attribute the high incidence of nonreporting of income and evasion of taxes in countries like France and Italy predominantly to corruption and complaisance in the bureaucracy . . . the law enforcement authorities are relatively powerless to alter the historically rooted attitude that only fools would "come clean" with the tax bureaucracy.[24]

Vito Tanzi argues that "the system of taxation is what it is *because* there is much evasion. It would be absurd to assume that it would be the same if taxes were not evaded."[25] It is definitely true that factors such as "culture" and "history" have a strong effect on compliance. But, this is as far as we can take any analysis based on these variables. Olson already showed why culture alone would not be enough to create or maintain voluntary compliance. There is an indispensable need for effective enforcement. Compliance affects implementation and is affected by it; it is a behavior that is determined both by rational choice calculations — the probability of being caught and the price paid for evading compared to the potential benefit derived from undetected evasion — and by "political and cultural variables" — the force of habit and tradition coupled with factors such as the regime's legitimacy and consensus on the way public monies are spent. It is necessary to look at both sides of the coin to get a correct picture of it.

The question of how compliance is affected by implementation is important to the issue of reform — what can be done to increase revenues by way of strengthening the administration's impact on compliance — and is taken up in Chapter Eight. At this point, suffice it to say that the ability to enforce the law determines how seriously it will be taken by taxpayers. A strong organization will command a higher level of compliance than a weak one and will achieve a greater degree of implementation.

The second question, how implementation is affected by compliance will be taken up in the chapters dealing with the process' tasks. All that needs to be said now is that low levels of compliance are typical of the poor countries and that this constraint exacerbates weaknesses in administrative capability. The consequences are gaps in implementation.

The next sections describe how the resources required for implementation and the content of the policies themselves affect the ability to carry plans into action.

Resources for Implementing Policies — The Effects of Poverty and Lack of Redundancy

In rich countries a weakness in one area can be overcome by calling upon idle capacity in other areas; there are policy options and administrative capability to seize them whenever the need arises. A variety of complicated schemes such as the value added tax, or elaborate presumptive methods of assessment can be implemented, when a simple income tax fails to produce expected revenue because compliance is low. Rich organizations, as Caiden and Wildavsky describe them,

> are characterized by largesse; they have ample reserves in case anything runs short. They have many ways to do things so that if one fails another takes over. They have a multitude of talented people so that there is always someone who can carry on, despite the fact that some men get sick, others go on vacation, and a few turn out to be incompetent.[26]

Poor countries suffer from insufficient supply of virtually everything that is needed to make a bureaucracy work. They lack wealth that can be taxed, political strength to tax what they have, and administrative ability to implement their policies. Weaknesses in policy are magnified by weaknesses in implementation. Problems are harder to solve because the tasks are greater while the means for carrying them out are skimpier. The level on which an agency operates depends on the extent of redundancy in each of the crucial components of implementation. Redundancy in procedures assures that if one proves deficient, another may be immediately plugged in to prevent breakdown. Information gathered in multiple forms by independent organizations ensures that if one makes an error of omission or interpretation, the others will not. More personnel than the minimum needed to run the organization assures that when something unexpected occurs, it will be dealt with without disturbing routine work. Surplus funds permit the agency to embark on more than one course of action when the best way can be found only through trial and error.[27]

Poverty, we are reminded by Caiden and Wildavsky, means much more than just low personal incomes. Poverty means not having enough of virtually everything that counts. A poor country has relatively few people with technical skills — there are not enough lawyers, accountants, bookkeepers and economists to fill available positions let alone create an overcapacity. A poor country has less information — it knows less about itself, about important activities that take place — and the data available is not sufficiently accurate to guide decisions.

When there is a shortage in the critical components of implementation the organization achieves less and what it does attain is of poor quality. Between the law and the treasury coffers stand men whose duty is to ensure that everyone who should pay does what he ought to when he ought to. The process of implementing tax policies is comprised of a series of sequential, mutually reinforcing functions: processing, audit, collection, and enforcement. Each of these tasks must be completed in a certain order and within a very limited length of time. When not done when, or as, they should, outputs — the amount of revenue collected — are immediately affected. The government will be losing potential tax revenue that would be very difficult to retrieve later. The combined effect of all functions is vital to achieve a level of implementation and enforcement that would have an effect on evasion — reduce or keep it at manageable proportions.

The processing of returns filed each year must be completed within a few months of the end of the filing period so that it will be possible to initiate collection of delinquent accounts before next year's taxes are due. If the collectors do not descend on delinquent taxpayers immediately after deadlines have elapsed, they foster the tendency to disregard deadlines and to postpone endlessly the payment of taxes. Worse yet, they make their own job harder because next year there will be two years' worth of back taxes to collect. Unless the majority can be convinced to respect deadlines, there will be more delinquencies than collection agents can effectively cope with.

Audit work is a race against time — auditors must be able to audit all the cases that have been selected before the statute of limitations goes into effect. They must start as early as possible to have a reasonable chance of finishing what they are commissioned to do. Melvin White and Andrew C. Quale of the technical staff of the Colombian Commission on Tax Reform observed that:

> the greater the delay in processing the returns, the more likely it is that the . . . statute of limitations will run out against the government. If the government has not succeeded in officially assessing a tax return within two years from the date on which the tax liability arose, the taxpayer's private assessment will become binding on the government. This occurrence is quite costly to the government, since the taxpayer's private assessment is often significantly lower than the official assessment.[28]

Impact of audit done years after the events examined have occurred is softened by the passage of time. An audit conducted a few months after filing period is more effective than one done two or three years later. First of all the taxpayer will treat the possibility of being audited more seriously and will not underreport quite as much as he would had he known that it will be years before anyone will come around asking questions. When the taxpayer feels that the agency has lost control of its paperwork he will take advantage of the situation and evade. Oliver Oldman describes this reaction well:

> The Argentine taxpayer felt that the tax authorities had lost control over their paperwork and over the taxpayers. This was a major factor in evasion. The tax office was swamped with millions of documents in disorder . . . months and even years elapsed before a check could be made to ascertain whether the taxpayer had filed his sworn return and paid the tax.[29]

Secondly, most of the information the auditor needs to determine the validity of a return is not formally recorded. It can be obtained through interviews and visual inspection. Therefore, the quality of the data deteriorates with the passage of time. A question that would have embarrassed a taxpayer, causing him to behave in ways that would indicate to the experienced auditor that he is lying, could be answered without the slightest inconvenience, a few years after the fact. Much of audit work is painstaking gathering of little bits of data; the main items in the return are likely to be correct; the little bits that count do not survive long in the minds of men.

Each element in this process reinforces the others, so, if one is weak it weakens the rest. An agency with the best auditors in the country will not go far in inducing taxpayers to limit evasion to marginal items if returns are not processed in time.

The problem of resource mobilization in poor countries is that the government reaches only a small number of its potential taxpayers, and even then does not succeed in getting what is due. Both the relative number of taxpayers and the amounts they pay are smaller than those in rich nations.[30] There is a large gap between policy and outputs. Effective rates — those actually paid — are lower than legal rates and the actual tax base is narrower than the legal base.[31] As Kaldor points out, the problem is not so much with the policy but with its implementation:

> The shortfall in revenue is largely a reflection of failure to tax the wealthier sectors of the community effectively. Though progressive income taxes and

> inheritance taxes exist on paper in most of the underdeveloped countries — sometimes imposed at high nominal rates, mounting to eighty percent or more on the highest incomes — there are few cases in which such taxes are effective in practice.[32]

This is why simple economic solutions aimed at increasing revenues — raise this rate, reduce that exemption, add this tax — will not solve the problem. Increasing the legal rate of a tax carries no guarantee that there will be a similar increase in the actual rate. By the same token, levying a new tax by itself contains no assurance that all of the revenue for which it was imposed will be obtained. Richard Bird explains why:

> Present poor administrative machine . . . will continue to function at the same low level no matter what changes are made in tax policy or in tax structure . . . it often seems to be easier to make drastic changes in tax policy than . . . to improve the administration of existing taxes. Once a policy change has been made, however, there is usually little reason to expect the new tax to be administered better than the old, for the same people must administer both.[33]

Conclusion

Beyond factors of wealth and economic structure, the amount of revenue that is obtained through taxation is determined by how much is being asked for, and by the extent to which policies are implemented. The revenue target set in the tax policy is determined by existing wealth, the government's desire to tax it and by the political feasibility of enacting fiscal policies. The degree of target fulfillment depends on two sets of factors, the first being the magnitude of the task that has to be performed which is a function of policy stability and simplicity, and the level of voluntary compliance.

Simplicity and stability in tax policy affect implementation by determining the degree of difficulty in execution. Two factors contribute to complexity and instability of tax policy in poor countries. First, an increase in revenue is easier to obtain through policy changes than through administrative improvements. Therefore, every time additional revenue is needed, a new tax will be introduced or some other change made in existing taxes. Secondly, political factors limit the extent of the changes that can be made at one time. The government must wait for a crisis to happen before being able to enact a policy that will increase the tax burden. Instead of formulating tax policy once a year and then sticking to it, the government starts with a structure which is insufficient hoping to improve it as things get worse. A vicious cycle is thus created in which frequent changes in policy are responsible for partial implementation, which in turn contributes to the need for more changes to raise the needed revenue. The more changes that are made, the more complex the structure becomes, the more difficult implementation will be and the greater the gap between expectations and outcomes. This is how policy makers end up asking for more and more while getting less and less.

The second set of factors which determine the ability to reach goals are the resources and means available for implementation. The critical resources are: information, personnel and expertise. The means of implementation are: audit, collection, and enforcement. Chart 3-5 illustrates the relationships between these factors in graphical form.

The purpose of this chapter was to exemplify the roles played by policy and implementation in determining the outputs of the taxing process. The existence of an economic potential does not in and of itself guarantee that effective policies to tap it will be enacted, neither does the existence of a policy guarantee its implementation. Furthermore, what cannot be achieved under normal conditions because political preferences overwhelm economic rationality may become attainable when a crisis occurs. Political as well as economic barriers to taxation are lifted, even if only temporarily, when the prospects of continuing with the existing policies seem darker than extracting more resources.

The main problem poor countries face in mobilizing resources is not with policy but with implementation. Their policies are usually grander than their achievements. The problem is not that they don't want, or do not need to raise more money, but that they do not succeed in making their policies work. There are too many difficulties and not enough resources to overcome them. A Filipino revenue official put it bluntly: "The main problem in taxation here is implementation. Our laws and procedures are fine, the trouble is that they are not carried out to the letter." The economic potential may be there, the policy tools for extracting it handy, and still, the treasury coffers will remain empty because a large proportion of the population refuses to comply and the administration is not capable of enforcing the laws.

CHART 3-5
The Determinants of Government Revenue

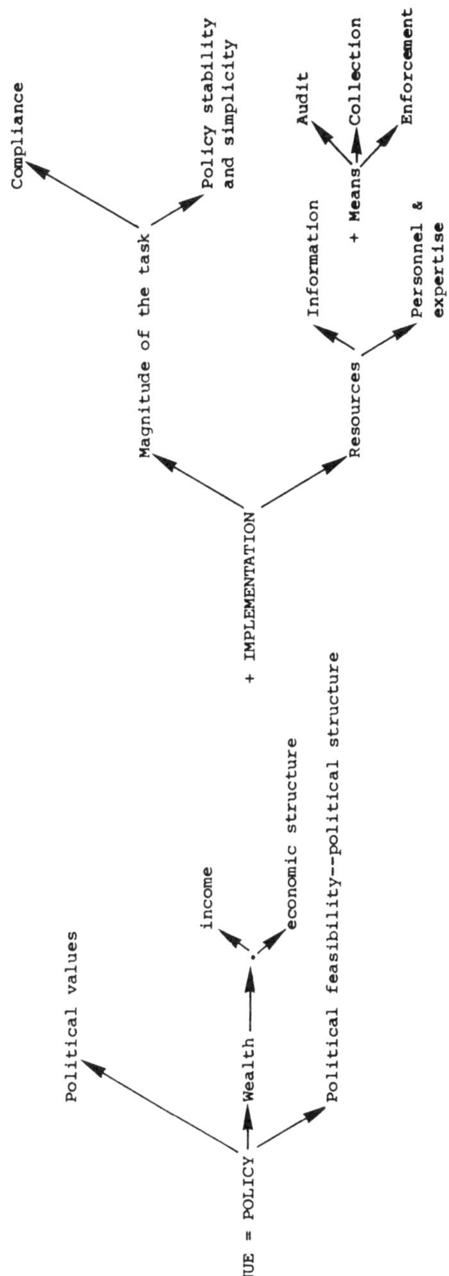

Notes

1. Raja J. Chelliah, "Tax Potential and Economic Growth in the Countries of the ECAFE Region," *Economic Bulletin for Asia and the Far East* XVII, 2 (September 1966), p. 44.
2. Arnold J. Melstner, *The Politics of City Revenue* (Berkeley: University of California Press, 1971), Chapter 3.
3. Ibid., p. 8.
4. Douglas S. Paauw, *Financing Economic Development — The Indonesian Case* (Cambridge: Free Press, MIT, 1960); Milton C. Taylor, "The Relationship between Income Tax Administration and Income Tax Policy in Nigeria," *Nigerian Journal of Economics and Social Studies* 9, II (1967): 203-15; C.R.M. Harvey, "Observations on the 1969 Zambian Budget and the Administrative Constraint on Further Tax Reform," *Zambia Law Journal* I, 2 (1969): 37-43; Edward A. Arowolo, "The Taxation of Low Incomes in African Countries," *International Monetary Staff Papers* XV (1968): 322-43.
5. Richard Musgrave, *The Theory of Public Finance* (New York: McGraw Hill, 1959).
6. Detailed descriptions of these rules are contained in: Gerardo P. Sicat, *Taxation and Progress* (Manila: National Economic Council, Republic of the Philippines, 1972); and Anan Lewchalermwong, *Taxation and Tax Reform in Thailand* (Bangkok: Kurusupha Ladaparao Press, 1972).
7. This pattern is described by Fred W. Riggs in Chapter Nine of his *Administration in Developing Countries* (Boston: Houghton Mifflin, 1964).
8. A.R. Prest, *Public Finance in Underdeveloped Countries* (New York: Praeger, 1962), p. 33.
9. T.B. Smith, "The Policy Implementation Process," *Policy Sciences* 4 (1973): 197-209.
10. Roy Blough, The Federal Taxing Process (New York: Prentice Hall, 1952), p. 12.
11. Cesar B. Abrencia, "The Budget and Development Policy from 1955 to 1966," *Economic Research Journal* XIV, 2 (1967): 108-09.
12. Taylor, "The Relationship . . .", p. 214.
13. Donald S. Van Meter and Carl E. Van Horn, "The Policy Implementation Process: A Conceptual Framework," *Administration and Society* 6 (1975): 480.
14. Martha Derthick, *New Sowns in Town* (Washington, D.C.: Urban Institute, 1970).
15. Jeffrey L. Pressman and Aaron Wildavsky, *Implementation* (Berkeley: University of California Press, 1973).
16. Edward A. Arowolo, "The Taxation . . . ", pp. 322-41.
17. I am using the concept of administrative routine as it has been developed by Ira Sharkansky in his *The Routines of Politics* (New York: Van Nostrand Reinhold, 1970).
18. S.M. Supersad, "Tax Administration Reforms in Trinidad and Tobago," paper presented at the Conference on the Administration of Income Tax in Commonwealth Caribbean States, University of the West Indies, St. Augustine Campus, (April 1970), p. 30.
19. Reorganization Panel on the Revenue System and Administration, "Report on Revenue System and Administration," mimeographed (Manila, Republic of the Philippines: Commission on Reorganization, 1970), p. 17.

20. M.L. Bahatia, "The Problem of Tax Evasion in India," *AICC Economic Review* XX, II (1967): 23.
21. Harry G. Johnson, "Self Assessment to Personal Income Tax: The American System," *British Tax Review* (1971): 81.
22. Norman D. Nowak, *Tax Administration in Theory and Practice* (New York: Praeger, 1970), p. 15.
23. Mancur Olson, *The Logic of Collective Action* (New York: Shocken Books, 1971), p. 13.
24. Arnold J. Heidenheimer, Hugh Heclo, and Carolyn T. Adams, *Comparative Public Policy: The Politics of Social Choice in Europe and America* (New York: St. Martin's Press, 1975), p. 240. The authors rely on the work of Gunther Schmolders.
25. Vito Tanzi, *The Individual Income Tax and Economic Growth: An International Comparison* (Baltimore: The John Hopkins Press, 1969), p. 84.
26. Naomi Caiden and Aaron Wildavsky, *Planning and Budgeting in Poor Countries* (New York: John Wiley, 1974), p. 49.
27. I rely here on Martin Landau, "Redundancy, Rationality and the Problems of Duplication and Overlap," *Public Administration Review* 29 (1969); and Caiden-Wildavsky's application of Landau's concepts to poor countries, in Ibid., Chapter 2.
28. Melvin White and Andrew C. Quale, Jr., "The Colombian Individual Income Tax: Rates, Exemptions, Deductions, and Administrative Aspects," in *Fiscal Reform for Colombia,* Richard Musgrave and Malcolm Gillis (eds.) (Cambridge: The Law School of Harvard University, 1971), p. 320.
29. Oliver Oldman, "Controlling Income Tax Evasion," in Joint Tax Program OAS/IDB/ECLA, *Problems of Tax Administration* (Baltimore: The John Hopkins Press, 1963), p. 374.
30. See Prest, p. 20.
31. See Oliver Oldman and Daniel M. Holland, "Measuring Tax Evasion" (mimeo), 1973.
32. Nicholas Kaldor, "Will Underdeveloped Countries Learn to Tax?" *Foreign Affairs* 4, 12 (1963): 410-19
33. Richard M. Bird, "The Political Economy of Tax Reform," in *Readings on Taxation in Developing Countries,* Richard M. Bird and Oliver Oldman (eds.), 3rd edition (Baltimore: The Johns Hopkins Press, 1975), p. 82.

The Instruments and Resources of Implementation

Chapter Four

How to Do a Lot with Very Little: Resources for Implementation

> After receipt practically all work is manually handled. Machines such as typewriters, adding machines, calculating machines, listing, posting and printing machines are few in number. Assessments, computations, listing, posting and correspondence are largely handwritten. This makes verifying and balancing difficult and time consuming.
>
> Foreign Tax Assistance Staff.[1]

At the heart of the taxing process are data and expertise to process and analyze it. Even small omissions or poor interpretations may cost the government a good deal in lost revenues. Here lies the difference between policy and implementation. The law levies a tax at a certain rate on a category of income, spending or goods; it does not specify exactly the names of those liable to the tax nor does it provide the necessary data regarding their taxable income. Implementing the law means generating these data and interpreting them correctly so that when the rules of calculating tax dues are applied the outcome, revenue collected, will come close to the legislator's goals.

Potential revenues are lost either because the data available for decisions is not comprehensive or reliable. But data by itself has no meaning; it has to be interpreted correctly. The fact that a company purchased a car is data which can be interpreted for purposes of taxing in more than one way. One possible meaning is that the car is an expense and should therefore be deducted from taxable income. The second possible meaning is that the car is part of the income of a certain individual and should be taxed accordingly.

Assigning meaning to bits of data has a far reaching impact on the scope of implementation.

How do participants make do when the information and expertise at hand fall short of what is needed to perform the tasks for which they are responsible? What are the effects of the paucity of data and limitations in expertise on the taxing process? What are the means available to overcome these constraints; how have the rich countries solved these problems when they faced them? Can these methods work for the poor countries today?

This chapter begins with a description of the problems of information in poor countries, proceeds to analyze attempts to ameliorate it by decentralization, and looks for explanations as to why they have not been very successful. The problems of personnel and expertise are discussed next. The entire government service suffers from insufficient expertise and technical knowhow; is there anything unique about problems of personnel in a tax agency? What means are available to ameliorate these problems and what difficulties are there in implementing them?

Obtaining Information by Decentralization

> A major impediment to tax enforcement in many parts of Latin America is the refusal of taxpayers to keep required books and records. A very large number of small merchants and peddlers are not competent to keep those required by the commercial code or tax laws. Others, who are competent, fail to do so deliberately or deny that they have any when an inspector wishes to examine them. These noncompliant groups constitute in many countries a majority, sometimes a very great numerical majority, of the merchants and traders.
>
> Joseph P. Crockett, "Common Obstacles to Effective Tax Administration in Latin America," p. 8.

> The taxpayer [in Indonesia] does not ordinarily submit statements of his income; rather, assessment of income is largely the responsibility of the tax authorities. Frequently, this becomes little more than a guessing game, with the taxpayer ingeniously attempting to obscure the size, and often, diverse components, of his total income.
>
> Douglas S. Paauw, *Financing Economic Development — The Indonesian Case,* p. 194.

Central governments in poor countries are ignorant of events taking place in their economy. They are, to borrow an expression from Henry Bretton,[1] blind. The central administration does not know who its taxpayers are, or how much they earn. Formal records from which this information can be extracted are nonexistent. Written records are being kept almost exclusively by the handful of large companies usually operating in the capital city. Most of the economic activity that takes place outside this small circle is not formally recorded. There are few records of purchases and sales, operating costs, losses and stock, and since in many cases prices are not fixed but bargainable, it is even difficult to obtain a rough estimate of profits.

Tax agencies in rich countries rely on elaborate networks of national statistics to obtain the information they need. The government has a tremendous amount of both aggregate and person by person data. It also has extensive storage capacity, powerful means for retrieving data and ability to conduct complex cross-checkings to discover hidden trends of evasion. What makes it possible to gather all this data is that a formal receipt or record is issued when opening a bank account, buying a car, a house or any large household appliance, installing a phone, attending school, in short there are not many things that a person does that are not recorded. Sooner or later this data ends up in one of the central government's information systems.

Not only is it possible to get a good bit of information on any individual taxpayer, a great deal of aggregate data is also available. National accounting statistics are elaborate, fairly reliable and comprehenive.Aggregate data is useful in determining what areas of economic activity deserve more attention than others, as well as formulating averages — of income, profits, turnover, operating costs — against which an individual's report can be compared to detect possible underreporting. Only when a more detailed investigation is called for does it become necessary to directly contact the taxpayer.

These sources of information do not exist in a poor country. The main source for information is the taxpayer himself, his close associates, friends, competitors and neighbors. The main methods for obtaining information on a taxpayer's income are the interview and the visual inspection rather than data analyses. Caiden and Wildavsky have a lively description of how information is obtained by means of visual inspection:

> An engineer who had worked in Pakistan described his task of estimating the amount of goods handled by a major port. The data on hand seemed to vastly underestimate the amount of goods that even a casual inspection of the port suggested. He discovered that taxes were collected on the amount of goods transported out of the port area. It was, therefore, in the interest of the shippers to underestimate the amount of material they handled. Since the tax figures were the sole basis for determining activity in the port area, the engineer decided he was better off taking several vantage points around the port and visually estimating the tonnage of goods that came in over a period of time.[3]

When information must be obtained through interviews and visual inspection, agents must be placed in direct contact with the taxpayers whose returns they have to audit, collect or investigate. Close contact with taxpayers is required not only in order to assess the validity of known information, but also to discover relevant information that is not on record — taxpayers who have never filed, economic activities hitherto unknown to tax officials. To enable officials to establish the close contacts they need to obtain information, the organization must be decentralized.

Sending agents from a central office to collect information outside the capital city will not do. Getting to the taxpayer does not in itself guarantee that the desired information will be obtained. To succeed the auditor must not only be able to ask the right questions — demonstrating that he already knows a good bit and, therefore, cannot be easily misled — he must also be trusted and respected. A stranger appearing one day in the town-square, asking delicate questions about the private affairs of important members of the community, is unlikely to receive the answers expected. He does not know where to begin or what exactly to ask, who he should talk to first to get the basic cues, who can be trusted and who should be avoided, whose support is essential, who are the friends and enemies of a certain taxpayer, and who may be prepared to disclose certain vital pieces of data about another person, as well as who is likely to give false information.

Caiden and Wildavsky describe another reason why traveling officials fail to attain expected results. According to their observations, the combined effects of hot weather and poor roads are so exhausting that by the time the official reaches his destination he has very little energy left to do his job properly:

> The problem [of data] is compounded when transportation is poor and communication inadequate so that it is difficult to get around and expensive to collect the required data. Central government officials who dislike traveling in the countryside are unlikely to make strenuous efforts to collect data. It is too hot, too tiresome, too uncomfortable to bother.[4]

Even in countries where distances are short, travel does not leave enough time to accomplish what the official hoped to achieve. A Trinidadian examiner describes his experience:

> We can't reach these people (in small town outside the capital city) from the main office in Port of Spain. Though distances in the island are short, driving is difficult because of the road conditions. Examiners do not want to travel and when they do, very little is achieved because most of the day is spent on the road and in recouperating from the driving.

Finally, in a survey on field organizations in Africa, Maddick found that decisions made by resident officials were better than those of traveling agents:

> It was British administrative experience in Africa that departments with officers in the field got more done and made far fewer mistakes than those who tried to operate their services purely through officers visiting areas from time to time.[5]

Historical evidence supports this logic. Today's rich countries relied on a decentralized organization when little or no information was available at the national level. Only after formal accounting developed was there a gradual shift towards centralization. This is how Sabine describes the process in England:

> The local administration of income tax, the local General Commissioners and the Surveyor's district was the direct result of a comparatively elementary transport system. Increasing centralization of income tax administration followed improvements in communications; . . . One of the dangers may be the comparative disappearance of the personal link between taxpayer and the Inspector, but some compensation may be derived from the improvement and increase in statistical evidence.[6]

Heller and Penniman found similar trends in state tax administration in the U.S.A. where decentralization at the beginning of this century was justified by "the need for an ear to the local ground and close contact with taxpayers as prerequisites to successful administration."[7] It was only after "objective sources of information became more highly developed" that a centralized organization turned out to be more effective in reaching the goals of audit and enforcement.

Finally, empirical evidence indicates that in countries where both central and local authorities collect taxes, there is a higher extractive capability than in nations that rely solely on central administration. When Lotz and Morss added "degree of decentralization" to the determinants of government revenue, the explanatory power of their formula was substantially improved. They found that "government decentralization has a direct impact on tax levels . . . a higher degree of decentralization is frequently associated with a higher tax revenue."[8]

Officials interviewed were in agreement that a decentralized structure is essential and that without it there will be little, if any, revenue collected outside the capital city. Chart 4-1 contains descriptions of the advantages of decentralization as perceived by senior revenue officials in Thailand, Trinidad, Philippines and Jamaica.

Creating field offices, designing procedures, allocating authority and assigning staff are all technical problems that are not especially difficult to solve. None of these actions, however, will make an organization work as planned. There may be a place carrying a sign reading "Income Tax Office Nowhere City," employing officials who make decisions according to predetermined procedures, and yet the purpose for which it was set up — making decisions on important issues based on information locally generated — may still not be realized. Accomplishing the first step requires merely personnel, budgets and facilities. Before the second step can be reached a relationship of trust must exist between head office and local officials.

Experience shows practice to lag behind aspirations — plans to decentralize have not quite succeeded. Years after a local organization has

CHART 4-1
Decentralization Would Improve Access to Information: Comments by Senior Revenue Officials

Jamaica:	The reason why I think we should have local branches is that the collector would in that case be familiar with the taxpayers under his jurisdiction. If for instance, a man owns a small fish shop the collector would know if he is making enough to pay tax. We here [at the Head Office] have no way of ascertaining that so we may be wasting our time with someone who really doesn't have it. The local collector could serve summonses; it would be very difficult for taxpayers to hide from him.
Trinidad:	Officers who live in the area know more about taxpayers than those who come down from Port of Spain. You send an officer from Port of Spain to collect tax from one John Brown in Tunapuna and he goes there and asks people where can this taxpayer be reached and he will probably be told that there are ten people with the same name and all sorts of things like that. This will not happen to an officer residing in the area because he will know this John Brown personally.
Philippines:	[The objectives of decentralization were:] to promote a higher degree of efficiency in tax assessment, collection and enforcement of internal revenue laws . . . to bring the revenue service closer to the taxpaying public; to insure a closer check and canvass of the tax potential of the provinces and cities . . .
Thailand:	The amphur (district office) office, where the taxpayer files his return is usually not very large and the tax agent there should know the people under his jurisdiction . . . From here at the head office there is not much that we can do except review the returns to see if they comply with the revenue code, if the proper rates were applied, deductions allowed, etc.

been set up and given the authority to act, important decisions concerning local cases are still being made at the center. In collection, for example the local offices do not do much more than what banks do — they accept payments, issue official receipts and, on occasion, send reminders to delinquent taxpayers. They do not engage in systematic searches for potential taxpayers nor do they send agents to collect payment from delinquent taxpayers. In audit the practice is to send large and complicated returns to the central office, retaining only the smaller ones at the local level. Almost no enforcement work is done by regional or district officials. Investigations and prosecutions are matters completely reserved for the central office. The exchange of information between the center and the regions is limited. Each region and district is expected to collect the same amount as in the previous year plus a small increment by pressuring the taxpayers on record a bit harder.

Officials in the field may be in a position to obtain better information than is available at the central office, but they are rarely allowed to make important decisions. Riggs describes such a situation well:

> A decentralized agency soon discovered that all the cases decided by its new regional offices were being appealed to headquarters. Headquarters regularly found regional decisions improper and overruled them, concluding that the local staff was quite unreliable. The regional directors . . . began transmitting all cases to headquarters for decision . . . Ultimately the agency remained as centralized in decision making as it had been before, but it was now encumbered with the additional expense of its regional offices.[9]

According to Riggs this happens when authority is decentralized without policy guidelines. If there are no clear decision rules, a local official undertaking a case, must do so on the basis of his own decision premises. The citizen, aware that there are no universal rules since seemingly similar problems have been resolved in different ways, appeals his case to the head office. Head office officials acting on their own decision premises may reach a different decision, making the appeal stand and thereby fostering a tendency not to comply with decisions made by local officials.

A government commission that assessed the success of various administrative reforms in the Philippines concluded that though field offices do exist they make few decisions on any matters of substantial importance:

> As early as 1955, broad powers had been delegated to Regional Directors including the assessment and collection of all internal revenue taxes and administration and enforcement of revenue laws . . . Over a period of twelve years of decentralized operations, however, the extent of delegated authority has been diminished so that . . . the Regional Directors' authority to act on assessment, collection, legal and other matters were limited. These limitations are expressed in the amounts of tax cases that may be given final

> decision at the region, beyond which amounts the cases have to be referred to the National Office for review and approval.[10]

The commission recommended that the field offices be given the authority to resolve cases irrespective of the amounts involved. This recommendation has not been implemented. The practice of referring most important cases to the head office was still in force in 1975.

Riggs is right when he says that lack of clear decision rules may lead to a shift in actual power, to make decisions, from field officials to the highest levels in the hierarchy. It is the inability to draw clear decision rules that created the need for a field organization in the first place. If the head office and the field officers could agree on everything, and reach similar decisions, there would be no need for, nor would there be any meaning to, a field organization. At the root of decentralization is the agreement that decisions made by field officers can and probably will differ from central office policies. But, in order to work efficiently, it is not enough to admit that better information may be obtained at the local level. The head office must be convinced that decisions made by field officers hold water. When there is a ladder of authority, taxpayers squeezed by auditors at lower levels will do everything in their power to climb it in the hope of getting a better deal from the higher echelons. The chances for success are good because senior officials do not fully understand how information is obtained and are not sure that it is sufficiently reliable. They do not trust the judgment of those who generate it, and may not be prepared to put decisions to test in a court of law. The risk of losing a case in court is greater than the cost of giving in at one point or another in order to prevent a showdown. It is precisely for this reason that the central office reserves the right to make final decisions on large returns — this is the area where the risks are greatest. The Philippine Tax Commission observed that the central office intervenes primarily when big taxpayers are examined.

> It is the current practice that the top thirty assessments from each regional district be elevated to the National Office for review. In most instances the Regional Director simply loses control over them, never knowing what happens to these cases. A pertinent example of this was cited by one Regional Director. According to him, the Commissioner often requests his regional office to submit a list of the assessment cases being investigated. The Commissioner then selects from among the list a number of cases that he finds interesting. He then returns to the regional office some of those included in the list but the other cases are simply taken over by the National Office.[11]

Returns that are highly complex — such as those filed by large companies with branches in a number of communities — are also excluded from the jurisdiction of the field offices. The list of exceptions, formal as well as informal, is long, and the unifying characteristic of all of them is that they include most types of cases where large scale evasion is likely to be found.

In this way the auditors in the central office skim the milk, leaving their counterparts in the regions with only low fat returns. This, in turn, affects the latter's promotion prospects. When you deal, for an extended period of time, with low potential returns, your record of assessments will be too poor to make a promotion likely. One common method to circumvent the rule that requires large accounts to be sent to the central office, is to make these accounts small enough so that they can be handled on the local level.

> The limitation in assessment jurisdiction . . . affords as inducement to the regional office to reduce the assessment so that the tax case would fall within its jurisdiction. This causes a decline in tax collection . . . Second, the initiative of the regional office to vigorously pursue a tax case for which the department is accountable might be dampened, simply because the former has no jurisdiction over the case.[12]

In an organization in which money, equipment and qualified personnel are insufficient to meet most basic needs, first priority is always given to the head office. It is to be expected that those making allocation decisions will first take care of their own interests. What is left after the head office is provided for will be allocated to the field organization. As a result the regions get less of everything that matters; they are the poorest among the poor. Those saying that the regions cannot really be trusted with much more than routine office audits and general service to the public, given present conditions in the regions, are right. It is this criticism, however, which prevents the regions from acquiring the resources and skills necessary for making decisions that will be upheld by their colleagues at the head office.

A strong regional organization cannot be set up when there are not enough resources to properly run the central office. Both Jamaican and Trinidadian officials explained the reasons for not having regional offices — though they could certainly use them: resources are insufficient to carry out even elementary activities at the head office. We should, first, they said, make sure that the head office is functioning satisfactorily before we start showing ourselves around the country. The size, or lack of it, of both countries allows them to indulge in this luxury. They can afford to limit their activities to the capital city because the tax potential in the rest of the country is low and the distances are small so that in a one day's drive an official can get to almost any community. Officials in these countries believe that even when the tax potential outside the capital city is not tapped, not much is lost because it is too low to make the effort worthwhile.

The collection of taxes from nonurban residents, which comprise the bulk of the society in poor countries, is possible only through the use of methods of audit, assessment and collection that depend on direct contact between tax agent and taxpayer. For these methods to work well the tax agency must be decentralized, and local branches established across the country. While local branches are indispensable, if the government is to collect something, using them effectively is hampered by lack of trust between central and local officials. Developing a relationship of trust between the head office and its field branches is harder in a poor country than it is in a rich one. In a rich country there are hardly any differences in work conditions, atmosphere and skills between a central and local office. In a poor country the gap between an office in the capital city and one in a local town is enormous. Virtually everything is different, including the types of problems that confront the official and the methods he uses to solve them. What created that need for decentralization is also the main reason why it is only partially accomplished.

Revenues from rural areas usually account for only a small percentage of total tax collections. Eighty percent of all taxes in Jamaica and Trinidad, for example, are collected in the urban areas. In the Philippines it has recently been decided to close down local offices where the annual tax yield was smaller than the salaries of the local officials who collected it. A decentralized organization is expensive and it does not seem to be able to produce as much revenue as the central office. Indeed poor countries keep exemption levels as high as they can to minimize the number of taxpayers they may have to deal with. Until about a decade ago the payment of taxes was limited to a small number of well-to-do professionals and businessmen who usually operated in the big cities. Recently for economic reasons (need for additional revenue) and perhaps political causes (desire for greater integration) many countries lowered exemption levels, thereby increasing the number of potential taxpayers, and were, therefore, forced to decentralize. This pattern of development is described by Carlos Aguirre:

> Income tax, at the outset, affects only a small number of taxpayers, mostly merchants and industrialists, who are almost always working close to the most important urban center. As time goes by it becomes necessary to increase the volume of collection . . . this leads to a marked increase in the scope and volume of the duties . . . and to an expansion of the geographic area in which they are to be performed. Consequently decentralization becomes one of the main devices available for the remodelling of the administration to enable it to cope with this very different state of affairs.[13]

Though decentralization is indispensable, it amplifies the already acute problems of personnel and expertise without substantially improving the nation's revenue situation. A recent assessment of the outcomes of newly established regional offices in the Philippines concluded that "they [the new offices] . . . added to already proliferated and uncoordinated activities, without . . . making any significant contribution to the productive capacity of the Bureau."[14]

Personnel and Expertise

> The ability to cope with sudden strains, unforeseen contingencies . . . is often connected with the existence of over-capacity. To this end organizations may tolerate idle machinery, build up stocks, and personnel whose time is not fully occupied.
>
> Naomi Caiden and Aaron Wildavsky,
> *Planning and Budgeting in Poor Countries*, New York, p. 45.

> The tax administrator on the one hand sees new burdens falling on his shoulders — new taxes are being imposed and existing levies become more severe. He must collect more taxes, at higher rates, and from an ever expanding body of taxpayers. On the other hand he finds himself saddled with a staff which is insufficient, inexperienced and poorly paid.
>
> Stanley S. Surrey, "Tax Administration in Underdeveloped Countries."

Shortage of well trained personnel is perhaps the most frequently cited[15] cause for administrative weakness in poor countries. Two factors contribute to personnel problems: one is the national shortage of people with technical training, and the second is the low salaries paid in the civil service. There are fewer trained people around and most of them do not work for the government because it pays substantially less than the private sector. The reason why civil service salaries are not competitive is because the government is poor and cannot afford to pay more. It is poor partly because its tax intake is low.

This logic is sound as far as most government activities are concerned, but revenue administration poses a different problem. Here we are dealing with one of the few government agencies that makes much more money than it spends. By adding auditors and collectors and improving the skills of those already working, revenues will be increased much above the additional cost of personnel and training. Revenue administration, as Harold M. Groves[16] points out, unlike other government agencies who only spend money, pays for itself by increased collections.

Experience shows that this theory does not work well in practice. Reflecting on his long experience as a tax advisor, Milton C. Taylor describes the problem thus:

> It is an anachronism that tax enforcement, which actually provides the recurrent revenue resources for most government services . . . is invariably

> given no special attention with respect to its needs for manpower resources . . . Although there is probably no better general way of improving tax administration . . . than to provide more and better staff resources . . . governments show no general tendency to establish a priority for tax administration, even when they are confronted with the hard fact that the employment of an additional tax inspector will result in an increase in tax collections of as much as twenty times his salary.[17]

This logic could not be foreign to practitioners. If it is so strong, why is it so weak as to remain unused? Even a poor government has the ability to upgrade the quality and increase the number of personnel in a certain agency. If it chooses to use its powers it is likely to succeed; it would not be able to equally affect the entire range of its activities, but there is evidence to indicate that if efforts are concentrated in one limited area, such as central banks, results are achieved. So the question then becomes one of priorities: important activities get first turn at the table; they get preferential treatment. But what if there are more so-called important activities than means to satisfy them? In that event, which is most likely the normal state of affairs, priorities are determined according to the rate of return. Scarce resources are invested where the likelihood of success is greater. But this is putting the cart before the horse. This question shall be returned to in the conclusion.

Officials interviewed repeatedly referred to insufficient manpower and poor skills as the main reason why the agency was falling behind in carrying out its tasks. The auditors were not sufficiently trained and experienced to cope with the evasion schemes designed by private accountants for their clients. Lacking the technical expertise of certified accountants they were hard put to unveil, let alone prove, evasion. Similarly, collection agents, with only a rudimentary in-service course on taxation, were at a loss when they had to apply enforcement measures against delinquent taxpayers. Chart 4-2 illustrates how senior officials view the technical ability of their subordinates.

The department not only has less of everything it needs, it also loses it rapidly and is forced to struggle to replenish diminished stocks. Unlike other departments, the Revenue is in tough competition with the private sector, which is always trying to recruit people with inside knowledge and experience in taxation. An accountant who worked for a number of years in, say, withholding, is a valuable asset for the payroll section of a private company, and he will be offered a tempting increase in his salary to leave government service. A senior Jamaican official describes how this problem affects his organization:

> The private sector keeps stealing our staff away. As we improve enforcement of PAYE the companies must improve their accounts, so they come to us looking for people familiar with the system. Our biggest problem is with the commercial banks, we compete for the same type of employees and they invariably win.

CHART 4-2
Lack of Skill, Not Will, Is the Main Weakness of Revenue Personnel

Thailand:	I believe that the technical know-how of our auditors is inadequate to cope with the tax evasion practiced by our taxpayers. We don't have a tax school or a serious training program; we don't even have a budget for these things. (a)
Philippines:	The competence of collection fieldmen leaves much to be desired . . . It seems that any person could be appointed as collection agent provided that he or she possesses some kind of civil service eligibility. No standard educational attainment is even prescribed. (b)
Jamaica:	It is becoming increasingly apparent that the most serious problem in the Income Tax Department is the need for sharpening the skills of management, particularly below the Commissioner and Senior Deputy Commissioner level . . . Most of the problems have as their root a shortage of expertise . . . I do not detect lack of desire or potential . . . It is simply a shortage of *skill,* probably existing because there has been little opportunity to train and develop . . . (c)
Trinidad:	Staff is not adequately trained and experienced, and there is lack of specialization and managerial skills. The situation warrants an expanded and intensified training program. (d)

Source:

a. Senior Thai official.
b. Joint Legislative Executive Tax Commission, *A Study on Tax Administration,* mimeographed (Manila 1965), p. 123.
c. U.S.A. Agency for International Development, Special Report on Executive Training, (Kingston, Jamaica, February 1971).
d. Board of Inland Revenue, Trinidad and Tobago, Background Paper on Trinidad and Tobago Tax Administration, (submitted to the Conference on Administration of Income Tax in Commonwealth Carribean States, St. Augustine, Trinidad, April 1970), p. 30.

A high rate of staff turnover is not unique to poor countries, it exists in all tax agencies.[17] But the drainage problem in poor countries has another more acute dimension — beyond that of losing experienced staff. Here the pressures from the private sector are stronger and their effects are worse because of the national shortage in trained people. The IRS should not have any serious problems in refilling vacant positions since there is a perpetual supply of newly trained people. In poor countries, since there aren't enough trained people around, if you lose one it is hard to find a replacement. The government is forced to recruit personnel with only basic skills, often merely high school education, and then invest time and money in bringing them to the minimal level of expertise that would enable them to perform required tasks.

> We [says a Trinidadian official] . . . are no longer trying to recruit qualified accountants, because we have learned from experience that we cannot train them . . . we decided to recruit people without professional qualifications and train them internally. They will never be as good as certified accountants, but they are more likely to stay and work for us.

Then, shortly after the new recruit has acquired the tools of the trade and some experience, he is snatched away by a private firm, leaving the government to start the recruitment and training process from the beginning. The financial loss can be regained (because private firms are required to pay the training expenses) but lost time cannot. The vacant position is likely to remain vacant for some time and the work will be left undone. In rich countries where there is a redundancy in expertise it is always possible to temporarily employ someone who is slightly less qualified than the person who left until a proper replacement can be found. In this way continuity of work is always preserved and no severe dislocations occur just because one individual has left his job.

Poor countries operate on subsistence level. In every echelon in the hierarchy of expertise there are only the minimum skills required for that echelon. Replacements are hard to find because everyone knows barely enough to do his own job. In Jamaica and Thailand a phenomena was encountered that demonstrates this problem well. Both countries produced annual reports based on statistics gathered from returns filed. They both ceased doing so. Jamaica has not produced a revenue report since 1965, and in Thailand, the department ceased compiling data in 1959. In both cases the reason given was that the person in charge of statistics had left his job and a replacement could not be found. As described by Anan, "The Revenue Department [in Thailand] ceased compiling statistics of assessable and taxable income after 1959. This was probably due to the fact that the officials who compiled them had left to work in another organization and no replacement was made."[19] In Jamaica, the official who was responsible for preparing the Department's annual report told me that after he was promoted to another job his old position remained vacant because the department could not find a suitable replacement. It took nearly ten years to revive the annual reports in Jamaica. Many important tasks are a one-man operation and if the person leaves, the function may simply be discontinued.

The high staff turnover exacerbates the department's problem with lower level personnel who are new to the job and need a substantial amount of training and experience before they can be useful. An old timer in the Jamaican department of income tax had this to say when asked why auditors generally fail to cope with their work load and carry backlogs from one year to another:

> Perhaps the problem is that our people are green, and maybe that's why they fail to cope with their work load. Maybe if people were more experienced they would have been able to cope with their problems without asking for help from other sections.

There is a quick remedy that has been recommended by more than one tax advisor. If officials lack know-how, train them! Nothing could be simpler. Taylor's recipe has been frequently offered: "This problem [poor expertise] can best be met by sending virtually everyone back to school."[20] If everyone is sent to school, who will be left to raise the revenue? Training is one of the least controversial issues in an organization; everyone can gain from it and there is almost nothing to lose. Agreeing that "more" training is needed is an easy matter, actually implementing an agency-wide comprehensive training program is not quite as simple.

The ability to develop expertise and specialization through training is dependent upon the existence of redundancy in personnel. Where redundancy is limited so will expertise be, not only because one person must do many things and he, therefore, never has enough time to learn how to do any one of them really well; unless there are more personnel than the minimum needed to keep the agency running, it is not possible to relieve an official for training because that will leave his job undone. Trinidad's Chairman of the Board of Inland Revenue explains why he has not been able to launch the training programs he desired: "The thinly spread staff could not be released for fulltime, or even part-time, training, because of the growing mountain of paper work which has to be processed."[21]

Therefore, even when the other constraints on training — lack of budgets and facilities — can be overcome it is unlikely that a sufficiently large number of officials will be released from their daily chores to enable them to participate. The department can afford to train only a handful of people at a time and therefore only the most promising and able stand a reasonable chance of getting a proper education. This again contributes to the shortage of talent and expertise in low and middle management ranks since those who made it to the training program rarely return to occupy their previous position. The usual pattern is for them to join the inner club of the department's top management, leaving middle and lower level positions in the hands of less skilled officers.

How are limitations in quantity and quality reflected in performance? Insufficient number of trained personnel are responsible for delays in processing paperwork and the frequent incurrence of costly errors: inability to deal with unexpected crises without disrupting routine operations. Finally the dominance of clerks over personnel with technical knowledge creates a tendency to emphasize paper work at the expense of action leading to results — additional revenue collected.

Consequences

Delays in Processing and High Incidence of Costly Errors

More paperwork flows into the department each day than existing personnel can cope with. It takes years to process one year's returns. In the Philippines lists of taxes paid and accounts outstanding are available no sooner than two years after returns were filed. Backlogs develop in other areas as well; auditors are often found, as in Jamaica, working on returns filed six or more years ago. Some departments have even lost control over their correspondence with taxpayers. Queries regarding refunds, penalties and tax obligations are answered long after they have been originally received. Once the agency falls behind, it is usually hard to get back on top of things, because while the original backlog is being cleared a new one is already growing. Taxing is a never-ending process; the mountain of paper that has to be processed is reborn every year and gets ever larger in size. Chart 4-3 contains illustrations of this problem.

When there is no other alternative but to use clerks to carry out technical tasks, such as assessment and processing, the organization will incur a heavy cost from errors made due to lack of know-how. S. M. Supersad, Trinidad's Chairman of the Board of Inland Revenue, describes what happened when clerks were in charge of processing:

> Prior to 1969 the staff in the division was clerical and had no accounting know-how. Clerks spent a few months on the job and were transferred to another ministry. They did terrible things, messed up the accounts beyond repair. When the Hollerith machines were introduced a few years ago the clerks simply discontinued the manual accounting and started Hollerith accounting with a clean slate. This destroyed the continuity in the accounts without which it is impossible to tell what is going on. This is why we have a lot of money in the government coffers that we can't link to anybody. We know someone paid it to us, but we don't know who. For all we know these people are still on our arrears lists. If we prosecute one of these people and this state of affairs is disclosed to the public, we would never be able to collect a penny again.

CHART 4-3
Tax Agencies Are Overwhelmed by their Paperwork

Jamaica:	Every year you get a new inflow of returns. We can never sit back leisurely and solve last year's problems. There are many cases where we know we could get more money but we must file them because of shortage of time and personnel. (a)
Jamaica:	. . . there is no follow-up on the return forms sent out to taxpayers each year . . . So many people don't file and so many returns are returned to us by the post office that it is quite impossible to have an effective follow-up with available manpower. (b)
Jamaica	We don't have the personnel to deal with all these [evasion] cases . . . We don't have audit capacity to deal with all the cases known to us . . . We could double the intake if we had adequate — quality and quantity — staff. (c)
Colombia:	The income tax administration is overburdened. As of . . . 67,000 tax returns (out of a total of 1,181,692) remained to be processed . . . As of June 1968, the Division of Taxes still had 100,000 1966 returns to process and would not be able to even begin on 1967 returns until October 1968 or later. (d)
Philippines:	The reason why we are having problems with the delinquent accounts is that our recording system is not accurate nor up to date. The last printout of official posted payments that we have [April 1975] is for the fiscal year, 1973. I have no listing of payments made after December 1973. (e)
Zambia:	. . . the department of income tax is woefully short of staff of all descriptions, having only about 75% of its authorized establishment, which in itself is out of date. As a result the department is already behind with its work. Between one third and one half of the 1967/68 assessments have not been made, and at the time of writing the 1968/69 assessments should be starting. (f)

Chart 4-3 (Continued)

Source:

a, b, c. Senior Jamaican officials.
d. Melvin White and Andrew C. Quale, Jr., "The Colombian Individual Income Tax: Rates, Exemptions, Deductions, and Administrative Aspects," in Richard Musgrave and Malcolm Gillis (eds.), *Fiscal Reform for Colombia* (Cambridge, The Law School of Harvard University, 1971), p. 320.
e. Senior Filipino official.
f. C. R. M. Harvey, "Observations on the 1969 Zambian Budget and the Administrative Constraint on Further Tax Reform," *Zambia Law Journal*, I, 2 (1969), p. 39.

On another occasion the department employed clerks in order to speed up the process of assessment. A few months later the number of objections filed with the department shot up. A tremendous amount of time and money was lost in resolving these conflicts. It took a while before it was learned that the assessing clerks took the liberty of increasing assessments at the slightest cause. Deductions that seemed to be excessive were disallowed without any further inquiry. If a receipt did not accompany even the most self-evident and minor expense claimed, the item was added to the taxable income. Taxpayers did not know what had hit them; neither did the department. When the cause for the astronomical increase in objections was discovered it was already too late. It was not possible to annul all the assessments that had been issued; there was no other choice but to examine thoroughly every objection filed and make the necessary corrections. An attempt to reduce the backlog in assessments led to the creation of a new and larger one.

Inability to Cope with Unexpected Crises: Up and Down on a Seesaw

Since there are never enough people on hand to do what must be done, whenever a crisis occurs in one area, personnel must be transferred from less affected areas. Many of these crises occur periodically making it worse for everyone since there is hardly a section that has all its staff on the job all the time. Some personnel are endlessly on loan. They orbit, as one official called it, moving from one place to another, rarely getting enough time for doing their own work. During the filing period, for example, it is common to take some collectors off their work to strengthen processing and taxpayer assistance (provided for taxpayers who cannot fill out their forms by themselves). Later, auditors are taken off their jobs to assist in classification and mathematical verification. They may be taken off their work again when during a certain month the withholding section is having trouble with processing returns. In Jamaica, collectors are used to deliver withholding forms to employers around the country because there is no one else in the department to do it and the post office cannot guarantee to deliver all the forms to all employers in time. When special projects, such as collection campaigns, are launched auditors are again loaned to assist collectors.

There is never enough manpower for a sufficient length of time to eradicate the cause of the crises. Collection campaigns must be undertaken time and again because it is not possible to do a comprehensive job on the department's records. While the flood is being stopped in one area where the dam has cracked, new cracks are developing elsewhere where the supports have been weakened by transferring personnel to the crisis area.

One official called this the seesaw effect; as problems are solved in one area they are already developing in others. Like a seesaw, you go up and down; you get a little bit higher in one area only by lowering the other. Never can both be raised at the same time.

> We can't do our work properly because of the constant shifting of staff from one section to another. This is what happens: the math verification section has a big backlog and we send a few officers there to help them clear it, in the meantime we run into a backlog here. The result is that no one makes any progress, when one section goes up another goes down.

A similar situation is described by Manuel Rapaport, a senior official of the Organization of American States.

> The administrator is obliged in times of crisis to concentrate the available resources in the affected sector at the cost of weakening those assigned to other departments (identification of new taxpayers, investigation of the real size of the taxable bases declared, etc.). What is being remedied on the one hand is distorted on the other. The consequence is that the evasion on the whole is stimulated by administrative incompetence resulting from insufficient resources to efficiently cover different fields at the same time.[22]

Attempts to improve the allocation of resources by careful planning — estimating what the needs would be and assigning available staff according to priorities — creates tremendous dislocations and need for additional reshufflings. There always seem to be too many people in one section and not enough in the others. Every director complains he does not have enough while his colleagues have more than they can use. The truth is that everyone is short of what he needs but things look particularly depressing when a crisis occurs and the amount of work that must be done overwhelms those who must do it.

> The imbalance of assignment of personnel has been a perennial problem in our organization. Year after year, we make reshuffles of personnel, aimed at sufficiently staffing the different offices. Enormous time and effort, as well as substantial amounts of money are spent for the transfers of these personnel, but after the reshuffle individual transfers are made, returning the transferred personnel to their old positions.[23]

People who acquired some technical expertise in a certain job dislike being asked to do something else. Professional auditors do not take great pleasure in doing math verification. Their own work is being neglected while they are working to save the neck of another section. The temporary work they are asked to do is not done well because they don't like doing it, because they are bored by it and because they don't have any stake in trying hard to do it well. As described by a Latin American observer:

> To all this should be added the demoralizing effect produced among qualified professionals or technical personnel on withdrawing them from technical tasks of fiscal audit and devoting them to making elementary mathematical calculations.[24]

The section that suffers most from temporary transfers is audit. Trinidad's Commissioner for Audit told me that almost thirty percent of his staff are permanently loaned to other sections and some of the people that are loaned are never returned. Audit is the section that receives the first call whenever something goes wrong because the auditors are usually the personnel with the best training and those who can be removed from their work without immediate effect on the Department's aggregate performance: "Our auditors are used to perform other functions in the department. They are moved around from one trouble area to another. The reason why we are using them is because they are our best men." Even the small number of qualified personnel the Department has cannot be used to create a strong impact in any particular area because it is not possible to keep them there long enough.

Too Much Paperwork, Too Little Enforcement

Riggs and Heady[25] dubbed it "formalism" — doing everything the book says you ought to do without really doing or achieving anything. Formalism consists of reshuffling paper instead of taking the steps necessary to reach results. Caiden and Wildavsky describe this form of behavior better than anyone else:

> Documents . . . are evidence of "work". The matter outstanding is resolved to the satisfaction of the participants when a report is filed, an order given, a letter sent, a number inserted in a ledger, no matter what happens to the piece of paper once it leaves the office, absolving its temporary owner of responsibility. Confusing paper for action is dubbed formalism for it substitutes form for reality. It is assumed that an order given is carried out; that passage of a law brings about the situation it enacts; that a satisfactory progress report means just that.[26]

A senior Jamaican official explained that everything works well until you get to the point of enforcement. There is no problem in issuing one reminder notice after another to delinquent taxpayers, the problem is to take the necessary action when no response is forthcoming. A similar observation was made by the Public Administration Service in its study of revenue administration in Thailand; here are two typical comments:

> Almost all returns are subjected to office inspection but few are subjected to field investigation. This is due to a lack of qualified personnel. The offices are staffed with an oversupply of clerical personnel and an undersupply of technical personnel.

> The preponderance of clerks over technical staff has contributed in large measure to emphasis being placed on office and clerical tasks, in order to keep the clerks busy, rather than upon technical tasks requisite to good tax administration.

Clerks do what they know best — writing letters, issuing reminders and processing incoming mail; results, as far as they are concerned, are not measured in amounts of money collected but in the amount of paper being processed. Clerks also lack the technical skills required for enforcement. Seizing property or preparing a file for court prosecution are tasks requiring specialized skills. Thus, much of the work done is actually wasted because there are not enough people around to follow up with the necessary action to close open cases.

If the Problem Is Acute and the Solution Handy, Why Do Difficulties Persist?

Why isn't something drastic done to upgrade the quality and introduce some redundancy in personnel? Specifically why doesn't the government create employment conditions that would attract capable people? The first thing to do to understand why practitioners are not doing what appears to be vital is to pose the question that they have probably asked themselves: supposing that the action has been taken, will the problem stay or vanish?

Civil servants everywhere, not only in poor countries, are paid less than equally capable people in the private sector; this is a universal phenomena. Yet this fact does not seem to impinge on the ability of governments in rich nations to recruit and retain capable personnel in their service. There are a number of factors — security, prestige, opportunity to influence important decisions (concerning large scale issues) — that make up for the lower pay.

This mechanism does not seem to be equally successful in poor countries. Though candidates for clerical and top management positions are in ample supply, many technical and supervisory positions remain vacant for years. When there is an acute national shortage of people with technical skills, differences in salaries offered by government and the private sector grow. The private sector is more flexible than the government; it can raise the salaries it pays to the point where they overwhelm the nonmaterial compensation attached to government service. Banks, for example, cannot function without bookkeepers and accountants and they will pay what is required to get first shot at available supply.[27] A senior Jamaican official describes why the government almost always loses in the competition with the private sector over scarce manpower:

> We can offer a university graduate a starting salary of $3,900 per annum; he can easily get twice as much in the private sector. We can't get good accountants for the same reason . . . even the people that we train ourselves leave us. Private companies can import foreign administrators; we can't because we cannot offer them a suitable pay. There is no real prestige in working for the Income Tax Department like you have in the U.K., so you can't count on that to keep people working for a smaller pay.

In exactly the same way Trinidad has lost nearly all the certified accountants it managed to hire a few years ago.[28]

Once again, if salary is as serious an obstacle to recruitment of capable personnel as these officials describe and, assuming lack of capable personnel is indeed a major constraint on successful implementation, why doesn't the government raise its pay scales? A Director of Personnel in Thailand explained that he is not the only one using this argument in justifying requests for budget increases. Other agencies can make an equally convincing case for increasing their allocations and there just isn't enough money to permit salary increases across the civil service; nor is it possible to authorize a substantial increase for only one department. Such action invites heavy pressure from those who have not been as lucky, the Commissioner of Internal Revenue is only one among many agency directors who would like to recruit more competent people. In his own words:

> The Civil Service Commission is thinking in broad terms, they say that they cannot raise our salaries without raising them across the entire civil service and they don't have the money to do that. The budget people pay more attention to the spending side, they are not oriented to revenue collection . . . they say that they must consider the needs of other departments, and there are others, besides the Revenue Department, who claim that with more people and better pay the revenue will be higher. The Department of Agriculture, for example, contends that if they will be allowed to improve the economic conditions of farmers they will be able to produce more and revenues from income tax as a consequence will go up. In other words, as you can see we do not have a monopoly on this argument.

In fact, the point raised by the Department of Agriculture is easier to go along with because it is more convenient politically to the Minister of Finance. Spending money to provide more and better agricultural advisors is likely to increase the Minister's popularity — something that cannot be said about spending it to hire more tax collectors who would make it harder to evade.

But there is more to the issue of personnel than budgetary strategies for obtaining additional funds when existing appropriations are insufficient. The poor may occasionally dream about what it would be like to be rich, but in daily decisions the constraints of the situation are taken as given. A rich man, if he has a good idea of how to make more money, will look for ways to surpass existing constraints to obtain the additional capital he needs to put his idea to work. Information from a number of personnel directors was convincing evidence that poor countries behave in the same way as a poor person does — they do what is possible with the resources they have, sometimes dreaming but rarely counting on major improvements to take place. A long comment made by a senior Trinidadian official provides a glimpse into this frame of mind and deserves to be quoted in full:

> This is what irked all the American advisors we had. They could not understand why our salaries are so low, office equipment antiquated and budgets stringent. They repeatedly recommended that the government improve our working conditions insisting that with a small investment collections will increase significantly. You must understand what it means to be a small poor country. Everything touches everything else. You cannot introduce modern equipment in one ministry unless you are prepared to do the same in all of them. What the Americans could not rid themselves of was their casual attitude toward spending. If you need something because that will enable you to do a better job, then you should get it. We just don't think that way, you do your job with whatever is available. The smallest improvement in work conditions and facilities takes years to achieve. Most of the improvements will usually be limited to the most vital needs.

The logic of spending a bit more to gain a lot more works well in rich nations. It does not function in a poor nation because there is just about enough to keep everyone hanging on. That little extra needed to obtain an improvement just does not exist. Even when there is a windfall, by the time the additional resources are distributed among the many claimants, too little is left for each to make a difference. It is not possible to upgrade the expertise and the pay of revenue officials without doing the same for the rest of the civil service and that task is beyond available means of any poor country.

Strengthening personnel by raising salaries and increasing the number of positions has an immediate cost in terms of money and pressure from other agencies to receive an equal share of increase, but it is not at all certain that there would be immediate benefits as well that would justify the expense. Even if the new personnel policies do succeed, the other problems which limit the effectiveness of implementation continue to exist. The new personnel will be just as constrained by poor information, lack of compliance and the paucity of bookkeeping skills as the old less capable staff. Expertise is at the root of many problems, but it is complemented from all sides by other factors. Strengthening expertise is definitely going to help, but participants are under the impression that achievements will be dwarfed by costs. At a great expense, the most they can hope to achieve is a drop in a vast sea of needed improvements.

This chapter does not have its own conclusion. Revenue officials in poor countries must make do with very little of everything they need; there can be only dim and distant hopes for improvements. Decisions however must be made; they cannot be postponed until a time in the future when more resources will be at hand, not only because no help is seen coming, but, more importantly, the collection of taxes cannot wait. So how do they make do and what effects do the means that they employ have on the results they are able to reach? Answers to these questions are contained in the following three chapters where the behavior of participants in performing the various functions for which they are responsible is described.

Notes

1. Foreign Tax Assistance Staff, "Report on Tax Administration in Jamaica," mimeographed (Internal Revenue Service, 1965).
2. Henry Bretton, *Power and Politics in Africa* (Chicago: Aldine, 1973), p. 305. Caiden and Wildavsky make similar observations in their *Planning and Budgeting in Poor Countries* (New York: John Wiley, 1974), and both authors cite W. Stolper, *Planning without Facts: Lessons in Resource Allocation from Nigeria's Development, 1959-60* (Cambridge: Harvard University Press, 1966).
3. Caiden and Wildavsky, pp. 55-56.
4. Ibid., p. 56.
5. Henry Maddick, *Democracy, Decentralization and Development* (Bombay: Asia Publishing House, 1963), p. 51.
6. B.E.V. Sabine, *A History of Income Tax* (London: George Allen and Unwin, 1966), p. 253.
7. Clara Penniman and Walter W. Heller, *State Income Tax Administration* (Chicago: Public Administration Service, 1959).
8. J.R. Lotz and E.R. Morss, "A Theory of Tax Level Determinants for Developing Countries," *Economic Development and Cultural Change* 18 (1970): 336.
9. Fred W. Riggs, *Administration in Developing Countries* (Boston: Houghton Mifflin, 1964), pp. 340-41.

10. "Report on Revenue System and Administration," mimeographed (report prepared for the Commission on Reorganization, Manila, Republic of the Philippines, 1970).
11. Joint Legislative Executive Tax Commission, "A Study on Tax Administration," mimeographed (Manila, Republic of the Philippines, 1965), p. 238.
12. Ibid., p. 64.
13. Carlos A. Aguirre, "Decentralization in Tax Administration" (Guatemala City, Guatemala: Inter-American Center of Tax Administrators, Seventh General Assembly, 1973), p. 127.
14. Joint Legislative Executive Tax Commission, p. 5.
15. The most comprehensive study of manpower problems in poor countries is: Frederick Harbison and Charles A. Myers, *Education, Manpower and Economic Growth* (New York: McGraw-Hill, 1964), see especially pp. 51-58.
16. Harold M. Groves, "Income Tax Administration," *National Tax Journal* XII, 1: 40-41.
17. Milton C. Taylor, "The Relationship between Income Tax Administration and Income Tax Policy in Nigeria," *Nigerian Journal of Economics and Social Studies* 9, 2 (1967): 214.
18. E. Pendelton Herring, *Public Administration and the Public Interest* (New York: McGraw-Hill, 1936). Herring describes how the IRS struggled with turnover at the beginning of the century and quotes Internal Revenue Commissioner Blair:

> Here is a fellow that comes in and devotes his time to his work. He goes to school at night and works like a dog and masters this income tax business . . . The taxpayer comes in and sees him doing the work, and how he handles it . . . , and says: "There's a bright fellow; he will be worth a lot of money in our business." We are paying him $3,000, and they will pay him $10,000. (p. 54)

19. Anan Lewchalermwong, *Taxation and Tax Reform in Thailand* (Bangkok: Kurusupha Press, 1972), p. 79, n. 37.
20. Taylor, "The Relationship . . .", p. 214.
21. S.M. Supersad, "Background Paper on Trinidad and Tobago Tax Administration," mimeographed (Paper submitted to the Conference on the Tax Administration of Income Tax in Commonwealth Caribbean States, April 1970), p. 30.
22. Manuel Rapaport, "The Collection of Tax Debts: Administrative Policies and Problems," (Buenos Aires: Inter-American Center of Tax Administrators, Second General Assembly, 1968), p. 97.
23. International Memorandum, Bureau of Internal Revenue, Republic of the Philippines, June 28, 1972.
24. Rapaport, p. 97.
25. Fred W. Riggs and Ferrel Heady, "The Philippine Administrative System: A Fusion of East and West," *Towards a Comparative Study of Public Administration,* W.J. Siffin (ed.) (Bloomington, Indiana: Indiana University, 1957), pp. 266-67.
26. Caiden and Wildavsky, pp. 60-61.
27. For a description of differences in pay scales and their implications on recruitment for the civil service in poor countries, see Albert Waterston,

Development Planning: Lessons of Experience (Baltimore: The Johns Hopkins Press, 1965), p. 253ff.

28. Supersad, pp. 20-22.

Chapter Five

Catch Me if You Can: Audit and Assessment

If an income tax is to be anything other than a poll tax — or at the most a tax based on occupation or profession — some attempt at assessment of individual incomes becomes necessary. This immediately raises serious difficulties in many underdeveloped countries.

A.R. Prest, *Public Finance in Underdeveloped Countries*, p. 31.

"The Tax Administration seeks to secure maximum compliance to the tax laws . . . by means of an annual audit plan."

Auditor's Manual

"The role of audit is to encourage and achieve the highest possible degree of voluntary compliance."

Auditor's Manual

Comprehensive Assessment and Selective Audit

Data fuels the taxing process. The more data there is and the higher its quality in terms of both accuracy and reliability, the greater the proportion of the policy's revenue potential that will be reached. The collection of taxes is based on the ability to identify taxpayers and to obtain comprehensive data on the multitude of items that form taxable income; or in the case of indirect taxation the value of the taxed good or service. Since data determines the amount of tax that would have to be paid, there is an irresistable incentive to omit some items and manipulate others so that the tax bite would be minimized. This is why control mechanisms are needed. The function of audit-assessment is to ensure that the data used to calculate tax dues is indeed reliable, accurate and comprehensive.

How is this task performed? What are the problems it poses? What do participants do to overcome them? What goals do these methods promote? Are these the goals that the agency (as opposed to individual auditors) wants promoted? How do they affect the ability to implement tax policies?

The root problem of audit-assessment is complexity. The number of taxpayers and taxed items is huge, the quantity of the data and the complexity of the rules of calculation defies any attempt at comprehensiveness and accuracy. Though it may be essential to check every individual and every item (as one expert suggests: "Check each return carefully and follow up on any item that suggests further investigation"[1]) it is not possible to do so. The government must choose between comprehensiveness and accuracy; the more you get of one the less you get of the other. Unfortunately a continuum does not exist so that the convenient middle of the road solution is not available. The government must choose between allowing the taxpayers to calculate their own tax and subjecting a few of the calculations to detailed verification or retaining the calculations in its own hands and thereby submitting every taxpayer to an official assessment. If accuracy is preferred then there is no other possibility than to limit severely the number of cases to which it will apply. If comprehensiveness is deemed more important, then accuracy must be sacrificed and no return will be intensively audited. Complexity is reduced either by limiting the number of cases where complicated calculations must be made or by simplifying the calculations themselves.

There are two known procedures for handling the task of audit-assessment.[2] The U.S.A. followed the principle of accuracy in developing its "self-assessment system." Taxpayers are supplied with forms and rules of calculation and are expected to calculate their tax, file their return and pay at the same time. The Internal Revenue Service accepts the payments made from the majority of the taxpayers without much more than a simple arithmetic verification. Then, a small sample of returns is selected based on criteria which enable the agency to reach those that have evaded in a significant way. These returns are subjected to a thorough and methodic audit aimed at getting as close as possible to reality.

No one doubts that a great number of returns contain inaccuracies, but the guiding assumption is that they are so small and numerous as to both defy detection and make it uneconomical. The reason why this assumption is tenable is that the accuracy achieved by audit succeeds in deterring potential evaders. According to Tanzi, "In the U.S. people do not evade taxes to any substantial extent because if they did the chance of being caught would be quite high and the consequences quite serious."[3]

There is no need for comprehensiveness — assessing every taxpayer; the procedure secures compliance with the requirement to report accurately through deterrence. Instead of influencing taxpayers through the assurance that their information will be examined, an appeal is made to their fear of penalties. Since only a small percentage of the returns is examined, the majority of the taxpayers has a good chance to underreport and get away with it. Why should anyone report accurately? Because the few who are caught are severely penalized. The agency is not satisfied with imposing deficiency assessments; it adds penalties to the requirement to pay back taxes. When the taxpayer decides whether or not to include certain items in his report, he must consider whether the probability of paying less tax is worth the risk of a heavy monetary penalty or in extreme cases a jail sentence.

To obtain the desired deterrence effect three requirements must be fulfilled in selecting the sample for audit. First, returns must be selected in such a way that evasion-safe areas will not develop. If, for example, it becomes known that stock brokers are rarely audited, there will be a remarkable increase in the number of those who wish to join that profession. To prevent this from happening, the sample selected for audit must be a representative sample; it must include returns from every type of profession, income level and geographic area. The relative weight given to each profession is determined by the degree to which it is evasion prone; there are certain occupations that are more amenable to tax evasion than others. It is relatively easy for a lawyer or a medical doctor to omit certain items of income because there is very little control that can be exercised on the number of clients or patients served.

The second requirement concerns the number of returns that are audited annually. It must be sufficiently high so that each taxpayer making enough money to evade will stand a good chance of being audited within a reasonable period of time. If persons who have the opportunity to evade are audited only once in say ten years they are not going to be strongly influenced by it.

The third criteria concerns the quality of the examination. Accuracy is vital. No taxpayer should come out of an audit with the feeling that he had the upper hand. Superficial audits are worse than no audits since they damage the department's reputation. The taxpayer learns that there is nothing to be afraid of. As long as he plans his evasion well, there are pretty good chances that it will not be discovered. Only by being able to unveil the smartest scheme does the department stand a chance of convincing people not to try.

If certain occupations are rarely audited, if the number of audits in relation to the total number of returns is so small that it will take more than six or seven years to complete an audit cycle, and if the quality of the examination is poor, there will be no noticeable effect on compliance. The harder the auditors work the more evasion they may unveil but no one including those caught will be dissuaded from repeating the same offence next year.

The second procedure developed in Britain is based on the principle of comprehensiveness. No return is accepted without some scrutiny. Taxpayers are required to appear before an assessment officer who examines the information supplied and calculates the tax. The assumption is that most taxpayers will cheat if given the opportunity, therefore it is vital that everyone be subjected to a direct if superficial assessment. The desired compliance is maintained through the certainty of examination.

While the American system conserves administrative resources of time, personnel and money, it makes serious demands elsewhere. It is heavily, almost entirely dependent on the ability or willingness of the taxpayers to comply with the requirements of information. If the taxpayer is to be trusted to calculate his own tax, there must be a verifiable base from which he will proceed. Without formal bookkeeping there is no basis for preparing the reports, no basis for accepting it on its face value and even fewer possibilities for reaching accuracy in the sample audited. There is much less processing to do but unless the quality of information is high, more might be lost than gained by conserving resources.

The British model, on the other hand, demands very little from the taxpayer; he may even be illiterate. As long as he appears before the assessing officer and can be interviewed, he will be taxed. Its weaknesses are buried in its principle — comprehensiveness. Since all returns must be assessed before payment is made, delays in processing returns are immediately reflected in the revenue; and, as the processing work load is heavy, there is a constant danger of slipping into backlogs which tend to perpetuate themselves.

The purpose of the control mechanism, however it is operated, is to convince most taxpayers to avoid playing a game of wait and see. If most taxpayers report only a fraction of what they are really making, then even the best detection method will crumble under the weight of the errors that it will be detecting. It is not enough to be able to detect errors; it is necessary to be able to correct them, and to convince taxpayers not to repeat making them. Once the process is working and most taxpayers comply, a good detection and deterrence mechanism will keep it going. The ability to detect errors and impose penalties on those who deviate from the rules is also the way to start the process working. The problem is that when you start from scratch results are not quickly obtained. Countries such as Britain and the U.S.A. which now have smoothly running processes have gone through long periods during which taxpayers continued to ignore the tax agency regardless of how hard it tried to convince them to go along.

It takes time to perfect the process and develop the necessary skills; it takes even more time for large numbers of taxpayers to realize that the tax department has the ability to make its word stick. Progress is achieved by making rules stand. The department may not be able to do all that it has to do right from the start, but what it does do must strictly adhere to the principles that it eventually hopes to achieve. If the principles are compromised before they are fully instituted they never will be.

Compromise with an evader once and he will be never convinced to change his ways.

Organizations overcome their complexity problems by choosing between accuracy for the few or a less strict examination for everyone, but there still remains the complexity encountered by the individual auditor. Whether he examines a few cases intensively or a lot of cases superficially he faces more calculations than he can hope to complete within a reasonable period of time. He may have too much information so that he will have to find ways for deciding which parts are more important than the others. Or he may be supplied with too little information and will then have to decide where to look to get what he needs to do his job. Worse yet, he may not have the time or the necessary expertise to make the required calculations. In making his choices the auditor posits goals against the constraints and opportunities of the situation in which he operates. The choices made have a direct impact on the amount of revenues collected and the ability to produce deterrence. Methods that are effective in obtaining, through audit, a bit more money this year, may destroy the prospects of obtaining a higher level of accuracy in reporting (and a resulting higher level of revenues) in the future. Methods that are effective in promoting compliance are slower, more cumbersome and frequently more expensive.

How then is the task of audit carried out in the poor countries, where both information and auditing expertise are severely limited; what methods are used to simplify calculations; why have these methods been preferred over others, and how do they affect outputs? The experience described here is based primarily on data from Jamaica, Trinidad and Tobago, Thailand and the Philippines, but whenever available, data from other countries was included as well.

The British assessment model instituted in many poor countries during the colonial era has recently begun to lose its attractiveness and is being rejected by an ever increasing number of countries. A method that has been working well in Britain didn't prove to be quite as efficient in most poor countries. The difficulties described by an Indian observer are typical:

> Arrears of collection are piling, completed assessments are being opened and reopened, the number of appeals and counter-appeals is mounting, collection of taxes is falling and petty refund claims are incredibly delayed . . . Our tax administration is rather like an ant heap. You go and look at it and you will see a great many ants all running about and they are obviously moving in one direction or another but it is very difficult to see where they are going to or what they are doing. The tax officials are no doubt on the move, but, in spite of the apparent activity, the administration seems to be at a stand still.[4]

A senior Trinidadian official describes how comprehensive assessment worked before it was replaced (in 1972) by selective audit:

> Tax productivity was minimal, they assessed the easy cases and put the difficult ones aside for a later date. At the end of the year they took all the remaining returns, gave them a quick review and made the assessment without really getting into the matter. The really difficult cases were thus never audited, most of the time and energy were devoted to the simple cases.

Auditors were expected to do a comprehensive job and that precisely is what they have attempted to do. As a result, they developed what one veteran auditor called the "assessor's mentality" — "if they see something that is wrong in a return regardless of how insignificant it is, they will proceed to correct it." That usually meant that it was impossible to assess all returns in the same year in which they were filed. Since there were no priorities auditors set their own. What was easy was done first. Difficult cases were put aside to be dealt with later when more time would be available. The most obvious errors, where the amounts involved are typically small, absorbed most of the auditors' attention and energy. There was never enough time to invest in the difficult cases. The complicated returns were dealt with hastily shortly before prescription went into effect. Things never got better, always worse. There never was less, always more work to do. There was no hope for unveiling carefully engineered evasion. Huge backlogs tended to develop as the number of filers increased (as a result of the expansion in business activity and the rise in salaries) at a rate faster than the number of auditors. backlogs in assessment made it even more difficult to terminate a case since taxpayers took advantage of the lapse of time and argued endlessly about every little detail. An Indian commentator describes what happened when officials had to make assessments four or five years after returns had been filed:

> Gone is the finality of assessment, gone too is the sanctity of the completed assessment, gone also is the 'judicious and not capricious' approach to an assessment. Assessments settled years ago are reopened to raise petty demands; more time is spent on minor reassessment resulting in accumulation of current assessments which if completed early, would yield far greater revenue than the reopened assessments.[5]

Since much of the data that is used in making assessments is not formally recorded, the further decisions are being moved from the occurrence of the events with which they deal — the more arbitrary they become, the more frequently will they be challenged. Backlogs in assessment create collection problems. Old debts are much more difficult to collect than current ones. A taxpayer assessed a few years after he has filed his report will not pay promptly.

Finally when assessments are made years after the reports have been filed they lose what impact they could have had on compliance. People do not take seriously an examination that may take place years after the events occurred. For one thing they know that much of the information that is material to proving evasion will by then have disappeared. Furthermore, even if the audit would be effective, the value of the money would have declined. Hence a deficiency assessment paid four or five years later amounts to less than what would have been paid had true income been reported earlier.

Late assessments also enforce the casual attitude with which the payment of taxes is taken. No one takes the law seriously because the tax agency itself is not able to implement it strictly.

Why assess thousands of returns when the same goal can be achieved perhaps even more effectively by auditing only a few? The American procedure has irresistable qualities. It is simple and has all the appearances of rationality and modernity that appeal to administrators and politicans anxious to show that they are moving along with the times. Thus, instead of attempting to improve the existing system, many countries including Jamaica, Trinidad, Thailand and the Philippines rejected it completely and adopted the American self-assessment model. The responsibility for preparing the return and calculating the tax due was shifted from the assessing officer to the taxpayer. Assessors were trained to do audit work; an audit plan was made and classifiers instructed to select, according to certain predetermined criteria, returns for audit.

Most if not all the deficiencies of the old system have been eliminated as if by a magic wand. There are no more backlogs because auditors have to do only as many cases as they can manage. Since assessment is no longer a precondition for payment, it does not matter if not all the audits that were planned are actually executed. There is less work to be sure, but has there been an improvement in production? To answer that question the audit process must be examined as it is carried out in practice. The selection of returns is discussed first. Secondly, the calculations that are made to determine whether the taxpayer's information can be relied upon are presented. Thirdly, the strategies used to obtain his cooperation and consent to the final findings are aired. Lastly, an attempt is made to assess the results and offer an explanation as to why they are as they are.

Separating Wheat from Chaff — Classification

In choosing who will be audited the classifier predetermines the outcomes of the entire audit process. Suppressed income can be unveiled only when it is there. If the selection of returns for audit is poor even the best auditor will not be able to obtain good results in terms of unveiling evasion. The classification of returns poses two problems. What are good indicators of evasion[6] and, second, how can a classifier scan a large number of returns in order to find the few that are in need of audit?

Since the process is not computerized (and will not be in the foreseen future — most poor countries are still struggling with computerization of return processing) and scanning must be done manually, complex selection criteria that are necessary for picking up carefully engineered evasion cannot be used. Since the classifier must often scan thousands of returns within a few months (in Jamaica, for instance, one classifier goes over some 10,000 returns in one year), he must use simple criteria. In the words of a senior Jamaican official:

> There are no written standards; we rely on the expertise of the classification officer . . . . The classification officer gets the taxpayer's file so that when he looks at a return he has the person's whole history in front of him.

The classifier draws on his personal experience and a few simple indicators. The common methods of evasion and the items most likely to be inflated or suppressed are known to any experienced auditor. He will also know from experience that evasion is more common in certain businesses (for example, nightclubs, restaurants, second-class hotels and gambling pools) than in others. It is this experience that simplifies the classifier's job and is used to carry the hunter to where the game is. The size of the return is perhaps one of the most important criteria used. The assumption is that tax potential is directly correlated with the volume of income. Hence the rule: *Look for the money where the money is.* In the words of a Filipino auditor: "first of all we classify returns by volume of income and concentrate our attention on those with the largest volume."

When you have to go over a large number of returns and you must therefore train your eye to catch the most obvious irregularities, you run the risk of overlooking the carefully engineered evasion. Indeed some audit directors have complained that

> classification is not working as it is supposed to. . . . The average adjusted tax is much too low. . . . The classifiers are classifying the small man, the little fellow; where are the big meaty cases?

The answer is that these cases are not going to be flushed out by looking at travel or entertainment expenses nor even by making a quick comparison between sales and profits. Again experience may partially compensate for the inability to carry out complex searches. In small communities people making money are visible, and in poor countries their numbers are relatively small. Thus some good cases may be selected by checking just how much tax these people are paying.

> We learned from experience, that a lot of people who appear to be small in reality are quite big. . . . You can't really tell what's behind a small tax return. It is therefore important that the classifier be a very experienced man, that he will know how much can be made in a certain business. Some of the more experienced officers know many of the taxpayers, they know what kind of standard of living they maintain and so they can spot underreporting when they come across it.
>
> (Trinidad)

This method can work only when the community is small enough to permit the classifier to develop the necessary "acquaintances." If the national community is large as it is in Thailand or the Philippines it would have to be divided into smaller units. Indeed, in the Philippines all returns are classified at the regional office and then assigned for audit to the district or national office according to volume of income and type of business (businesses operating on a national level are audited at the central office). In Thailand classification is again at the regional level while the Head Office is responsible for the entire Bangkok area.

Limitations in classification impose constraints on the capability of audit to affect compliance. As long as selection is done manually only simple criteria such as type of business, size of income, profit or turnover and ratio of profit to sales, can be used. These criteria will lead to the selection of returns with the most obvious errors that typically involve small amounts. Experience — ability to discern that something may be wrong when everything seemingly indicates that all is in order — and personal acquaintance with many taxpayers help to overcome some of the difficulties. But, neither experience nor the personal acquaintance can replace the complex cross-checking that is required to flush out a carefully doctored return. Identifying these returns and unveiling the hidden income is the first condition an audit program must satisfy before it can develop any hopes of securing results in terms of improved compliance.

Not all the returns that deserve to be audited can be audited. Revenue potential cannot be the only criteria for selecting cases. Some returns are more complicated, more difficult to audit than others. Investigating a bank or an insurance company is infinitely more complicated than a contractor's company. The first will take a lot more time and require special skills that the auditors may not have.

> It would be ridiculous for the Bureau of Internal Revenue to assign an examiner without sufficient background in mining accounting to determine the correct tax liability of a mining concern.[7]

A Thai auditor tells of his experience:

> The mining companies [are the most difficult to deal with in my district], because they have so many different kinds of expenses. It makes it very difficult to verify.

Returns that are selected for audit must not exceed the level of expertise available in the department. The department would become the laughing stock of the business community if it undertook to audit a return and then was forced to close the case without being able to reach worthwhile results. S. M. Supersad, Trinidad's Chairman of the Board of Internal Revenue, summarized the problem thus:

> Lack of the required competence could lead to lower standards, unnecessary prolongation of audits and, perhaps, harrassment of taxpayers. . . . if auditors are not available to conduct quality audits, it might be advisable not to undertake audit of certain returns. It would merely expose weaknesses and might provide scope and incentive to taxpayers to evade.[8]

Accountants with specialized expertise in banking, mining, insurance or shipping industries are extremely scarce, and are usually working for the private sector and not for the tax department.

The complexity of a return is often directly related to its size. The bigger it is the more complicated and hence more difficult to audit. An internal departmental study cautions against emphasizing size:

> It is the experience both in the U.S.A. and in Canada that the larger income returns yield the highest tax adjustments and show a high frequency of change in examination. No study has been made to determine whether the experience in Trinidad has been similar. There would however appear to be some correlation between the size of the income and the accounting and reporting complexity involved in auditing large income returns.[9]

In rich countries the classifier may choose any return that he thinks should be audited; in the poor he is restricted to those with which the auditors can be expected to cope. If audit capabilities are limited it may be wiser to concentrate on the simpler returns. The small amount of defifiency assessment that can be obtained from each return will be partially compensated for by the greater number of returns that would be done. The advantage of auditing a large number of simple returns is that better coverage can be obtained. Whatever limitations there are in the quality of audits, they can be compensated for by the increase in quantity. Though every department selects some simple cases, the milestone of any audit program is the big return. It is more convenient to audit a few known cases where behavior is basically predictable and results are assured, than to run around in an open and vast field, looking for something that is not easily distinguishable from its environment. Increase in quantity requires a decrease in quality. To achieve a greater number of audits without increasing the number of auditors, the examinations must be less thorough. There would be heavier reliance on intuition and general impressions than detailed examination of formal records.

Professional accountants will object to a policy that forces them to depart from their professional standards. They will argue that their professional reputation may be damaged. The junior examiners, lured to the department by the promise that though the pay is lower than what they can get in the private sector the job is on a much higher level, will be even more frustrated than their senior colleagues if asked to spend their entire day examining small fry. Trinidad's Chairman of the Board of Internal Revenue explains why it has not been possible to increase coverage by lowering quality:

> These officers were promised, when recruited, that they will have a glamorous career auditing all these big firms. How can you tell them that for the next five years they will have to satisfy themselves with audits of grocery stores and street peddlers. We will be in trouble up to our necks with the Unions if we did that and many of the auditors will probably resign.

There is a strong feeling especially in the smaller nations that in fact the task is not as complicated as it may sound. It is possible by elimination to drastically reduce the number of returns that are worth a second glance. This attitude is reflected in a speech delivered by Trinidad's Chairman of the Board of Inland Revenue:

> In practice, many returns do not require examination. The majority of taxpayers who file returns pay their taxes under the PAYE withholding system. Many are so small that the tax recovery potential would not justify, . . . the cost of examination. . . . of the others, not all could be fully audited with the limited resources at [our] disposal.[10]

Along the same lines, a Jamaican official commented that "there are so many cases that require audit that we don't need any plans." No one will deny that this is true. The point is that if only obvious returns are selected very soon there will be no more obvious evasion. No selection rule can be exclusively relied upon since, once it becomes known, taxpayers will doctor their returns to prevent them from being picked up. For example, if returns that exceed a certain amount are the only ones that are selected, it will not be long before everyone will report income below that amount.

What do the auditors do with the returns that are selected? The first rule they are expected to follow is "work as fast as you can." The larger the number of returns that are audited the greater the chances that audit will have an impact on compliance. The second rule is "follow all leads and do not leave many stones unturned." The taxpayer should be impressed that the auditors are capable of finding suppressed income even when it is well hidden. The third rule is "refrain from drawing a deficiency assessment that is not well grounded in acceptable evidence." There is no use in imposing large assessments that later on would not be collected because the taxpayer filed an objection.

It is not possible to follow all three rules simultaneously, especially when the level of expertise is low and the quality of the accounts examined poor. The rule that says work fast is incompatible with the rule that requires comprehensiveness. The compromise that auditors will strike depends on the inducements they receive in terms of promotion and whatever other rewards that are valued in their particular organization. Motivation is important, because, unable to follow all rules simultaneously, auditors may be tempted to prefer the one that is most convenient to them. If what they should do is not sufficiently clear, they may decide to take things easy and sit on cases endlessly, claiming later that they have presented severe difficulties or that the taxpayers refused to cooperate. A senior official in Thailand complained that "they [auditors] could do their work faster and more effectively, too. Some cases take up to three months . . . the majority take three weeks. This is too slow." By way of comparison audits in Jamaica and Trinidad take only four to six days.

When auditors are hard pressed to complete examinations rapidly, they may ignore the quality criteria and draw arbitrary assessments. When the criteria by which auditors are evaluated is the amount of assessments they draw, there is the danger that they will impose unreasonably high assessments, sacrificing feasibility of collection. A senior official describes what happened, when, in his organization, amount assessed was made a major criteria for promotion.

> I think that auditors make unreasonably high assessments that cannot be realized later on, i.e., cannot be collected. The reason for this is that auditors are promoted on the basis (among other things) of . . . . the amount of tax added to the original return. The result is that they are constantly trying to assess taxpayers as high as they can.

A similar problem was observed in the Philippines "when assessors are left to do their work they make arbitrary assessments that turn out to be too high and cause us problems in collection."

The way to achieve a balanced approach is by emphasizing feasibility of collection. The auditor should work fast and do a thorough job, but the results of his examination are not worth much unless they are accepted by the taxpayer. The auditor must resolve whatever differences of opinion there are between himself and the taxpayer. He is not allowed to finalize an assessment unless his supervisor is satisfied that everything that could be done has been done to convince the taxpayer to accept it. Differences of opinion must be resolved at the lowest possible level. Only when a case is air tight and the taxpayer challenges basic principles is permission granted to send it up the ladder. In this way, a safeguard is introduced that ensures that auditors will not impose arbitrary assessments. In the Philippines for example:

> BIR (Bureau of Internal Revenue) Policy is to count only those assessments which have a legal leg to stand on. Assessments made are subject to review by supervisors. If the supervisors will really do their job of reviewing the assessments made by their examiners, the latter will be discouraged from unduly inflating their assessments.[11]

None of these procedures is complicated or difficult to follow. Yet introducing them does not guarantee the expected results. Successful implementation depends on the existence of a middle management level that has the skills and experience to supervise. Only the supervisors of small groups of auditors can detect and correct, in time, deviations from prescribed norms. Typically the middle is the weakest level in bureaucracies in poor countries. Capable and well trained persons are scarce and therefore quickly sucked from lower to the top levels, either skipping middle levels completely or spending a relatively short time there. This is a problem that has no immediate or apparent solution. It is safe to assume that no significant improvement can or will be achieved before levels of education are raised and the entire public and private sectors reach saturation. Until that happens methods must be devised to live with this constraint.

When it is difficult to directly control an entire population, the alternative is to select a random sample. In Trinidad, for example, "the reviewers are examining a sample so that the auditor does not know whether his audits will be reviewed or not. This keeps them on their toes.

A small group of highly qualified auditors subjecting a sample of audits to a detailed quality review may be able to do the job that the supervisors are suppose to do. Technical review serves other goals as well. It helps as a Trinidadian senior official pointed out "to maintain standardization in audit. Different auditors treat certain items differently. The reviewer's task is to ensure a uniform interpretation of the law." Technical review can also be used to limit corruption. A study conducted in the Philippines concluded that

> the reason why examiners have not been deterred from conniving with taxpayers is that they are secure in the knowledge that their report may not be reviewed .... A minimum fixed percentage of all closed cases may be auto-

> matically subjected to review to determine whether sound judgment or discretion was exercised.[12]

As auditors are under pressure to work fast and since frequently they cannot rely on the records the taxpayer submits, certain aids to calculation are used to render manageable the task of determining how much more the taxpayer should be asked to pay.

Aids to Calculations

> Our goal here is to get tax money and as much of it as possible; so if a case takes too much time, get out of it.
>
> (Audit Director)

It is a mistake to think that audit is solely or even primarily accounting work. There is that, of course, but as a veteran Internal Revenue Service auditor said, "Audit is eighty percent psychology and only twenty percent accounting." The books of accounts, even when they are available and are fairly detailed and comprehensive, can at best only indicate that expenses were inflated or income suppressed. To discover exactly how much, the auditor must get additional information that almost by definition cannot be found in the books. No one steals and leaves fingerprints behind. This is true for rich countries where record keeping and accounting procedures are sophisticated and widely spread. It is even truer in poor countries where documents submitted by taxpayers are frequently unreliable because recording procedures are either too crude or completely nonexistent. Says a senior auditor in one of the poor countries:

> We are at a disadvantage when we confront a taxpayer who has not kept adequate records. We can't assess him arbitrarily; it will be illegal and would not hold in a court of law. Yet, to get even a rough idea of his income will require a large investment in time which we cannot afford because of the shortage in trained auditors.

Auditors do not have time to spare, so they must use methods that work well without demanding a big investment in time and expertise.

Pick the Odd One Out

The first rule is, as a Trinidadian auditor put it: "We go in and try to hit the taxpayer on the most visible things and close the case." What is a visible thing? Anyone walking into a room where auditors are at work will see them bent over piles of documents, moving their eyes up and down long columns of figures. What are they doing? They are engaged in the familiar game called "pick the odd one out." They are looking for a figure that does not fit with the rest. Something that is unusually large or exceptionally small. Compared to what? Compared to what they know from experience to be reasonable. After a year or two in this work you know what is reasonable, what is acceptable and what is not. You learn what questions should be asked. Here is an example described by a Filipino auditor: "The taxpayer says that he employs this many stenographers. The question to ask is who do they serve? No one would employ twenty stenographers for one or two executives." An experienced examiner should know what are the average profit ratios for different types of industries. Now if a reported ratio is too low, he would have to look for explanations.

Another good lead is the tendency for too many details in the accounts. Oftentimes this is a means used to duplicate expenses. Along the same line, books of account that are too tidy and clean may serve as an indication that they are not in daily use but have been specially prepared for tax purposes.

These irregularities, deviations from the average, indicate the need for further search. Alone, they cannot support a deficiency assessment. Irregularities merely suggest that taxable income may have been lowered. A Filipino described it well: "The basic thing in this work is to find something that will draw attention to something else that will lead the examiner to hidden income."

There is, however, no guarantee that a more detailed examination will produce results.

You Know a Return by Looking at Who Submits It

To minimize that risk the examiner attempts to assess the taxpayer's credibility. Every taxpayer will be able to offer some explanation to the irregularities found in his return. This, however, puts the auditor back in square one. In most cases a time consuming investigation is required to determine the validity of the explanations. The auditor can save a lot of time and effort if he has a simple decision rule which will help him accept or reject explanations on face value.

Instead of verifying the validity of the information supplied by the taxpayer, the auditor tries to determine to what extent he himself can be trusted. A Jamaican auditor describes how it is done: "You test the man's credibility. . . . If a man's answers are elusive, if he takes time to answer your questions, if he gives you tentative answers then you know he is trying to hide things from you." Another auditor provided a more detailed description:

> He will tell you how careful and honest he is. He has never been in trouble with the Income Tax Department. He assures you that you will find all his records in good condition. While he is telling you that, even in an airconditioned building he is perspiring. When you ask for essential records he will

> say that his wife who is a very meticulous person threw that particular one out when she dusted his desk. He will be able to remember and produce insignificant details, but when you ask him about the important ones that you want, he is blank.

Establishing credibility is even more important with companies because their accounts are more complicated and hence more difficult to verify. The first thing to look for is the company's history. The best description is by a Thai audit supervisor:

> The history of the company serves as a guide: how they keep and have kept their records, do they have an internal auditor, is he a serious man with a good reputation . . . how many times has the company changed its accountants? If there have been frequent changes it could indicate that accountants were asked to betray their professional code and have refused to do so.

The reputation of the firm of accountants that prepared the accounts is also valuable, says a Jamaican auditor:

> Some accounting firms are known to be more reliable than others. So when you get an account that has been certified by them, you can pretty much accept it. Other firms have a bad reputation and when you get something from them you double-check everything . . . sometimes, to protect themselves, accountants will qualify their certification by saying, for example, that stock is estimated rather than actual; that is an indication that there may be something wrong.

Auditors agree that the most important thing to know is who is the manager. What kind of reputation does he have? Is he a shareholder or an outsider (as an outsider his interest in interfering with proper accounting may be lesser than that of a manager who is also a major shareholder)? The manager's personal history may also be indicative. What is his reputation among fellow executives? What kinds of companies did he work for in the past? A description of how this information is obtained is the best way to demonstrate how it is used:

> I have been here for twenty years and I keep my own records. I keep track of the first ten men in every business, at least the first ten big men. These people's reputation is fairly well known; I will have quite a bit of details about each of them in my files. In this group of people it is not difficult to find out who can be trusted and who cannot, who is honest and who is a crook. . . . frequently you get a manager who is too young to be known. In that case you can get an idea from looking at who is on the board of directors. The latter are going to be familiar, if not all, at least a few will. If these are crooks with no reputation at all, they are unlikely to choose an honest man to manage their company for them. So by looking at the board of directors you can decide whether to trust or to suspect the manager.

How Small Is Small?

When the taxpayer's credibility is not sufficiently strong to act upon, the auditor will have to resume the search for information. The best place to start is the place of business. A Trinidadian auditor describes what can be learned from visiting the business premises:

> In one place you find that the owner is always busy, there are a lot of customers in the store and he seems to be doing well. This type of place is worth looking into. In the other place you hardly see a customer, the owner just sits there doing nothing and the place is neglected. This type of place is not worth your time.

Such a visit also allows the auditor to verify quickly a few major items in the return such as number of employees, capital assets, repairs. This is also the best place to interview the taxpayer. Here the taxpayer can speak his own language and the auditor can actually see the items he refers to. A Jamaican auditor describes his practice:

> Even if the interview is held at the accountant's office I like to visit the business place. I go there early in the morning before I go to the interview . . . . I check to see how many people are actually employed. Sometimes they claim that they have a dozen employees and at no time can you find more than six . . . . You can learn a lot by interviewing the taxpayer at his business, at the accountant's office he can get help, the accountant can signal him to stall, or not to answer a particular question . . . .

Questions and Answers — The More He Talks the Deeper He falls

Useful information often comes from the least expected source, the taxpayer himself. Ask the taxpayer what he may think are leading questions and he will clam up. Ask him to talk about his business, the kinds of problems he has and how he solves them and you will be surprised how quickly he will tell you the secrets of his trade. The more he talks the more the auditor learns about the business and its operating practices. The more he knows the easier it becomes to "pick the odd one out." You can't see the odd one unless you know what the regular ones are.

The taxpayer, unless he is exceptionally well prepared, does not remember exactly what information he has put down in his return. Thus as he talks he may disclose something that he had intended to keep from the auditor. He may indicate, for example, that his wife has her own bank account, something he did not mention before because he has been using that account to deposit cash that has not been recorded in the books. A Jamaican auditor described his experience:

> I don't bother with the accounts at all, I ask him about his sources of income. I try to get him to talk about his operation. Just a friendly discus-

> sion of his business. In the process of this he may mention a source of income that he didn't report. Many people here derive their income from three or four sources.

If You Want to Learn about Profits, Talk about Losses

One topic that taxpayers like to delve on are expenses. The higher the expenses, the lower the profit ratio, the smaller the tax due. But large expenses are also an indicator of a high turnover. Expenses usually go up with the scale of business and vice versa. Up to a point, by inflating expenses, the taxpayer can reduce his taxable income. But, when the delicate line between what is reasonable and exaggerated is crossed, large expenses indicate that something is wrong, that either they are inflated or that profits are suppressed. A Trinidadian auditor describes how he uses this mechanism to discover hidden income:

> People are always complaining about their expenses; this is something they like to talk about because they think that this way they will provide you with an excuse for their low profits. . . . The best thing is to let them talk; you learn more than by asking questions.

The auditor shows an interest in expenditures, and the taxpayer quickly responds; the alternative, he knows well, is to talk about profits, and that he would like to avoid. Then the question arises: "If your profit is as low as you have claimed it is, how come you are spending so much money to make it; wouldn't you be better off by putting it in a bank and collecting the interest?"

Most of these aids to calculation can be used when the taxpayer has some records of his business transactions. But, what if there are no records? Small traders in poor countries, as a rule, do not maintain books of account. Audit manuals prescribe, for these cases, indirect methods. Net worth and bank deposit analysis are the most commonly used. In the first method the auditor prepares a list of assets and liabilities at the beginning and the end of a tax year. The difference between the taxpayer's worth (assets minus liabilities) at the beginning and end of the year is his added net worth that serves as a basis for calculating the tax due.

In the bank deposit method the auditor tries to reconstruct the taxpayer's income and expenses from the records of his bank drawings and deposits.

The indirect methods are time consuming and more difficult than the direct ones. Auditors, if they can, will avoid taking cases that require the use of these methods. If they are saddled with such a case, they will prefer the method — usually bank deposits, that yields the quickest results. The net worth method is not used frequently because it requires the auditor to obtain information that is not readily available. One important type of information are the taxpayer's personal possessions. Asked if he visits the taxpayer's residence, a Jamaican auditor responded, "No, we don't do that. The taxpayers will become very annoyed. In general you don't want to put the taxpayer into too much trouble, you must keep good relations, we are a small island."

Similar answers were given in the other countries. Entering a man's home for purposes of audit is not acceptable. For these reasons, even when the indirect methods are used, the investigation is far from being comprehensive.

Ask for More — When It Starts to Hurt, the Taxpayer Will Let You Know

Some countries prefer to shortcut the process by using what is commonly called "estimated assessment." Instead of trying to get to the taxpayer's actual income and expenses, the examiner tries to reach a rough idea based on a few obvious and visible indicators. In Thailand, for example,

> the estimated tax is determined on the basis of human intuition . . . . if you don't have any idea at all about a certain kind of business, you go out and watch the shop for a few days. . . You look at the electricity bill, you look for any luxury items such as a big modern refrigerator, how many people are employed.

Once an estimated assessment has been made, it can be used as a base to which small increments will be added each year. The taxpayer will not be allowed to pay less unless he can prove that his income has fallen. The advantage of this method is that it requires very little effort. Managed properly it can yield good results. So long as the taxpayer pays what he is asked to without complaint, it could be taken as a sign that the estimate is far below actual income. The auditor can count on the taxpayer to come in screaming and yelling armed with every piece of information he can lay his hands on when he is asked to pay more than he thinks he should. If the annual increments to the base are substantial, many taxpayers will find it in their interest to maintain books of account.

In practice the use of estimated assessments is limited. When taxpayers are squeezed by arbitrary means, they file objections that are difficult to settle, since there was no clear-cut evidence to begin with. When they are not squeezed hard enough, the department will be losing money.

From the calculations that are made to determine how much the taxpayer should pay, we now move to the strategies that are used to obtain his consent to comply.

Strategies

> "Taxpayers make every effort not to follow through, not to allow the auditor to complete the audit quickly."

> "We will do everything possible to reach an agreement with the taxpayer so that he will pay the deficiency assessment and close the account."

> "I am not trying to force my figures on them; we must compromise because we don't have strong evidence against the taxpayer."

The auditor cannot succeed in carrying out his task without the taxpayer's cooperation. Though taxpayers rarely refuse to cooperate, they often use every means available to protect themselves, making it difficult for the auditor to complete his job. The taxpayer has all the time in the world; the auditor must finish the job by next Wednesday.

The auditor must find ways to get the information he needs quickly. Most auditors agree that the best thing to start with is "known things and a friendly approach. Get the man's confidence. Give him allowances he didn't ask for, build a relationship. Act like big brother, better tell me what you have, we don't want to put you out of business" (Jamaican auditor). Says another Jamaican auditor, "The first thing I do when I get there is set the taxpayer at ease. I make it a point to arrive on time! Jamaica is a country where people rarely come on time. In this way I create the impression that I am a businesslike person."

If the carrot doesn't work, the stick will. The second method is to convince the taxpayer that you already know enough to nail him: "If you get one piece of evidence on something that the man has, this is your key card. Without disclosing exactly what you know, you may get information on the rest of his assets" (Jamaican auditor).

The third method is to convince the taxpayer that loss of time and nerves can be mutual. Just as the taxpayer can employ delaying tactics, so can the auditor resort to harrassment. Instead of spending a day or two on the business premises, he may hang around for a whole week, question the employees, interview clients and generally make everybody aware of the fact that the business is being investigated. The rule of "let's get it over with" seems to work with even the most reluctant taxpayers. Nobody enjoys having an income tax auditor around when doing business.

When everything else has failed and the taxpayer perseveres, the best method to bring him running to the tax office is to impose an arbitrary assessment.

> The two most effective means of getting the taxpayer to come up here and answer our questions is first a personal visitation by one of our examiners,

> and second an arbitrary assessment: we choose some of the most obvious errors on the return, increase the assessment and mail a deficiency assessment notice; the next thing you know the taxpayer comes running up to protest.
>
> (Philippines)

This method, however, must be reserved as a last resort for the most stubborn taxpayers.

Unless judiciously and carefully applied, these last two methods — "let's get it over with" and the arbitrary assessment — can easily backfire. Innocent taxpayers may be unduly harassed. A taxpayer who thinks he is harassed may take his complaint to the newspapers or the courts. One thing that tax departments can do without is bad publicity.

Auditors, unless they are carefully trained and supervised, have a tendency to become overaggressive. When the thin line between judicious use of strategy and harassment is crossed, the department stands to lose what public esteem and court support it has. The auditor's job will become more, rather than less, difficult. A senior Filipino official describes the situation well:

> Fear will not get us anywhere; an examiner who bullies his taxpayer may only find that the latter keeps fooling him whenever his back is turned. A taxpayer, even here, is usually quite worried, if not scared, when he finds out that his return is going to be audited. The examiner must do his utmost to alleviate this fear and make the taxpayer feel at ease. If the taxpayer feels that the examiner is out to get him by hook or by crook, and that he will make a big case out of the smallest error, he will only try harder at hiding his income.

The mechanism that can keep the auditor within bounds is the requirement to obtain the taxpayer's approval of the deficiency assessment. This is what makes the auditor's job a difficult one, for it is not enough to reach good assessments in a short period of time. It is also necessary to obtain the taxpayer's consent. The higher the deficiency assessment, the more difficult it is to convince the taxpayer to accept it. The taxpayer gives up when he thinks that he won't be able to get a better deal by taking his case to higher administrative levels or the courts. At the auditor's level a number of methods are commonly used to reach agreement with the taxpayer.

Man is adaptive. Given time and lack of choice he learns to live with the worst. The auditor capitalizes on the fact that the taxpayer is faced with uncertainty as to how much he might be asked to pay. The rule is that if you are led to believe that you will have to pay say fifty dollars, you get used to that idea during the few days or weeks that elapse between the time the price has been quoted and the day payment is made. Then, just as you fish for your pocketbook, you are informed that the price has been dropped to forty dollars; not only do you pay more willingly, you leave believing that you saved ten dollars.

The auditor, as he goes along in his work, drops a hint here and a word there about how much the taxpayer could expect to be asked to pay. The taxpayer has no idea how far the auditor will succeed in carrying the examination. Hence the slightest hint is a relief that leads to the conclusion: "Well, if it's only that." The auditor tries to establish a base that will be acceptable to both parties and around which the final bargaining will take place.

The process is governed by the fact that the auditor, for all practical purposes, has unlimited discretion. He may choose to see certain things, overlook others and no one would ever know. He can comb the area clean, picking up the smallest detail, or he may go through it gathering only a few of the most obvious items. If the taxpayer cooperates by furnishing the information the auditor is asking for, a few stones can be left unturned. When difficulties are piled in the auditor's way, he can use his discretionary powers to squeeze the lemon dry. The smallest item will go into his report; the taxpayer will be kept in the dark throughout and slapped with a high deficiency assessment at the very end.

Agreement is reached in stages. Its essence is developed during the audit itself while the final details are worked out during a bargaining session that almost always follows the audit. In Jamaica informal sessions are often held even before the official assessment notice is issued. In other countries the notice of assessment is issued, the taxpayer files an objection and only then is the session held.

A bargaining session can lead to a compromise that will close the case only when the taxpayer has already accepted the base. If the auditor's discretion was virtually unlimited during the examination, it is extremely narrow after the report has been completed. He can give in only in areas where the added assessment rests on interpretation or incomplete documentation. At this level it is impossible to give in on a point of fact. A Filipino auditor told me, "We give in on some items, and we don't on others. For example, we can give in on representation expenses, even if they cannot be fully substantiated, provided that the amount in question is reasonable."

Reasonable is the magic word that allows the auditor to maneuver; it gives him the extra little elbow room that he may need. How does he determine what is reasonable and what is not? The most detailed description comes from a Filipino official:

> We make comparisons with other similar businesses. Much will depend on the explanation that the taxpayer can give us. Is he able, for example, to specify exactly on what has the money been spent . . . . [another factor is]

> his reputation. His reputation will affect his credibility; it will assist us in determining what is a reasonable amount for him.
>
> We try to learn as much as we can about the background of the taxpayer before going into conference with him. We will try to see whether there is a pattern in his behavior and reporting; it will be used as a basis for our decisions.

If the taxpayer has accepted the general line of the audit and wishes merely to lower the amount at the margins, the conference will lead to a mutally acceptable compromise and the case will be closed. When the auditor has failed to convince the taxpayer to accept the base, no bargaining could lead to a compromise and the case will probably have to be litigated in court. What if bargaining is not permissible for political or other reasons? Officials criticized for conniving with taxpayers and accepting bribes may refuse to bargain because that will only expose them to further attacks. Auditors in Thailand told me bluntly that they cannot afford to lower a deficiency assessment, because if they do it will immediately be assumed that it was done for money. When a taxpayer tries to challenge our findings, they said, we tell him that if he wishes he may go to court. Yet the number of objections reaching the courts in Thailand is extremely small. How then are agreements reached outside the courts? An audit director explained why the auditors can refuse to bargain without worrying that every other assessment that they make will get stuck in court:

> When we investigate someone we are quite lenient, we take into consideration the ups and downs of business. Even when we impose an added assessment we will leave the taxpayer with a certain margin in his favor; we would not try to squeeze him dry. So we do not negotiate with the taxpayer . . . . he will not take us to court because he knows that he has evaded, he knows that we have left him with a margin, and he knows that for these reasons he will not be able to get the sympathy of the court.

This is another example of the philosophy guiding the entire audit program in poor countries: better have a little bit today than a lot more tomorrow. If you can't bargain with the taxpayer to keep him from going to the courts, you lower your demands to begin with. The alternative of insisting on payment of the full amount is not even seriously considered. If the explanation for why tax departments compromise is true, then the system will break down if bargaining is taken out without tailoring deficiency assessments to what taxpayers are prepared to pay. The following account, quoted from an internal report on audit practices in the Philippines, supports this claim:

> A taxpayer who does not agree with the examiner's proposals is allowed

> five days to appear at an informal conference . . . . In practice, however, the procedures are frequently disregarded and the taxpayers receive an assessment notice without having been given the opportunity to present his protest. The failure to observe this procedure is attributed to the examiner who may be exasperated with the taxpayer's failure to agree with his findings . . . Assessment Department is bogged down with appeals from taxpayers who demand reexamination of assessments.

When the taxpayer is dissatisfied he doesn't pay; he protests. When a lot of taxpayers protest the process by which objections are resolved courts get clogged and the list of outstanding amounts mushroom. As time passes, bad debts tend to develop since people move around and can no longer be found while others have completely forgotten that they owe tax and will be reluctant to pay. Says a senior Jamaican auditor:

> The appeal procedure is very lengthy and cumbersome; if we let the taxpayer go into it, it would take a long time before we would see any money from him . . . . Right now we have enough objection cases to keep the revenue court (one judge) busy for the next hundred years.

Auditors reach results by compromising. They may compromise before finalizing the assessment by keeping it sufficiently low so that the taxpayer will not be motivated to try his luck in court. Or they may compromise after the assessment has been made by retreating from certain demands that they have made. Either way they must reach a middle ground between their demands and the taxpayer's expectations. If that is not done and the auditors insist on having their own way, assessments will get stuck endlessly in the courts and no results will be reached.

Outcomes

> "Audit merely causes the taxpayer to change his means of evasion. Probably after he is audited he will design a better way for evading . . . . As long as they don't have proper records there is no sense in talking about voluntary compliance."
>
> Auditor

The selective audit program, as every audit manual reads, is intended to promote voluntary compliance. The four countries studied have had selective audit for varying lengths of time: since 1970 in Jamaica, 1972 in Trinidad, and almost two decades in Thailand and the Philippines. What have they produced? Improvements in the accuracy of reporting, which is the program's main goal, cannot be measured directly; no outside researcher will be allowed to examine returns as this is a violation of the rules of secrecy that bind every tax department. Two surrogates on which some data are available can be used. One is the total number of filers, the other the number of filers reporting taxable income. A selective audit that is effective should lead to an increase in the number of filers that exceeds the normal growth. For the second surrogate it is safe to assume that some taxpayers comply with the filing requirement but reduce their income to below the taxable level. If compliance is being improved, then there must be a decrease in the percentage of nontaxable returns.

The data that is available does not show that the desired changes have been attained in any one of the two surrogates. In Jamaica the number of filers not only did not increase, it even dropped sharply immediately following the introduction of self-assessment. Table 5-1 shows that three years after the reform the number of filers is still substantially lower than what it was in the last year of comprehensive assessment. Table 5-2, based on data from the Philippines, shows a pattern of increase in the number of filers and taxable returns, but it is rather stable and does not seem to show any radical change that could be said to have been a result of the introduction of selective audit in the late fifties. The sharp fluctuations that occur between 1947 and 1952 can be related to the effects of the Second World War. The leap in the number of filers and drop in taxable returns that took place between 1971 and 1973 is clearly a result of the tax amnesties that were instituted during this period. The only other significant deviations from the pattern occurred between 1958-1959 and 1964-1965. The first change need not concern us here since it is a drop and not an increase in taxable returns. The second change, a sizable thirty percent increase, could be a result of a comprehensive study on tax administration conducted during 1964-1965 by the Joint Legislative Executive Tax Commission.[13] This was a time when everyone in the Bureau of Internal Revenue wanted to look nice, since it was expected that among other things the Commission in its final report would make recommendations on new job classifications and pay scales. There is an average annual increase of roughly fifteen percent in the number of taxable returns, an admirable achievement in itself, but the trend is stable and does not reflect any major increases that could be related to a change in the methods of audit.

Not one of the officials I have interviewed was willing to sign his name on a statement saying that selective audit brought about an improvement in the accuracy of returns. To the contrary, it is a matter of common knowledge that underreporting is still as widespread as it has been in the past and involves large amounts of money. Filipino auditors told me that even when they audit the same person year in and year out, the attitude toward reporting remains basically unchanged. One Jamaican senior auditor went as far as suggesting that the only way to bring an improvement is to return to the old procedure and start assessing taxpayers systematically. Selective audit, he explained, works well when most people

TABLE 5-1
Jamaican Taxpayers Fall Out of the Tax Net When Self Assessment Is Introduced

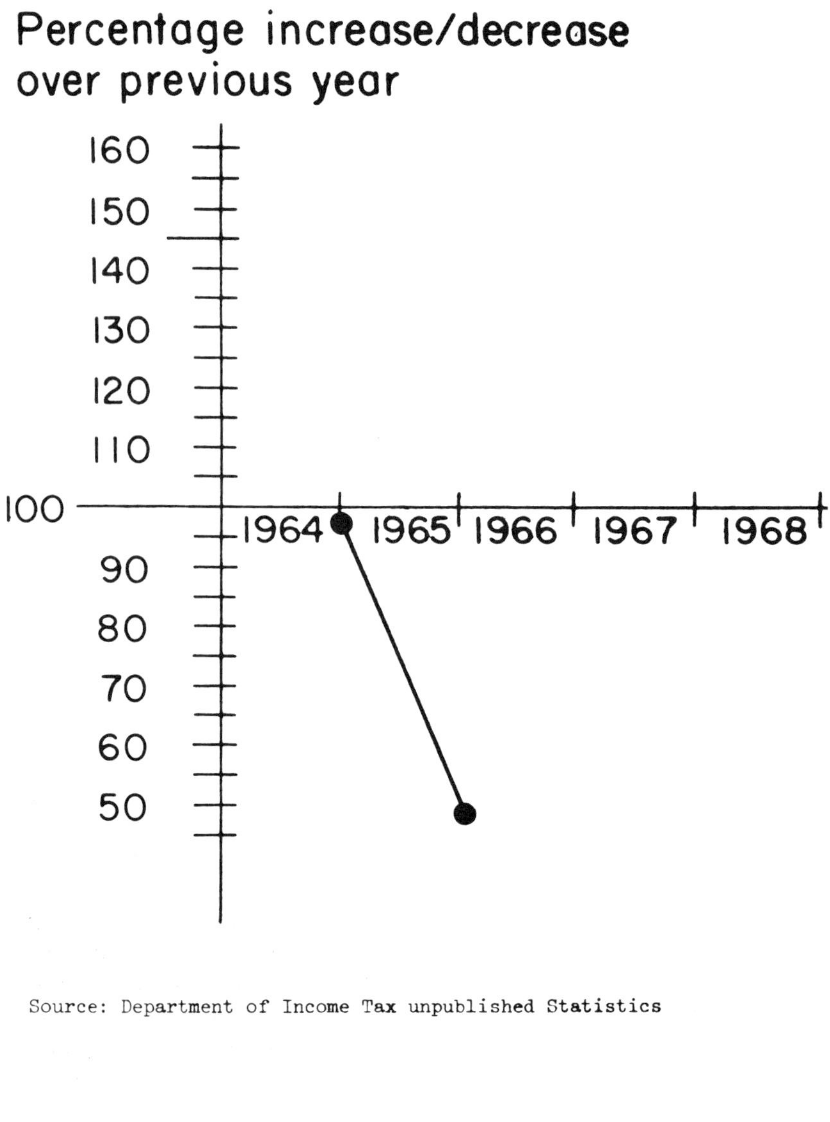

Source: Department of Income Tax unpublished Statistics

Table 5-1 (Continued)

	YEAR	No. OF FILERS
	1964	78,359
	1965	78,217
YEAR OF REFORM →	1966	
	1967	
	1968	
	1969	
	1970	NOT AVAILABLE
	1971	37,825
	1972	58,721
	1973	75,381
	1974	57,076

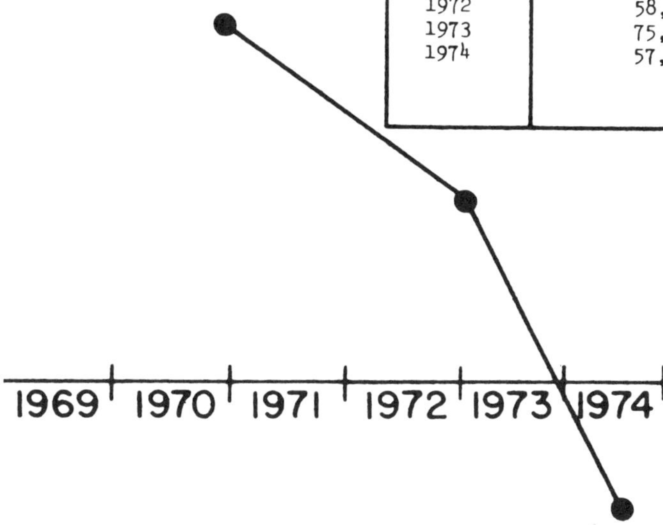

TABLE 5-2
Changes in Number of Filers and Taxable Returns Is Independent of Audit Methods

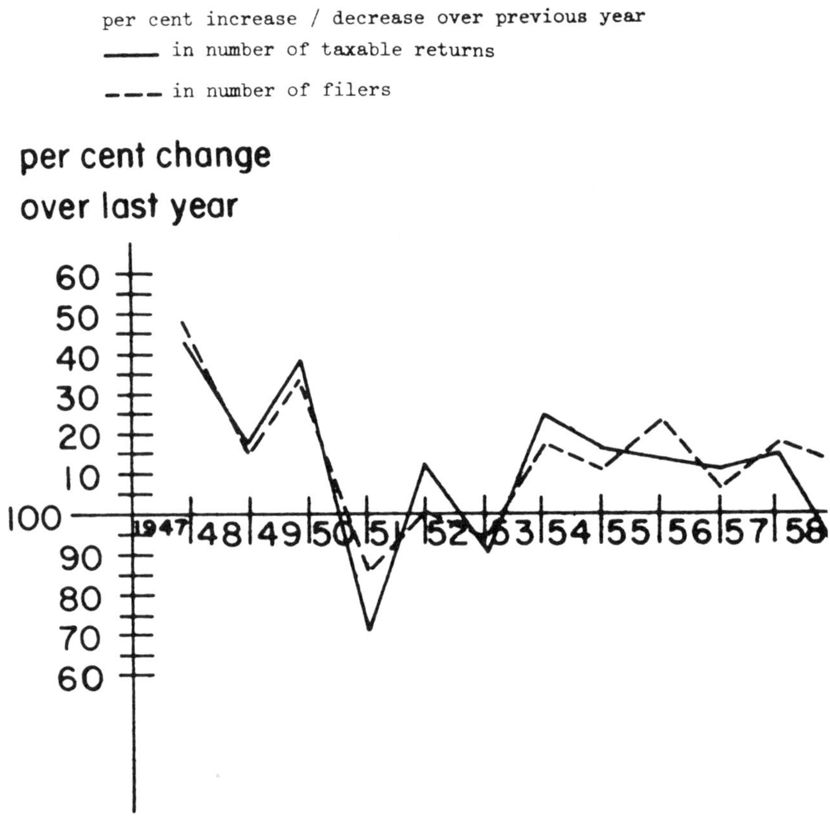

Source: Bureau of Internal Revenue Annual Reports, Republic of The Philippines

---

report more or less what their real income is. But in our case most people do nothing of the sort; many don't file at all and those who do report, report only a small fraction of their income. While we are fooling around with five hundred taxpayers, the other sixty or seventy thousand are going their own way. What is done in audit does not seem to affect the general public. He concluded, "Actually we must now get back to the old system that we have discarded and start assessing people and impose our estimates on them."

Self-assessment did remove some of the problems associated with

Table 5-2 (Continued)

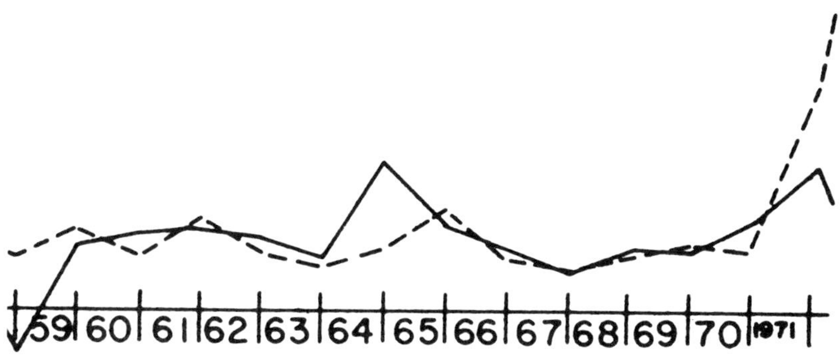

comprehensive assessment, but it does not seem to have succeeded in elevating the tax agency to the road leading to voluntary compliance.

The methods that are used to carry out the examinations, though quite effective in squeezing a bit more from some taxpayers do not succeed in inducing the majority to report true income. What should be done to obtain voluntary compliance is not done and the question is why? The answer can be found by comparing what auditors are required to do with the constraints that determine what they can reasonably be expected to do.

The main reason why audit fails to affect compliance is compromise. The compromise that comes at the end of the audit process puts an end to any hopes that may have been harbored that audit will improve reporting. Only when there is absolutely no possibility of gaining something from underreporting can there be hope that audit will induce taxpayers to report their true income. If it is possible to compromise then it pays to try your luck and underreport, for even if worse comes to worst you would not have to pay all the tax that you would have had to, had you reported accurately. With compromise the game of audit remains for the taxpayer a game of "heads I win, tails I do not lose."

Yet compromise is not an evil trick that is pulled out of the sleeve at the last stage of the examination to make it easier for the auditor to close the case. Compromise is the common denominator of all the methods that must be used to reach any results at all. If compromise means settling for less than what could, in theory, be obtained, then classifiers compromise when they do not select certain promising returns, because there is no one in the department who could audit them successfully. Auditors compromise when, instead of examining accounts that do not exist, they rely on impressions and secondhand information that is hard to verify properly and even harder to use as evidence to prove evasion in a court of law. What else is there at the end but to compromise on an amount that itself is a product of compromises.

The choice that auditors face is between working hard to improve compliance without reaching noticeable results within the foreseeable future and working hard to obtain revenue, a secondary goal but one that is much more tangible. To no one's surprise, more often than not the second alternative is preferred to the first. It would have been nice if the same procedures would have produced both results; in practice, however, one goal can be obtained only at the expense of the other. Under the least favorable conditions some results may be reached if certain shortcuts are taken. Even on the flimsiest evidence it is possible to convince a taxpayer to accept and pay a deficiency assessment. The taxpayer will be willing to give up something rather than risk a more thorough examination. Hence, immediate, tangible and quantifiable results are achieved.

What would it take to convince this taxpayer and many others not to repeat the same offence next year? Three conditions must be fulfilled before the auditors can expect to have reasonable chances of affecting compliance.

1. Coverage of occupations, income levels and geographic areas. Good coverage is hard to achieve because of limitations in classification and audit capability. Since classification is done by manual scanning, only simple selection criteria can be used. Experience and personal acquaintances can help the classifier in going a bit beyond obvious errors, but they are not sufficiently strong to enable him to flush out carefully planned evasion. Coverage is further limited by the ability of the auditors to examine certain types of returns. Government auditors usually have only elementary training in accounting, which, though sometimes compensated for by a substantial amount of experience, does not give them the upper hand in the confrontation with big company accountants. Most departments prefer not to audit certain returns at all when the skills for conducting a high quality examination are not available.

2. *Number of returns audited in relation to returns filed.* To convince taxpayers that the probability of being audited is a real one, the number of returns examined each year must be high enough so that a full audit cycle could be completed within the prescription period, usually five or six years. Most tax agencies are undermanned; many of the positions are vacant because there just aren't enough qualified accountants in the country. Furthermore, the high turnover of the staff leaves the department with newly trained examiners, since those who acquire enough experience leave. Unexperienced auditors are slower than experienced ones. Shortage of staff and limited experience combine to keep the number of returns that are completed annually at below the two percent mark. Within five years only ten percent of the filers will be audited. Thus most taxpayers will continue to act on the basis of the feeling that there is a very remote chance that their return will be selected for audit within the prescription period.

3. *Comprehensive examination.* The limited proliferation of formal accounting procedures and the limited accounting skills of the government's auditors puts the achievement of this goal outside the realm of feasibility. In areas where accounting procedures have been introduced, usually foreign corporations and large enterprises, their complexity is such that the government's auditors are hard put to reach any results at all. In areas where business records are not available or are not sufficiently comprehensive, the examination cannot produce information that could be used as evidence in a court of law. Therefore while the taxpayer should be confronted with findings that would convince him that the best thing is to comply, in practice he is left with the feeling that the auditor didn't learn enough and what he has gotten will not carry him far if they went to court.

No amount of will power can enable tax agencies in the poor countries to perform all these tasks sufficiently well. Virtually all the audit directors spoken to complained that regardless of how hard they try they don't seem to be able to do more than, as one of them put it, "scratch the ground." It is doubtful whether much more than scratching the ground can reasonably be expected. If the department would decide to put a greater effort into upgrading the professional capabilities of its auditors, it will have to cut down sharply on the already small number of audited returns for the length of training. If it decides to increase the number of returns that are audited, it will have to lower the standards of examination and hence compromise on the third requirement of compliance.

If it would select for audit only those returns that are supported by proper accounts and instruct the auditors to carry out a comprehensive examination that would eliminate the need to compromise, the result will be that the majority of the business enterprises in the country would not be audited at all. If compromise is ruled out without changing the quality of the examination and record keeping procedures, a great number of taxpayers will file objections, jamming the courts.

The alternative is to do neither and aim at increasing the revenue yield of the examinations. When revenue and not compliance is the main goal of audit, it is no longer necessary to satisfy the coverage requirement and struggle with all sorts of complicated returns where the chances of reaching any results are small. First, only those returns where high deficiency assessments can be quickly obtained need be audited. Second, the examination need not be comprehensive. It is carried only as far as it is economically worthwhile. Even when you know that there is more hidden income out there, you don't go after it unless the effort required is likely to be smaller than the revenue that might be obtained. Going after revenue and not compliance saves the department expensive and time consuming litigations in court. Perhaps the most important gain is the fact that by setting revenue as the main goal, the department can function with the skills that its auditors have and the procedures that the majority of the society is used to. Even if the department could recruit, train, and retain top-notch accountants in its service, the task of introducing formal accounting practices to the society at large cannot be completed with the resources that are available.

This, then, is the difference between the methods that are used to squeeze a bit more out of a taxpayer and those that must be used if he is to be convinced to report accurately. Examiners with just elementary training in accounting will find it very nearly impossible to penetrate deeply enough the accounts of a large corporation to convince its directors to pay a substantial deficiency assessment and to refrain from committing the same offences next year. The same examiners will quickly learn how to obtain the information they need to convince a smaller taxpayer that it pays to compromise and close the case. The only problem is that this leaves reporting a game played by the rule "catch me if you can" with both sides knowing that there are too many on the taxpayers' side and not enough on the government's side.

Notes

1. Joseph H. Murphy, "Selecting Income Tax Returns for Audit," *National Tax Journal* XII (1959): 232.
2. A good comparison between the American and British systems is Harry G. Johnson, "Self Assessment to Personal Income Tax: The American System," *British Tax Review* (1971): 78-85.
3. Vito Tanzi, "Personal Income Taxation in Latin America: Obstacles and Possibilities," *National Tax Journal* XIX (June): 156.
4. S.K. Agarwal, "Tax Collection and Administration," *The Economic Times* VII, 78 (1969): 5.
5. Ibid.
6. I have not been able to obtain specific information on the criteria used for selecting returns. These are highly confidential and for obvious reasons. As long as the taxpayer is kept in the dark about exactly what is used as an indicator for evasion, he cannot manipulate his accounts so that his return will not be selected.
7. Joint Legislative Executive Tax Commission, "A Study on Tax Administration," mimeographed (Manila, Republic of the Philippines, 1965), p. 65.
8. S.M. Supersad, "Present Problems in Organizing and Carrying Out a Balanced Audit Programme: Perspective for the Future," mimeographed (Trinidad, 1973).
9. Board of Inland Revenue, Trinidad and Tobago, "Internal Memorandum on Immediate Assessment Program" (1965).
10. S.M. Supersad, "Some Recent Developments in the Trinidad Tax Administration," mimeographed (Port of Spain, 1974), p. 5.
11. Joint Legislative Executive Tax Commission, "Feasibility of Joining the Assessment and Collection Functions of BIR in One Department, with Respect to Income Tax," mimeographed (Manila, Republic of the Philippines, March 3, 1972), p. 5.
12. Joint Legislative Executive Tax Commission, "A Study on Tax Administration," p. 128.
13. The Study's results are reported in the "Seventh Annual Report," Joint Legislative Executive Tax Commission (Manila, Republic of the Philippines, 1966), pp. 20-40.

Chapter Six

Waiting for the Taxpayer to Come and Pay: Collection

Take the case of the collection agent in Marikina. He is assigned a small cubicle on one end of the treasury office. He appears to be a part of the entire treasury force. An ocular survey shows that there is only one door provided for the office of the municipal treasury thereat. In entering the space given to the collection agent, one has to get through by crisscrossing the area being occupied by said treasury personnel. Worse, whether he likes it or not, the collection agent has to leave the cubicle after office hours at 5:00 p.m., otherwise he has to break through the windows for egress. How about taxpayers coming in the late afternoon? Who is there to attend to them? And according to the collection agent there are a number of them like businessmen and office workers coming during the late hours. Perforce, under the circumstances collection efficiency is impaired.[1]

Q: Can you please describe to me how you collect each and every internal revenue tax?

A: Well, our usual practice is to wait in the office for taxpayers to come and pay.[2]

Since assessment procedure has largely been relegated . . . to an audit function, it is important that the significant thrust in most tax administrations should be made in the area of collection procedures. Significantly this area of tax administration does not receive the type of attention which it so richly deserves.[3]

I do not know, where along the process of organizing collection units in the BIR, to direct efforts, necessary to effect collection of receivable accounts, was neglected and no specific unit organized to perform the responsibility. Collection agents . . . in our scheme of collection were set up merely to perform tellering functions.

(Philippines)

Tax collection is what tax agencies did in the past. The tax collector was, perhaps, the best known, most feared and hated of the central government's representatives. His task was to travel from one village to another to exact payment from the residents. Throughout history it was taken for granted that taxes must be collected or, more accurately, extracted from the citizen. There were only few exceptions where the government relied solely on the benevolence of its taxpayers. Tax agencies today do not collect, they accept what taxes are paid.

Why is it necessary to collect taxes? Or, why is it not sufficient to inform taxpayers of their duties and of the penalties that will be imposed if they will not comply? To Americans the question must seem foolish. Most of them pay almost routinely. As a British commentator observed:

> The system mobilizes a variety of motivations for getting the tax revenue in on time — the relief of getting it over and done with, the social value of sharing a collective burden, and the democratic appeal of being allowed to calculate one's financial responsibility to the state according to one's own lights.[4]

Most Americans and Britishers have never met a collection agent and they are probably not even aware that a small number of them exist.

So why is it necessary to collect taxes? A Jamaican collector describes her experience: "Writing a cheque for the Income Tax Department is something that you postpone until you absolutely must do it . . . so they wait till I come to collect it." The same view is expressed by a Filipino official in an internal memorandum: "We have forgotten somehow that there are still taxpayers who need prodding and will not voluntarily pay their tax liability without a persuader telling them to pay."

In the old days the taxpayer did not have to pay. In fact, he could not pay until after the assessment was made. So it was possible to combine assessment with collection. There was a direct, person to person contact between taxpayer and tax agent. The assessor, who dealt with more or less the same people year in and year out, knew or could quickly find out who was tardy in paying. This was lost with the advent of self-assessment. Thousands of taxpayers who previously belonged to small (usually geographically or occupationally based) groups now became anonymous. They felt it and took advantage of the new protection they acquired. This created the need for a systematic activity for the collection of delinquent accounts and returns.

Tax collection is the main business of the tax agency in a poor country because only a small part of the population files or pays voluntarily. There is no satisfactory methodology for arriving at the number of individuals and legal entities that should, but do not, file returns. Estimates based on the experience of informed practitioners run as high as sixty percent and often revolve around forty to fifty percent.[5] An informed Jamaican senior official indicated that if all those who should file were indeed filing, the number of returns would be double what it is. In the Philippines recently, as a result of a tax amnesty program, the number of filers leaped from one to four million. In other words, until 1974 there were no fewer than three million nonfilers, triple the number of filers in

1971. There is no assurance that the amnesty brought them all to the surface.

Nonfilers are only one side of the problem; the other side are those taxpayers who have accounts in arrears. In the Philippines in 1972 there were 177,039 cases involving P 237,750,317 — the total amount of Income Tax collected in that year was P 1,351,693,000. The amount outstanding was about twenty percent of annual collections. In 1970 outstanding accounts in the Kingston corporate area (Jamaica) amounted to J$ 22,443,000 (the amount outstanding in the parishes is unknown), while total income tax collections for the financial year 1970-71 were J$ 62,882,469, or roughly one-third of total annual collections. In the Bangkok metropolitan area outstanding accounts are estimated at ten percent of annual collections (exact figures are not available).

In most of the countries studied (three out of four) collection sections provide their departments with little more than banking services — they accept and post whatever taxes are being voluntarily paid. Tellering and note collection is the main occupation of most so-called collection agencies. Tellering is a function unknown to tax departments in rich countries where payment of taxes is done by checks that are sent through the mail. In many poor countries payment is made in cash, not by checks, and in person, not through the mail. The use of checking accounts is very limited, and has not yet proliferated beyond a small group of westernized people who are usually concentrated in the capital city. The mail poses another problem. The service offered by the post office is notoriously poor. It is not only terribly slow but, more important, not very reliable — letters have been known not to reach their address. Foreigners visiting poor countries are often cautioned not to put valuables, such as checks, in letters sent through the mail. In Jamaica, for example, the distribution of P.A.Y.E. (pay as you earn) forms to employers is carried out by the collection agents of the income tax department. The department simply does not trust the post office to deliver the forms to all of the addresses on time.

Since payments are made in cash, official receipts must be issued. The result is that the department must maintain offices around the country staffed by officials trained to perform banking services. This not only imposes a heavy drain on the limited manpower that the department has, but people trained to be bank tellers do not make good collectors. The requirements for the jobs are so different that it is rare that a person would do both well. Bank tellers sit in an office. Collectors are permanently on the move; the only time they can be found in the office is when they fill out their reports or get a new list of accounts. Tellers are handed the money, collectors must struggle to get it. Tellers serve whoever comes and need not worry about those who do not. Collectors must find and chase the taxpayer; they have a specific list of people from whom they must collect, and they cannot afford to overlook accounts that they have not been able to close.

Collection sections that are up to their necks in tellering work and must recruit and train people suitable for the job find it difficult to pursue their other tasks equally well.

> The number of personnel assigned to each local office was big enough to just barely handle the tellering work; there was no staff available to go out and make field collections. If the officers went out to collect delinquent accounts, they had to close down the office and there would be no one to do the tellering work.
>
> (Philippines)

Tellering consumes what manpower talent and energy there is in the collection agency; not much is left afterwards for delinquent accounts.

Compared to audit, collection seems such a simple task. There is no need to conduct complex investigations to find out how much a taxpayer should pay. All that has to be done is to locate the delinquent taxpayer and exact payment or the return from him. It does sound simple, doesn't it? If the figures on delinquent returns and accounts are correct, then perhaps achievements in this field are not that easy to obtain.

Nowhere are there heard complaints that the collectors lack the legal powers necessary to carry out their jobs. It is the other way around in most countries, where there is far more authority, more legal means for forcing tax payers to pay, than is actually used. If it is not for lack of authority, what is it? The best way to understand how collection works, the conditions under which it is going to be more successful and those under which it is not going to function at all, is to follow the collector and observe what he is expected to do, how he does it, and why he behaves as he does.

Collection can be studied only where it exists. In two of the countries that were visited collection activity was limited to tellering and withholding (Thailand and the Philippines). In the third (Trinidad and Tobago) a real collection section complete with detailed written procedures and a dozen well-trained agents was found. But as one of the agents said, "We just sit there and do nothing." The section simply did not function. There was one country (Jamaica) left where it could be studied not only why collection does not work, but how it does work. This is a limitation in the data over which there was no control. It is important to note that three out of four countries do not have a systematic field collection. It means that there are constraints that go beyond the idiosyncrasies of individual countries that make collection a difficult task, so much so that no one wants to do it.

Almost without exception, collection is treated as second to audit. It is a fifth wheel, not the major preoccupation of the tax agency. Says S. M. Supersad (Trinidad's Chairman of the Board of Internal Revenue):

> In many agencies collection is relegated as a function ancillary to the more glamorous audit function. Perhaps tax collectors have not yet lived out the stigma which the ancients attached to them.[6]

A former Commissioner of Internal Revenue in the Philippines puts the blame for poor achievement in collection on its inferior status in the department.

> Because of the wrong attitude of attaching more importance to assessment than collection, more credit is given to accomplishments in the former than in the latter, and big assessments are rewarded with promotions in rank or salary while collection accomplishments, no matter how outstanding, are ignored and overlooked. Consequently those performing collection functions are not given proper incentives and motivation, such that in most cases they turn in mediocre, if not below par, performance.[7]

Auditors can always laud themselves and be praised by others for what they have achieved. The only measure for evaluating their performance is last year's results. So all they have to do is aim at obtaining a small increment. There is no objective way to determine what they should have done. No one can criticize the audit section for not doing enough audits, for who can say with confidence that 500 is not enough, while 700 is. In collection, what is not done can be more important than what is. No matter what they have been able to achieve during the course of a year, collectors are always under the burden of the outstanding accounts. Anyone opposing tax increases, trying to justify his own delinquence, or simply looking for an easy way to criticize the department, keeps his eye trained on the outstanding accounts. Liberal congressmen in the Philippines have used, time and again, the argument that as long as the BIR is not collecting all existing taxes there is no justification to increase rates or impose new ones.

The Manila Times of April 18, 1967 reports that

> liberal leaders in the Senate . . . opposed the passage of the new tax measures . . . [and] urged the administration instead to intensify and improve tax collection before asking Congress to pass more revenue bills.

Another news item reads:

> Chairman of the Senate committee on finance said that the administration has yet to prove that its collection of taxes is already "at peak efficiency" and that it has collected all the revenue that could possibly be collected under present laws.

Achievements are overshadowed by what is being left unfinished. Therefore anyone going into a tax department and caring about his career will try to stay away from collection. In audit you can build a reputation; in collection you collect criticism. Anyone having the minimum qualifications that are required for auditors would not willingly become a collector. An American adviser observed (in 1955) that in the Philippines "many of those that are placed in the collection group feel that they have been demoted."[8] Twenty years later, when the present interviews were conducted the same feeling was expressed by agents in the collection department. A Regional Chief of Collections said no one wants to do this job because not only is it unpleasant, it also involves limited discretion. It is difficult to stay on good terms with the taxpayer because there is so little you can do for him; you are coming to collect a fixed amount and that's that.

> The problem in collection is that no one wants to do this work. Most people prefer to be in assessment, it is considered more interesting. There you can stay on good terms with the taxpayers, they will try to be nice to you because you have a certain amount of discretion. In collection you have no discretion, you are coming to collect a fixed amount which has already become delinquent, so right from the start there is hostility. Nobody wants to confront angry and abusive taxpayers day in and day out.

Asked to describe the difference in attitude toward audit and collection, the Director of the Department of Collection had this to say:

> If you want to get an idea of what is the difference here between collection and assessment, compare my shabby looking office to that of my counterpart in the Assessment Department; his is twice as large, nicely furnished, with curtains and all that and I have only this cubicle that is not even a room separated from my secretaries. I once told the Commissioner that the Minister of Finance couldn't possibly be interested in assessments; what he wants to know is how much money has been collected, but no one listens to me.

And since the quality of personnel in collection is usually lower than that in audit, control mechanisms have to be used to ensure that the agents will spend their time doing what they are being paid for. According to the Jamaican chief of collection, without detailed time report sheets (that are filled out by each collector daily, weekly and monthly), agents will not do what they are supposed to do.

Directors of collection need control procedures to protect themselves against the criticism that they are not trying hard enough to cut into the mountain of delinquent accounts. When detailed data can be produced showing what the agents have done with their time, it is no longer easy to say that they haven't done enough. Only the expert can tell that the amount of time spent on a case is exaggerated. Useful as they may be for protecting the department against its critics, control procedures do not make agents work harder. Quite to the contrary, control procedures may be exploited to rationalize low productivity by showing that it is average. The reports can be doctored (and as far as practitioners can tell, indeed they often are) so that the group average, the criteria by which everyone is judged, will remain comfortably low. All senior officials questioned on this matter expressed the same opinion: it is doubtful whether control procedures improve productivity; it is quite certain that they damage what morale the agents still have.

> Don't need that sort of thing. They treat the collection officers as if they were children. It does not encourage pride and responsibility in one's work. I am also quite sure that the time reports do not reflect reality. (Jamaica)

> I don't think that they are necessary, in fact many agents have complained to me about them; they feel that they are wasting their time . . . From looking at the reports it is clear that they are either fabricated or that something is wrong with the agents because too much time is required to close a case. (Jamaica)

> Collection agents feel depressed or frustrated at the practice of being forced to submit numerous collection reports on time which are subsequently left unacted upon. (Jamaica)

> The report forms . . . are not being used, the collectors don't fill them out because they know that nobody is looking at them. (Trinidad)

Collection is a new phenomena that started to take shape following the shift from assessment to selective audit. The Jamaican collection section is only three years old. The Trinidadian was set up in 1973 and by 1974, when these interviews were conducted, it still had not started to function properly. As this was being written (November 1975), I was informed by a senior Trinidadian official that, "so far there have been no further developments in the Department although we now have between ten to twelve people actually carrying field collection operations. We started this just a few weeks ago and time is too short to make any real evaluation." The Philippines has the oldest collection department, dating back to 1954. Thailand only has tellering services but no field collection. What was there before collection agencies were set up, and how were taxes collected? An American adviser describes the situation in the Philippines (which is typical).

> The Collection Department is a new department within the Bureau. Prior to 1953, the Bureau had no collection group, but left the collection of taxes entirely to the provincial and city Treasurers. As a result many taxes were never collected. Assessments were made and because of lack of follow up, were often forgotten and not paid.[10]

Implementation did not come easily. If after more than twenty years collection in the Philippines is still so weak that a tax amnesty trebled the number of filers almost over night, what can be expected of countries that have just started two or three years ago? Developments in this area are slow. At the beginning in the Philippines collectors were not even given authority to collect. The American adviser to the government at the time observed that

> the officials of the collection department are not authorized by law to collect money. All . . . [they] can do is urge the taxpayers to pay their taxes to the local treasurer, and assist the treasurer in locating the taxpayers.[11]

Why does it take longer to set up a collection activity than it does to put selective audit in motion? Audit has a relative advantage over collection because it is a natural successor to assessment — the basic skills are the same. The same people who have been assessors all their lives can, after a short period of training, start working as auditors in a selective audit program. Collection is an entirely new activity that must be built from scratch; it has no predecessor except in ancient times. There is no past experience to build on; no one knows exactly where to begin, what can be done and what should be avoided. In fact, as many officials told me, at the beginning no one even recognized the need for collection. In the words of a senior Trinidadian official:

> They never recognized the importance of collection. The attitude at the start of the reform was that people will pay because they must, because the law says so. No one at the time recognized the importance of collection and therefore steps were not taken, for example, to create technical positions. My staff till this very day is all clerical, nonprofessional. The Board never assigned enough staff for collection work because they didn't recognize the importance of this work. Only now they are beginning to see that without a strong collection force everything else that you do — audit, processing and the like — is worthless, it is a waste of time, we are not in the business to audit, we are in the business to collect tax revenues. To many people here, this is a revelation.

The reform started with assessment, leaving collection for later because everyone knew what should be done in audit while no one knew where to start in collection. When there is no past experience to serve as an indication of what might happen in the future, processes that might otherwise quickly be initiated take a longer time to evolve. Yet time is what tax departments do not have in abundance. The day after self assessment is instituted, delinquent accounts will start piling up unless there is something to convince taxpayers to go along with the new regulations. If something is not done immediately to hack down the current delinquencies before next year's start pouring in, the system of internal records will break down and with it the public's confidence in the agency's ability to collect debts. When the incoming flood of data is not immediately processed, it becomes impossible to know exactly who paid, how much and when. Far more important it becomes difficult to say precisely who has not paid. The reason why any organization that collects money imposes a fee on late payments is because they wreak havoc in record keeping. Instead of doing one thing once, you have to do it at least twice. When payment is not received by the time the deadline has expired, the "not paid" entry must be made; when payment is made the entry must be corrected. If the list is to be kept current it must be updated periodically. The more changes that must be made, the higher the incidence of errors. When deadlines are not taken seriously (since no penalties are imposed on late filers) and are not observed, lists have to be constantly updated and are never reliable — corrections will always be flowing down the pipeline. It will not be possible to produce a definitive list of all those who have and those who have not paid their taxes for a certain year, except by a gradual elimination of errors that may take years. By then many accounts will no longer be collectable. Accounting has a peculiar nature: once its internal order is seriously disturbed, it becomes terribly difficult to put back in shape. If something has gone wrong it will stay there for a long time to come. Caiden and Wildavsky caution policy makers not to introduce new accounting procedures since it will take an inordinate amount of effort and time before the confusion caused by the change will be straightened out.

> New accounting procedures have incredibly high start upcosts. It takes years to get them to run properly while whatever benefits were possessed by the old ones are lost. Accumulated experience from the past depends on getting data in certain ways, and the people who use it will be thrown off their bearings by a different format.[12]

Three observations can be made on the internal records of tax departments in the four countries studied: they are in a state of disorder, they have been in that state for some time and they don't seem to be getting much better. An anonymous Filipino official describes the data problems in the Philippines:

> We are informed . . . that included among the collectables are accounts where taxpayers alleged they have already paid . . . BIR cannot entirely disregard these allegations because DPC (Data Processing Center) reports there are thousands of official receipts which cannot be credited to any particular taxpayers for the reason they are illegible.

The Philippine Tax Commission made a similar observation:

> The regional offices are . . . compelled to review all of their past transac-

> tions to determine with greater accuracy which of their listed taxes are undisputed. Unless this is done (which is not always the case) field collectors hesitate to press payment for fear of being embarrassed and antagonizing taxpayers.[13]

Trinidad has a similar problem. The Chairman of the Board of Inland Revenue told me that it is difficult to tell exactly who has and who hasn't paid: "We are groping in the dark trying to separate the defaulters from the honest taxpayers by trial and error."

One way to straighten out the accounts and to bring them to a current basis is to forget the past and start with the present. This advice has been often given but has rarely been implemented. What may be administratively simple is not feasible politically. Explains a Trinidadian senior official:

> In my view the only way to get collections under way is by writing off our arrears and starting from scratch . . . We can't deal with the current arrears until we have wiped off the old ones. The Americans [advisers] told us to forget about the old arrears and concentrate on the current ones. It's a very good advice but we can't just ignore the old arrears — it is not legal.

Forgetting the past sets a dangerous precedent since it rewards all those who have not complied.

The methods that are being used to clear the accounts are the write-off and the collection campaign. The write-off is a legal method by which the tax agency can get rid of certain outstanding accounts that it has not succeeded in collecting, and which are deemed uncollectable. It differs in scope only from the first method. Though some accounts are written off every now and then when it becomes evident — by the death of the taxpayer for instance — that they have become uncollectable, write-offs have never been sufficiently exhaustive to put the accounts on a current year basis. The reason, explains the Trinidadian Commissioner, is that too much preparatory work is required before permission to write off can be secured.

> To get permission to write off we must convince the government that the debt is uncollectable. This has to be done for every single item . . . in each case extreme caution will have to be taken so as not to embarrass the government. Can you imagine what the opposition will do if they found out exactly what is going on here, that we are groping in the dark trying to separate the defaulters from the honest taxpayers by trial and error.

At the time this was said (December 1974), Trinidad had some 50,000 accounts in arrears and a collection section with fifteen recently recruited and trained agents. Even if all of them could have been relieved of all of their other daily duties — taxpayer assistance and tracing refunds that have not reached taxpayers on time — it would have taken them close to two years to cover terrain (at the rate of ten accounts daily, five days a week and ten months in a year). By the time they finish, thousands of new accounts will have been opened.

In a collection campaign the department assembles what staff it can from its various branches; everyone is assigned a list of accounts and sent to the streets. If sufficient manpower is used and the effort is kept up long enough, it is reasonable to expect that the campaign will produce the desired results. The list of delinquent accounts will be broken down into bad debts, which must be written off; accounts closed; part-payment agreements; hard-core delinquents (taxpayers blatantly refusing to pay) and accounts which were paid in the past but not posted.

The procedure has been initiated a number of times in the Philippines, but no significant changes were achieved in the state of accounts in arrears. The then commissioner of internal revenue exclaimed at the end of one of these campaigns, that, though results were poor, he would not accept the accusation that the officers didn't try hard enough or lacked competence.

> It is disheartening to note that from the initial and unofficial report received by my office, the general impression gathered was that the operations produced no tangible results, and your overall performance went far below our most conservation expectations. If at all, very little headway was made in closing or clearing delinquent accounts. . . . I will refuse to believe that the failure of that collection campaign which you launched last year is traceable to your personal shortcomings.

If it is not personal failings, what is it? A clue to the problem can be gained from a description of how these campaigns were conducted:

> We went from house to house and asked taxpayers to show us their receipts of payment; we told them that we are putting our records in order once and for all. The people were very helpful as everyone hoped that this is an opportunity to have all his problems with the BIR settled. The following year we get a delinquent list from the DPC with the names of those whom we have canvassed and who have produced receipts in the hope of avoiding any further harassment still in. Now these names are again assigned to collectors who again pay the taxpayer a visit. "I thought you said you are putting your accounts in order, so how come my name is still on the list?" says the dismayed and angry taxpayer, and what can the poor collector do but demand to see the receipt again; after all he cannot go back to the office and tell his supervisor that the taxpayer said that he showed the receipt to another collector last year. Naturally both taxpayers and collectors get angry and frustrated in the process and collection work suffers.

Collection campaigns fail to bring the department to a point from where it can start working normally because the internal record keeping procedures are faulty. What brought the list of delinquent accounts to where it is, also keeps it there. Pagarigan found in her study that

> during collection campaigns the field units are asked to update their list of delinquent accounts — a task which they do not do because they failed to do so on a regular basis and the workload has therefore become too voluminous to tackle.[14]

The collectors are quick to grasp that no matter how hard they work this year, the same cases they thought closed will be handed out to them again next year. The more they work, the more work they generate. No one likes to do the same thing twice, especially when it is as unpleasant as confronting a taxpayer you solemnly promised last year that he would never have to set his eyes on you again.

The fate of any new data that goes into the records is similar to that of the old; it gets twisted somewhere along the line and comes out as inaccurate as before. The effect of disorder is so strong that it engulfs any small improvement. Small bits of good data are lost in the general chaos that prevails. A comprehensive collection campaign that produces a great mass of new data adds yet another heavy burden to the already over taxed processing capabilities.

The confusion in the accounts persists even in the face of repeated attempts to eliminate it. The phenomena is so bewildering that an exasperated Filipino official told me that he believes no one really wants to see an improvement in this area: "You know when I think about it I begin to believe that the confusion in our accounting is deliberate, that someone up there doesn't want it to be straightened up. It is easier to hide evasion when things are in confusion, not so when everything is orderly." Confusion may have not been deliberately created but once its there it certainly becomes difficult to get rid of.

When data about delinquent taxpayers is poor it is not possible to get to them early enough to prevent further postponement of payment. The longer a taxpayer procrastinates the more difficult it is to extract the tax from him. A taxpayer is like the child who carefully starts reaching for something he knows is prohibited; when he sees that no reaction is coming he goes further than originally planned. If there is no immediate result, it is easy to be convinced that one will never come. A taxpayer who merely decides to postpone payment for a month or two since he is short of cash may be tempted to persevere if during the initial period there is no real attempt to make him pay. A taxpayer who has not paid this year is not likely to pay or even file next year. This is how small problems are turned into big problems. Collection is immensely more difficult when it is initiated a few years, rather than a few months, after deadlines have elapsed. The offence is a more serious one, and there are penalties and interest to be added to the bill. The tax bill itself has grown; an amount the taxpayer may have had some difficulty in paying is now four maybe five times bigger and that much more difficult to pay. When the agent gets to the taxpayer soon after the deadline has elapsed he convinces him that deadlines should be taken seriously. He is also in a better position to demand full and prompt payment. When the amount in question is comprised of a few years of back taxes the only feasible collection method is the part-payment agreement.

What can the collectors do when the information they need is not reliable or altogether not available? Are they to limit themselves to whatever collections can be initiated on the basis of what is available, or should they, in addition to collections, gather some of the data they need themselves and verify the accuracy of the rest? The answer is that they must do both and at the same time. A collection director claiming that his task is limited to collection based on existing reliable information will find himself with very little work to do. The information he thinks should be coming from processing never will.

Nonfilers can be unveiled only if the collector looks for them while out in the field doing routine collections. The Jamaican Chief of Collections described the duties of a collection agent thus:

> The collection officers are supposed to keep an open eye in the course of carrying out their duties. They should look around to see if there are any new businesses, houses, etc., and then check with our records to see if the chap is filing.

When collection agents are assigned to small geographical areas where they can develop a personal acquaintance with most of the residents, the simple method of "looking around" works well. A veteran rural collector summarizes his experience:

> I see them doing business and to my knowledge they are within the taxpaying group. The runners (his assistants who perform the actual collection) are my eyes and ears; they report to me when someone moves out of the parish, when someone dies and so on. That's how I know.

Other collectors added some details as to exactly how that knowledge is acquired:

> Pure knowledge of the area. People, you know, like to talk about how they live and how much they spend and the collector listens. A very good collector should be a man whom the people respect. He should be a prominent figure in the parish.

> The runners don't go to the details of income. They try to get an idea about a particular taxpayer's affairs by talking discreetly to his friends and neigh-

> bours, then he passes the information to the Income Tax Department who would then make a detailed investigation.

It takes time to develop this type of knowledge; it is only after you are no longer considered a stranger that people are willing to discuss their private affairs with you. Time carries two disadvantages: the longer one stays in one place the more he tends to identify with the interests of the local people. The other problem is promotions. During the colonial era it was possible to keep a person in a job for as long as the government wished. Nowadays civil service regulations that provide for transfers and promotions make it almost impossible to keep someone in the same place (the only exception to the rule is the capital city where everyone wants to serve) for a long time.

Methods that work well in small communities are not equally effective in urban areas. In a big city it is no longer possible to rely solely on the personal acquaintance approach, not only are there more people to be acquainted with, it is also more difficult to develop acquaintances. More formal methods are needed to obtain information. The most comprehensive but also most expensive and cumbersome, is the door to door survey. This is a dramatic tool that governments employ every now and then when they want to impress certain people that something serious is being done about those who do not file. There is no need to examine the entire population when less comprehensive methods may produce similar information. Those who make money, enough to pay tax, spend it. It is therefore possible to find them by studying telephone directories, car and property registers, lists of people who traveled abroad, membership lists in exclusive clubs — these are just some of the main sources of information that may lead to people who have money. A simple matching between the names pulled from these lists and the taxpayer roll should produce a list of people who may be potential taxpayers but who are either not filing at all or submitting a return for an amount too small to afford their spending habits.

The agents should spend part of their time looking for nonfilers, but do they actually do it? Here are a few of the most typical answers received whenever it was asked, "What do you actually do to unveil nonfilers?":

> Theoretically there is a force of collectors whose job is to go around and locate those who do not file. But in practice their time is consumed in running after those who do file but don't pay in time. (Jamaica)

> The Revenue Department concentrates its efforts upon the enforcement of tax laws against those taxpayers who are attempting to comply and are a matter of record through the filing of returns. There is little effort made to seek out those individuals who attempt to evade all taxes by never becoming a matter of record. (Thailand)[15]

> Attempts to locate . . . delinquents through field canvass has not been as productive as it would have wanted to be. Examiners were initially asked to submit lists of potential tax filers, later found to be erroneous.[16]

In the few rare instances where vigorous attempts at uncovering nonfilers were made, results were so disappointing that it would be long before they are tried again. Why does something that sounds so simple on paper turn out to be so difficult in practice?

Knowing does not equal doing. The collector may find that someone in his jurisdiction is not paying; how useful that knowledge will be depends on what the department allows him to do with it. In countries where civil liberties have any meaning at all, agents cannot be sent to the streets without specifying exactly what they are and are not allowed to do. The agent will not only antagonize taxpayers but will probably waste his own time if he walks around and demands receipt of tax from anyone that he suspects is evading payment. Before a citizen is approached, there must be reasonable evidence supporting the suspicion that he has not filed.

This is the beginning and the end of the collector's interest in unveiling potential taxpayers. He quickly loses interest in this type of activity because he is a man of action, and here there are no immediate, if any, results. A senior Filipino official describes the process:

> Suppose a collection agent finds out that a certain taxpayer in his area has not been filing . . . he can't just approach the taxpayer and demand that he file. He has to send a memo up to the Head Office where it will be sent to the Assessment Department that will investigate the matter and will later instruct the collector on how to proceed.

A Trinidadian collector describes his view of what is expected of him: "I can't start doing something without being asked to do it by my supervisor. I can't do anything on my own initiative." His director told me that "we here in this section do not initiate. If I get lists of defaulters from the boys upstairs [arrears section], I proceed to collect subject to the availability of staff. I am not looking for nonfilers." The last thing that a collector wants to do is to generate more work than he already has, and that does not produce results that will be credited to him. Why waste time and energy when someone else reaps the fruits of work you have done?

There is more to collection than preparing and mailing a few reminder notices to taxpayers that have not paid on time. People discount mimeographed letters they receive from the government regardless of how strongly worded they are. A senior Jamaican official describes the experience his department has had with written reminders:

> Suppose that this taxpayer is on our lists and we send him a notice to file a few months after the deadline has expired. He gets it and will say to him-

> self: "I'll get around to it." Another couple of months pass by and somebody here remembers that he hasn't filed yet and immediately sends him another notice which the taxpayer again ignores.

It is different when the taxpayer receives a personal visit from a collection agent who first explains cordially why he is there and later notifies him that he has no intention of leaving without something in his hand. Most people are convinced that the government means business if it bothered to send an official to their home. Since the visit is expected, the agent must appear. He must go out there, discover why the taxpayer has not paid, describe the consequences that would follow — such as, penal interest rates, seizure of property — and attempt to get all or part of the tax. Later on he must keep track of the case and make sure that the taxpayer has stood by his promises. The smallest slip of attention is immediately noticed and exploited.

The amount of work that this entails is enormous. The task calls for repeated scanning of large quantities of data to discover deviations. Most poor countries are still far from the stage where the computer periodically issues a list of delinquent accounts. At present, information concerning taxpayers is kept in files or on index cards, and only at great cost in time and energy is it possible to discover who has and who hasn't kept his promise. When the information finally reaches the collector, it comes too late for him to initiate preventive action. It is no longer a question of informing the taxpayer that three or four months have passed since the deadline expired, and convincing him to pay before the penal interest rate to be imposed adds a sizeable increment. When a taxpayer has accumulated two years worth of back taxes plus penalties and interest, the task of convincing him to pay becomes that much more difficult. It is not easy to insist on full payment simply because the amount is too big. When there is so much that must be done and so little that can be done, energies are turned elsewhere, to easier and more productive pursuits. Rather than engaging in preventive work, agents prefer to go after known delinquents. Since even here there are more cases than the entire collection force combined can hope to complete, priority is given to those where the prospects of reaching results are the best.

The collector has no special interest in any particular taxpayer. He thinks in aggregate terms — how much money he collects and how many cases he has closed. Therefore, agents prefer to work on accounts that can yield the quickest results. When agents come across a hard nut — unless it is an exceptionally big nut where the loss of time and energy is compensated by the amount obtained and the satisfaction that comes from nailing a big guy — they will just drop it and move on to the next case. The following is a sample of the comments made by collection officials on the rules that guide their behavior:

> Collection agents do not like to deal with old accounts . . . because they are more difficult to collect . . . They want to work with cases that yield the fastest results. (Philippines)

> . . . if a taxpayer gives you trouble you leave him and go to someone else. It's not very conducive to our morale to know that the bullies get away without paying and the honest man is sacked. (Trinidad)

> As for collection, they spend most of their time on withholding cases. I don't think that they should do that; what they should be doing is go after those who don't file and those who did file but had not paid. Even in withholding I'm not sure that they are going after the hard core cases. They want to show results so they are going after those cases that will yield the most revenue at the least effort. (Jamaica)

> . . . there is a tendency to drop any case when the slightest degree of difficulty develops or there is resistance on the part of the taxpayer to pay. The collectors will tend to collect the easiest cases, "skimming the cream" as it were. This, in turn, creates "aged accounts" and it is axiomatic that the older an account becomes, the more difficult it becomes.[17]

Relatively fresh accounts (usually two or three years old) are preferred to old ones. Withholding accounts are preferred to individuals. Cases where the taxpayer responds immediately are pursued more vigorously than those where the taxpayer is more stubborn. Most of all, collectors prefer to collect from those who pay willingly, rather than pursue those who ignore the reminders sent to them. When I showed interest in field collections I was usually told that "they [the collectors] don't want to get out of the office, they wait for the taxpayers to come to them" (Thailand). The Philippines Tax Commission made a similar observation: "The collection agent employs desk system of collection only. In other words, he merely waits for the taxpayer to come to his office to pay."[18]

I told a chief of collections in the Philippines that I could not understand why his agents prefer to spend their days in boredom at the office instead of going after taxpayers. His somewhat lengthy answer deserves to be quoted in full.

> The problem is that in most instances the taxpayer is hostile even before the agent has begun to say his piece . . . Since we can't be sure who has and who hasn't paid, it happens quite frequently that a collector informs a taxpayer that he has a delinquent account while in fact that account has been paid on time, a year ago. Naturally taxpayers don't like this; our collectors get a bad reputation and hence encounter hostility. When the taxpayer bullies you even before you have opened your mouth and if furthermore you are not too sure that the account is truly delinquent, it is difficult to continue with the job. This is the predicament of the collection agents. Many come to me and tell me that it is really futile to go out in the field . . . . They'd rather be bored in the office than encounter the taxpayer's ire compounded by the inability to realize any substantial collections at the end of the day.

The collector either collects or spends his time verifying data; he will not do both. His rewards depend on the amounts he has collected; so, if he can't do enough in field collections because he must devote part of his time to checking the accuracy of data he is given, he will prefer to work in office collection, tending to those who come to pay. The alternative, going into the field without assurance that those you are sent to collect from really owe the government money, is not feasible. Nothing can be more embarrassing for a collection agent than to approach a taxpayer, with all the earnestness that comes from the feeling that you've finally found your man, and be handed a tax receipt showing that the tax you are after has long since been paid. After falling on his face a number of times, the collector may decide that it is not only safer but perhaps more productive to spend his day behind a desk. Even in the event that the department is prepared to absorb public humiliation that comes from mistaking an honest taxpayer for a delinquent one and force the collectors to go into the field, they may not agree. It is always possible to return to the office at the end of the day and announce that nothing has been accomplished because taxpayers were uncooperative.

Problems of poor data are compounded by the difficulties in extracting payment. In poor countries, collection is an exasperating job because the average taxpayer is either not aware that he has to pay or if he is, does not understand why.[19] Therefore the collector must first succeed in convincing the taxpayer that he does indeed owe the amount in question, that it is correct and not arbitrary, that the penalties and interest added are according to the tax code and that he does not have the authority to make changes. Only then will it become possible to collect. The collector in a rich country rarely does more than inform the taxpayer of what he owes and requests a check for the amount, initiating enforcement procedures if results are not otherwise obtained. The Jamaican Chief of Collections describes what agents must do in addition to collection itself:

> Our collection officers are instructed to increase tax awareness. They must convince the taxpayer that whatever he is paying is the right amount, that we don't steal from him.

A collection agent adds:

> You have to explain to them how you arrived at the figures . . . Many of the people we get are not too aware of the law and the penalties on delinquent accounts. You have to do a lot of explaining. (Trinidad)

> With those who are not aware of the law it will take a lot of explaining before you can make them pay. (Trinidad)

The agents must contend with taxpayers who feel that they have been asked to pay too much. In their daily life the first price is always higher than the last actually paid. They cannot be easily convinced that the tax they are asked to pay is a result of a formal calculation where universal predetermined rules have been applied. It is not arbitrarily determined and therefore cannot be arbitrarily reduced. The collector cannot simply proceed with enforcement measures because if he does, the taxpayer will go to court and obtain an injunction. Pagarigan found, and experience in the other countries is corroborative, that:

> when the collection agent attempts to collect the tax which the taxpayer believes to be unjust, he is required to review the case file and determine whether the assessment is valid and whether the case should be reexamined. If he files a seizure notice the taxpayer may resist the collection through injunction procedure or appeal to the National Office. More often, the collection agent takes the course of least resistance when confronted with the protesting taxpayer and does nothing.[20]

Another hurdle to overcome after convincing the taxpayer that he should pay, is convincing him to pay the entire amount at one time. Usually these amounts are substantial since they are sometimes allowed to grow for a number of years before action is taken. Taxpayers usually start by saying that they cannot pay at all because they had lost money in the past year; their second line of defense is to offer to pay their debt in small monthly installments. So, after convincing the taxpayer that the amount he is being asked to pay is the correct one, and that it is his duty to pay, the collector is expected to determine how much can reasonably be expected of the taxpayer each month. Here is how a Jamaican senior official describes this task:

> They [collection agents] are supposed to find what the man's ability to pay is. Accordingly they can make a part-payment agreement with him. The purpose is to facilitate payment, we don't want to kill the goose that lays the golden eggs.

It is hard to convince the taxpayer to agree to pay; however once he accepts that fact, whatever he offers must quickly be grabbed before he changes his mind. A Jamaican collector explains:

> It is better to take the money offered than drive the man off by insisting that the full amount be paid on the spot. If you find a willing taxpayer don't drive him off.

The rule guiding the collector is: Try to get the full amount first, settle for a part-payment later, and never leave without something in your hand.

> We try to get all the amount owed when we are there, if the taxpayer is unable to pay all at once we make a part-payment agreement but we will not leave him until we have something concrete in our hands. (Trinidad)

> Even though the runner has a stated amount to collect and the taxpayer may owe two or three years' taxes, if the taxpayer offers to pay only part of his debt the runner will take it. We try to be flexible. (Jamaica)

A part-payment agreement that is stretched over a long period of time may prove to be no achievement at all. It is like carrying a box of ice cream ten blocks on a hot summer day. The box is full when you leave the store, melts down as you walk, leaving very little to enjoy by the time you get home. How does the collector get the taxpayer to accept a reasonable agreement? By sympathizing with him. A Jamaican agent explains:

> They have their tail up when you go in so you have to do something to calm them down. You have to find the reason why they are anti, why they didn't pay . . . you must accept a lot of blame that you are not responsible for. I think that it is better to coax him into paying rather than bully him into it.

Collection agents in the Philippines seem to go by the same rule. The director of collection describes what the agent must do to obtain good results:

> If a collector wants to be successful in his job he must exercise extreme patience and tact in dealing with the taxpayer; if he does not, the taxpayer is most likely to ball him out and send him to hell.

A Jamaican collector summarized his work succinctly: "A good collector is one who gets along with people."

The collector's discretion is limited. Under no circumstances is he allowed to reduce the assessment. There are also departmental regulations that set floors — minimum ratios — for part-payments. If his discretion is limited and threats of enforcement reserved for special occasions, how is the taxpayer convinced to do something he dislikes? Some leverage may be obtained by asking the taxpayer to pay more than the floor and then settling for less. That usually means that the floor becomes the ceiling. No one is willing to settle for less than what the collector has to offer. Since floors must be set sufficiently low to induce most taxpayers to prefer part-payments over litigation in court, the end result of delinquent collections through the part-payment method is the ice cream syndrome — very little remains at the end compared to what could have been had the taxpayer paid on time.

Some progress can be made by sympathizing with the taxpayer and allaying the fears and embarrassment that are naturally aroused by the confrontation with a tax agent. However, the effect is limited not only since it is primarily effective with small, rather than big, taxpayers, but also because when the chips are down and the taxpayer must choose between the worst of evils, there is less to be afraid of by going to court than by saying no to the collector. Agents admit that experience shows that courts impose settlements that are often lower than the department's floor. The reason most people go along with part-payment agreements is that the arrangement is convenient and saves the expenses of litigation in court.

Tax agencies must be flexible, they have no other choice. They cannot demand from the public what they themselves fail to practice. A request for full and prompt payment of back taxes does not sound particularly convincing when it is sounded for the first time, years after the debt was incurred. When the government does not operate on a current basis, it is hard put demanding it from its citizens. If the government does not succeed in enforcing deadlines, it encourages taxpayers not to comply, and will not be in a position to make serious demands when it finally catches up with them. Therefore, if the collector insists on getting everything the taxpayer owes — tax, penalties, interest — he runs the risk of receiving nothing. He compromises with the taxpayer because he wants to reach results. The alternative, threatening the taxpayer with legal action, is usually not open to him. There are too many delinquents to permit the department to effectively carry out that threat. The single case found where the courts were used to force taxpayers to pay only validates the assumption that guides collectors — don't count on enforcement to help you out.

Taking people to court has proved to be an effective method in the rural parts of Jamaica, first because the number of taxpayers there is very small, and secondly because being hauled in to court mars one's reputation. When people are convinced that they will indeed be called to appear in court they rush to pay. A local collector describes what happens when summonses to appear in court are issued:

> It is easy to follow up on accounts right up to the court stage because the numbers are so small (as a result of the breakdown into parishes and districts). People in the rural areas don't like to go to court. They live in small communities. They would run to pay me even in the last minute before the court convenes. In the urban areas they couldn't care less. They would offer me ten dollars a month on an outstanding account of say two or three hundred and if I refuse to accept it they say, "All right we'll go to court and offer that to the judge."

Jamaican officials observed that almost half of those summoned to court pay after they have received the summons and most of them do so during the last few days before the court convenes; some rush in to pay on the very last day. People go along only when they are fully convinced that if they don't they will indeed be hauled in to court.

This method does not work equally well when the number of taxpayers is large. In a small community it is difficult to hide the fact that a person has been summoned to court. In big cities no one knows, therefore no one cares. If the mere threat of court action is not enough to induce most people to pay, the court method will not work since it would still leave the department the task of enforcement. A Jamaican official explains:

> Prosecution will not necessarily result in a return being filed. What the court will do is fine the taxpayer . . . We would still have to go after him to get the return.

If less than the full amount is demanded and a part-payment agreement drawn, it becomes more difficult for the taxpayer to throw the collector out emptyhanded. There is everything to gain, and nothing to lose from signing a part-payment agreement. You write a check for ten percent of what you owe and the rest may or may not be paid, and anyway you need not worry about it at present. By contrast, by refusing to sign, you take the risk that your case will be among the few where strong enforcement action will be taken.

So something is better than nothing. Solving problems incrementally has the advantage of getting some of the benefits right at the start. In a comprehensive solution you have to wait until the very end of the process before you see any rewards. Tax departments pressed for revenue may not have a better way than the incremental approach.

The problem of collection is essentially the failure to prevent the rapid accumulation of delinquent accounts. So one solution is to collect the tax before it even reaches the taxpayer. This is the essence of the various schemes for withholding tax from salaries. The employer deducts the tax before salaries are paid and forwards it to the government. In this way, in principle at least, collection becomes unnecessary. The British have perfected a method where the amounts withheld each month add up at the end of the year to the total tax the individual has to pay, and there is no need to file returns. Deficiency assessments or refunds are nonexistent, except in a few extraordinary cases. When the process works as it should, it does away with a huge amount of paperwork that would have resulted if employed taxpayers had to file returns. There is a much simpler scheme used by the Americans, in which a certain fixed percentage is withheld without taking into account various deductions and expenses the taxpayer may claim. At the end of the year the taxpayer files a return and receives a refund or pays the balance due. Withholding is heavily relied on as a means of collection, as evidenced by the fact that approximately seventy percent of income tax collection in the U.S.A. is attributed to it.[21]

The method is particularly appealing to poor countries since, in principle at least, it makes evasion virtually impossible and "provides the government with a flow of revenue which is smooth and predictable."[22] Predictability is vital for those who are running the treasury. To be able to make budgetary decisions, budgeters must have a pretty good idea of the amounts and dates in which they become available.[23] A workable withholding system increases the otherwise low level of certainty in the collection machinery. Given such merits, it is hardly surprising that most poor countries invested a great deal of effort in adopting a withholding system in one form or another. (Jamaica and Trinidad have a British version, while Thailand and the Philippines opted for the U.S.A. model.) Like so many other innovations introduced in the past decade, withholding is far from producing the expected results. A disappointed withholding director in Trinidad describes his main problems:

> PAYE was introduced among other things to deduct the right amount of tax from employees so as to do away with refunds and arrears. The system is not achieving this goal. We still have 60,000 refunds a year . . . employers do not keep proper records, some deduct tax but do not remit it to us, others do not deduct at all.

His colleague in Jamaica described a similar situation. To avoid payment, employees move around, frequently changing jobs. Employers are not quick to report the hiring of a new employee, and by the time the withholding official arrives on the scene, the employee has left leaving no tracks and no tax. In his own words:

> Often the employer does not inform us that he has hired a new employee or perhaps we are just slow in processing the forms. It could be that some of the staff are inexperienced. At that level we usually have temporary staff and weak supervision . . . while this is going on the employee leaves his job and moves to another employer and the whole process starts from the beginning.

One type of evasion has been replaced by another which is even worse. If in the past some employees failed to report their income, their employers now do the same; they deduct the tax but keep it for themselves. Even government ministries in three of the countries where I conducted interviews are among the culprits. A senior official in Trinidad described the difficulties he has with government departments:

> This morning I interviewed a number of paymasters in government departments. They don't read our circulars, many of them have no idea of what they are supposed to do and in a few cases salaries have been paid and tax was not deducted.

An employer may frequently find himself in a situation where money is tight, and the tax withheld from his employees is the easiest thing to fall upon. In Jamaica, for example, many firms operate on overdraft; only the net amount that has to be paid to employees is drawn from the bank. Similarly, under conditions of inflation firms have an incentive to stall.

Every day that passes and the money is still in their bank accounts is a net gain for them, and a loss for the government. The profit made this way may be substantial when the number of employees is high. A senior Jamaican official describes his experience:

> Some firms will pay regularly every month so that we will not visit them. At the end of the year, when they file their returns we find that the list of employees and salaries paid to them is much larger than what they reported in the course of the year. To avoid trouble, these firms even send us a cheque to cover the difference so that there will be no penalties, and they kept PAYE money in their accounts for a couple of months. We know that some firms are doing this but we don't have the machinery to keep up with them. . . . A lot of tax escapes that way.

Stalling can be made less profitable by imposing stiff interest rates on late payments. But penalties must be methodically implemented before they start to induce employers to forward withheld taxes on time. To be able to impose penalties, the department must know who is stalling. This is not as easy as it sounds. Data problems in withholding are even worse than those in personal income tax. Returns are filed each month instead of once a year. In addition the complexity of each return is far greater than in individual files. Without the aid of computer processing, it is practically impossible to carry out the cross-checks necessary to spot evasion when it occurs. Anyone walking into a withholding section will see mountains of paper that a handful of clerks are desperately trying to process and file away before next month's load starts coming in.

Verifying the information that was used by the employers to deduct the tax is rarely undertaken. Yet, that information is often inaccurate. According to a Jamaican agent, "Taxpayers do not report changes in their status unless the change is favorable to them and we have no means of updating these codes ourselves." In the Philippines, as well as in the other countries that were studied, the government accepts withholding tax from those who volunteer to pay, without ensuring that all employers do the same. An internal memorandum describes what should be, but is not done, in the withholding area in the Philippines:

> Withholding tax enforcement program was never initiated . . . there are no means of identifying employers who do not file withholding tax returns. Examiners are supposed to examine withholding tax liability during income tax examinations and are required to include a statement in their reports . . . but this has never been complied with.

No one expected withholding to be flawless. Given its problems, how effective is it? The following table shows that it is quite a powerful tool.

FISCAL YEAR 1972

	Total Personal Income Tax	Withholding from Wages	percent
Jamaica	J$ 41,753,098	8,438,927	22%*
Philippines	P 276,000,000	166,000,000	60%**
Thailand	Not Available	Not Available	80%***
Trinidad	Not Available	Not Available	

Source: * Department of Income Tax
** Bureau of Internal Revenue, Republic of the Philippines, *Annual Report*, 1973.
*** Confidential World Bank Study.

Withholding works because in each country there are a few large prominent employers practicing an advanced stage of record keeping who deduct taxes from their employees according to withholding requirements. No practitioner spoken to seriously believed that withholding has reached the great mass of small employers (not as visible as the large companies) that do not have formal payrolls, but do have a strong interest in shielding their employees (often family members) from the tax authorities. So the percentages are high compared to the U.S.A., not because withholding works well, but because collection from the self-employed does not.

Why is the ratio in Jamaica so low compared to Thailand and the Philippines? The reason could be that while the latter employs a United States type withholding procedure, Jamaica has a British type system. The British Pay As You Earn is based on a complicated process in which information flows from employees to their employer, and from him to the department and back. Since the amounts withheld monthly must add up at the end of the year to the exact tax that the individual has to pay, a substantial amount of information must be supplied by the taxpayer to his employer and the tax authorities. There is also a need for periodic updating to adapt the tax calculations to changes in personal status and income. Complexity makes compliance harder and evasion easier. Some employers may not be able to do what they should, and therefore ignore requirements altogether. Others, looking for ways to make a little profit, will have plenty of opportunities to add or omit bits of data.

The opportunities for evasion are much more limited in a simple withholding procedure where the employer is required to deduct a certain fixed percentage without having to take into account each employee's allowable deductions.

It seems that in poor countries where bookkeeping procedures are rather crude — and many do not know how to keep a payroll — the method that works best is the method that requires the least.

Conclusion

> "The core of our effort in 1969 will be directed to ensure that revenues due are in fact collected."
>
> Dr. Eric Williams, Minister of Finance, Trinidad and Tobago, Budget Speech 1969

> Efforts are being made to recover amounts due for the years 1959 to 1961 and numerous requests and reminders for payment of tax have been dispatched to taxpayers. No real approach has been made in the past to keep the arrears list current, owing to shortage of staff, consequently a large number of bad debts is included in the accounts.
>
> Report on the state of arrears, Board of Inland Revenue, Trinidad and Tobago 1969

"We are here to collect, not to assess; everything else that is being done will be worthless unless we can get the money flowing into the government coffers." This statement, in various forms, has been made by virtually every collection official interviewed. Yet almost all of them acknowledged that they are not doing what they know they should to ensure that all revenues due will be in fact collected. The amounts in arrear are large everywhere and do not seem to diminish. Furthermore the number of those who have never filed may be well exceeding the number of those who do.

Not one of these officials complained that he lacks the authority to do what he must, or said he does not know how to go about solving the problems of collection. Still with just one exception, no regular action is taken to prevent the accumulation of accounts in arrears and to collect those that are already delinquent. Most departments spend what energy and resources they have on tellering — receiving payments from those who volunteer to pay. Some departments do not even have procedures for the collection of delinquent accounts. It is vaguely assumed that the agents who do the tellering work will also carry out the task of field collection. That however rarely happens either because the tellers do not have the time to do both tasks, or because they have not been trained to do delinquent collections and they don't want to find out. Delinquent collection is an entirely different job and it is not theirs.

Those few departments that do have a separate branch for delinquent collections are having difficulties in making it work properly. In some, collectors are not enthusiastic about leaving the comforts of the office to work with hostile taxpayers in the field. The information showing from whom they should be collecting is either altogether not produced or not sufficiently reliable to act upon. Thus, the collector's job entails more than collection; he must also do the preliminary work of generating and verifying data. Required to do two jobs, while being rewarded for doing just one, many opt for the easiest solution and do nothing. Collection work is exasperating in itself, without having to ensure each time before approaching a taxpayer that indeed he is delinquent. The knowledge that taxes must be paid and the understanding of how the tax is determined for each individual has not yet been fully disseminated. Many do not lie when they say that they simply have no idea what the collector wants from them. A substantial amount of time and patience must be invested in almost every case before there begins to be hope for collecting something. Even more time will be needed later to reach an agreement with the taxpayer as to how much would be paid monthly. Back taxes are collected through the part-payment method, a monthly installment plan. Though losing money, the government rarely insists on full and prompt payment of the entire debt, partly because it did not do enough to prevent arrears from accumulating in the first place, and partly because it is more convenient to reach an administrative compromise than to litigate in court. The courts do not act rapidly or strictly enough to provide a better alternative to the administrative compromise.

Since collectors are under pressure to collect as much as possible, they tend to lean towards those cases that promise the best results. Their first preference will thus be to work on withholding cases; these usually involve large sums and are easier to collect because the employer hands over money that is not his own. If they deal with self-employed at all, it will only be with those who offer the least resistance. Taxpayers who persevere in their refusal to comply are quickly abandoned. Old arrears are pushed aside because they are known to be difficult; old debts are harder to collect than current ones. Very recent accounts are not liked either because the amount involved is usually small. It is better to wait a year or two, permitting the account to grow so that it would be worthwhile to send a collector to collect it. Looking for nonfilers is the last thing that the collectors will do if they still have some time left and absolutely nothing else to do. This is the area where achievements are hardest to come by. It is not enough to suspect that someone who should is not filing. Before any action can be taken it is necessary to prove that the person indeed is a potential taxpayer and this requires an investigation that collectors are not equipped to conduct. There is no sense of urgency around this task. When you deal with delinquent accounts you always carry the burden of those that are still outstanding. Nonfilers are anonymous: no one knows exactly who and how many they are; what is not known does not hurt.

This behavior magnifies and perpetuates the problems of collection —

too many delinquents to effectively cope with and inaccurate and overburdened internal records. As collection is carried out — part-payment agreements, action initiated years after the original deadline for payment has passed — it fails to create the incentive to respect deadlines and comply with regulations. The taxpayer is given all the encouragement he needs to stall until an agent calls on him to pay.

Collection, to be done well, must be prompt, strict and comprehensive. In poor countries, it is neither. Collectors do not get to the point where they can be on top of things because they always do too little too late. They are permanently busy clearing away accounts that accumulated in the past, never having enough time to prevent them from growing so rapidly.

Though seemingly irrational, there is nothing wrong with the way collectors behave. Given the magnitude of the task and the means at their disposal to tackle it, collectors are doing what is most feasible. No amount of talking will convince a determined delinquent to pay. Therefore, from the time he is discovered, every additional minute the collector spends with him is wasted. Certain accounts cannot be closed unless the agent can effectively threaten the taxpayer with enforcement. Not being able to do that, the only feasible alternative, if any results are to be reached, is to work on those cases where the taxpayer is prepared to pay. By the same token there is no point in insisting on payment in full of all back taxes. In the absence of effective enforcement, that will merely drive the taxpayer away and instead of collecting something, the government will get nothing.

The Jamaican official who said that "the policy is not to waste too much time with one taxpayer, not to go to him a million times. If he is really stubborn you come back and recommend enforcement," was right. But because enforcement does not wait for the difficult cases at the end of the line, what is good for each individual collector is bad for collection as a whole. For a collector, under pressure to reach results, the rational thing to do is to pursue only those cases where results are the easiest to reach. No one will appreciate if instead he would devote his time to cases that require more than he has got. But in doing that, the collector makes it possible for another taxpayer to disregard deadlines and to avoid paying. In this way the problems of collection are perpetuated.

Notes

1. Joint Legislative Executive Tax Commission (JLETC), *A Study on Tax Administration in the Philippines*, mimeographed (Manila, Republic of the Philippines, 1965), p. 128.
2. Ibid., p. 133.

3. W.R. Devonish, "Significant Aspects of the Need for Administrative Reform," *The Caribbean Tax Administrator* 2 (July-Sept. 1972): p. 9.
4. Harry C. Johnson, "Self Assessment to Personal Income Tax: The American System," *British Tax Review* (1971): 79.
5. See, for example, Nicholas Kaldor, *Tax Reform in India: Report of a Survey* (Government of India: Department of Economic Affairs, Ministry of Finance, 1956).
6. S.M. Supersad, "Collection Policy and Strategies," (1974, mimeo), p. 1.
7. Benjamin Tabios, "Operations, Collections," *Philippine Tax Journal* (August 1964): p. 442.
8. Roy E. Davis, "Terminal Report to the Bureau of Internal Revenue, Department of Finance," mimeographed (Manila, Republic of the Philippines), p. 94.
9. JLETC, *A Study on Tax Administration,* p. 116.
10. Davis, p. 9.
11. Ibid., p. 10.
12. Naomi Caiden and Aaron Wildavsky, *Planning and Budgeting in Poor Countries* (New York: John Wiley, 1974), pp. 314-15.
13. JLETC, *A Study on Tax Administration,* p. 160.
14. Priscila B. Pagarigan, "An Analysis of the Assessment Functions in the Bureau of Internal Revenue" (Unpublished Ph.D. Dissertation, Centro Escolar University, Manila, 1973), p. 402.
15. Public Administration Service, "Report on Organization and Administration of the Revenue Department, Kingdom of Thailand," mimeographed (Thailand, March 1963), p. 38.
16. Pagarigan, p. 442.
17. Ernest Grayson, "Collection of Delinquent Accounts," *The Caribbean Tax Administrator* II, 1 (1972): 7.
18. JLETC, *A Study on Tax Administration,* p. 140.
19. Joint Legislative Executive Tax Commission, "Second survey on Tax Consciousness in the Philippines" (Manila, Republic of the Philippines, 1969).
20. Pagarigan, p. 402.
21. John C. Chommie, *The Internal Revenue Service* (New York: Praeger, 1970).
22. Peter S. Griffith, "Current Payment of Taxes on Income," Study Prepared for the Harvard-Chile Tax Project, 1970.
23. For a thorough analysis of this problem see Caiden and Wildavsky.
24. Lyle C. Fitch, "Concepts and Administration," in *The State of the Nations: Constraints on Development in Independent Africa,* F. Lofchie (ed.) (Berkeley: U.C. Press, 1971), p. 466.

Chapter Seven

Taxation and Evasion Are Twins: Compliance and Enforcement

"If the wealthy in the country pay that little, what can the government expect of the non-millionaires? . . . The Bureau of Internal Revenue list reminds us once again of the startling and shameful fact of life here: that hardly one percent of the population files income tax returns and scarcely one third of one percent declares taxable income."

Philippine Free Press, January 11, 1969.

"Make the evasion of taxes an even more painful process than paying them. In this, as in many areas of national policy, it is far more effective to work on . . . predictable reactions to pain and pleasure, rather than on such elusive factors as patriotism."

Roman A. Cruz, Jr., "Obstacles to Revenue Administration in the Philippines," p. 5.

Evasion is the scourge of taxation. This is where the greatest gaps between policy goals and implementation achievements are created. No matter how fine the tax laws are, how high the rates, if many taxpayers evade, government coffers will stay empty. High levels of evasion also reduce the effectiveness of audit and collection (resulting in further loss of revenue) since there never are, nor can there ever be, sufficient resources to handle large numbers of evaders. When too many people disregard rules and regulations, the organization is overwhelmed by the number of deviations it must discover and correct.

How can enforcement influence compliance? How should this function be performed so that evasion will be kept at manageably low levels? How does enforcement function in the poor countries? Why does it function as it does and how do these patterns of behavior affect existing levels of evasion and compliance?

The key to compliance is enforcement. Tax laws that are not enforced are not obeyed. Since taxpayers stand to gain money from evasion it is not possible to rely solely on national, patriotic, altruistic motivations to pay taxes. A situation must be created where most taxpayers will voluntarily pay what they should, not only because they believe they ought to, but because they know that they have no better choice.

The enforcement mechanism is based on simple rational choice calculations. Taxpayers are induced to pay voluntarily by turning payment into a less painful practice than evasion. A person who is in a position to gain from tax evasion is a person who has a lot to lose: circle of friends, business associates, a reputation, family. Being convicted and sentenced to serve time in prison for tax evasion hurts these valuable assets. Therefore the knowledge that there is a chance, even remote, that he would go to prison, would in many cases be enough to convince the taxpayer, if not to go straight altogether, at least to limit evasion to marginal amounts.

If the knowledge that some people have been harshly penalized for tax offenses has a restraining effect, the certainty that no evader is ever sent to prison encourages evasion. Though enforcement may not be enough to create compliance where it does not exist, it is essential to maintain it. Informants emphasized that a substantial proportion of evasion in their countries is a result of lax enforcement. Taxpayers take advantage of the fact that the risks involved in evasion are very limited. Chart 7-1 illustrates this view.

What conditions must exist for an enforcement program to succeed? The idea that evasion does not pay is a result of the experience the taxpayer has had with the tax agency. Taxpayers will be convinced to comply voluntarily with their duties when they see that few other choices exist; the agency detects deviations shortly after they occur, advises the person concerned of the situation, informs him of the penalties that will be imposed and implements them without any hesitation when he fails to respond. Soon the taxpayer learns that no matter how he turns he will bump into a wall and it will hurt, so he might as well go straight.

To begin with there are technical requirements that must be met. Enforcement is no different than audit or collection; it needs information and expertise and it cannot function well when there is a culture of evasion — a situation in which a person who complies is more promiscuous than an evader. When the entire taxing process works well, enforcement is directed at a relatively small group of deviant cases. Size (or lack of it) is essential to success. Since the goal of enforcement is deterrence, every case handled must receive careful and detailed attention that would enable the agency to convince the courts to hand out conviction and an appropriate (deterrent) penalty. Accuracy and comprehensiveness cannot be extended to more than a handful of cases.

If size is vital, why should an agency have difficulties in selecting a small sample of strong cases out of the multitude it has information about. Here implementation gets entangled with political issues. If enforcement is to be selective, then it can no longer be neutral. How will this selectivity affect the courts' "behavior"? The question becomes, who do you enforce the law upon? How is this choice going to be made, given

CHART 7-1
Lax Enforcement Breeds Evasion

Thailand:	The present system gives a strong incentive to taxpayers to risk tax evasion in the hope that if they are caught they can still make a deal with tax officers. (a)
Jamaica:	Taxpayers usually make a return for the smallest amount possible or don't file at all and wait to be assessed. Self-assessment was a gift to the Jamaican. Here is a man who will not send in his accounts under the previous system and suddenly you tell him not only to file accounts but also to assess himself and pay at the same time. This is ridiculous. The man will sit down and complete the form; when he reaches the end and finds that he has to pay a few hundred dollars he will simply put it aside and say to himself let them come to me, I'm not going to pay it. Now we here wait for him to file and he waits for us to come and get him and the result is that nobody moves. (b)
Trinidad:	Most taxpayers are not afraid to underreport income, even to claim expenses that do not exist, like claiming allowances for four children while only three are living. They know that nothing will happen to them if they do these things; the most that could happen if they are caught is that they will have to pay what they owe plus a small interest. The risk is worth taking. (c)

Source:

a. Anan Lewchalermwong, *Taxation and Tax Reform in Thailand,* (Bangkok, Kurusupha Press, 1972), p. 81.
b, c. Senior revenue officials.

---

that it will determine whose support the politician is likely to gain or lose? In countries where everyone is related to everyone else or where tradition and social status are cherished values, it may be very difficult to treat every evader equally, disregarding who he is or to what he belongs.

Enforcement has benefits, but is has its costs, too; it does not come free, since it alienates those on whom it is applied. Therefore the politician must weigh the benefits likely to be reached against the difficulties encountered and the price that would have to be paid. The worst decision he could make is to underestimate the difficulties of implementation. He would find himself in the awkward situation where the price has been paid in full, while few, if any, benefits received. The administration, hard as it may try, cannot guarantee the full-fledged support of the courts. And without the courts, no enforcement program can succeed. So the prospects for overcoming the technical difficulties are a prime factor in the decision to encourage administrators to enforce. But more than that is at stake. In a system where the only hope for introducing certain tax policies is the shared understanding that it would not be seriously implemented, tightening enforcement and eliminating flexibility in implementation may leave the government with fewer workable policies. Flexibility in implementation is one of the important strategies policy makers have for mobilizing support for tax programs. Thus, unless they have a very strong reason — such as an assurance that enforcement will be so successful that they would not have to introduce new tax measures in the near future — they would not do something that would amount to sawing off the branch they are perching on.

How is the process of enforcement carried out in the poor countries? What are the common difficulties, practices and outcomes? What is being achieved; how and why? There is a good reason for putting the end at the beginning. The end is that there are no results. As one observer bluntly put it, "On the matter of deterrence, a glaring fact stands out, which is that no one has, so far, been sent to jail for tax evasion."[1] The story is short, though tax codes normally contain provisions for enforcement which include financial penalties and prison terms, they are rarely and, in the case of prison terms, virtually never implemented. There is an enormous gap between what could (and should) be done and what is carried out in practice. Even the very term "enforcement" is used only with reference to routine audit and collection activities. The criminal aspect of tax evasion is generally overlooked. The conclusion that was reached by the Philippine Tax Commission holds equally well for the other countries studied:

> The emphasis on tax enforcement had always been on the assessment and collection of taxes. The criminal aspect of tax violations had been overlooked, as long as violators paid the taxes assessed against them. Thus the Bureau had been unable to generate the deterrent effect of convictions for tax evasion.[2]

Another official study was even more specific

> The record to date shows that there is only *one* truly successful instance of criminal prosecution for income tax evasion . . . it is to be noted, however, that this case took nearly ten years to conclude, and for income tax evasion dating back to 1946.[3]

In Thailand where the income tax code imposes a maximum penalty of seven years imprisonment or a fine not exceeding 200,000 Baht, no one could recollect even one instance where these provisions were used.[4] Jamaica and Trinidad do not differ. No one has ever been imprisoned, and the record of successful prosecutions still waits to be written. Most of the serious court cases are ones that have been initiated by taxpayers against judgments made by the Department.

It is certainly not for want of evasion that there is so little enforcement. Existing evidence points to the fact that there is more, not less, evasion in poor countries than in rich.[5] Poor countries require more enforcement than is needed in the rich but produce less. How can these results be explained? Why are there so few prosecutions being launched and even fewer severe penalties handed out?

The explanation starts with the problem. Enforcement in poor countries must be carried out in an environment of evasion, a situation where a large (some informants preferred to say "a majority") proportion of the population does not comply either because it doesn't want to, or because it cannot. The problem of compliance as practitioners see it is illustrated in Chart 7-2.

More must be done to achieve less. Evasion taxes administrative capability by increasing the demands of its tasks. The mere announcement of regulations and deadlines is not sufficient. To actually collect taxes the administration must prod, remind and remind again, threaten with penalties and occasionally carry them out. Still, despite everything that is done, low compliance persists and large numbers of people continue to defy the law — they do not file returns, file false returns or do not pay on time.

There are not enough auditors to unveil all or even most large scale evasions. There is not enough expertise to challenge sophisticated evasion schemes. There are not enough collection agents to collect all delinquent taxes within a reasonable period of time. There are not enough prosecutors and investigators to enforce the law and create the deterrent effect that is needed to preserve whatever level of compliance already exists. No matter how hard the agents work, they only manage, to use one of their favorite expressions, to scratch the ground. What is unveiled is merely a small fraction compared to what remains hidden. Large amounts of taxable income are left untapped because evaders continue to evade since their risk of losing is smaller than the chance of winning. All this effort goes into collecting what in rich countries is paid almost automatically. All the effort that can be made is insufficient to substantially expand the circle of taxpayers who pay voluntarily without being directly forced to do so.

The problem of compliance is made worse by the inability of a great

CHART 7-2
Low Compliance Accounts for Poor Results in Implementation

Philippines:	It is unfortunate though understandable that many people pay their taxes only upon prodding and threats of legal action . . . This attitude is partly due to their lack of understanding of tax laws, to their lack of belief in the integrity of tax collectors, to the habits developed during the occupation and, perhaps, to a general apathy to public affairs. (a)
Trinidad:	Our problem is that people traditionally didn't pay, nobody really cared that much for if there was a deficit in the budget the mother country bridged the gap. (b)
Philippines:	Normally, taxpayers avoid or resist payment of taxes. As more people do this, delinquent tax accounts necessarily mount . . . (c)
Jamaica:	A notice of assessment means very little to the average Jamaican. (d)
Trinidad:	Until nearly a decade ago Trinidad and Tobago was a colony and in keeping with its status was psychologically dependent on the Mother Country. The effect of dependence is evidenced by existing chronic attitude on the part of taxpayers that taxing is a form of oppression. (e)
Philippines:	The low level of tax compliance among taxpayers . . . principally accounted for the situation . . . where tax yields were quite meager and unable to cope with the mounting expenditure requirements of the government. (f)
Turkey:	Turkish officials have told us that only one fourth to one third of income subject to tax is reported on returns. Tax evasion seems to be an accepted business practice. (g)

Source:

a. Government Survey and Reorganization Commission, "Reorganization Plan and Report — Revenue System and Administration," (Manila, Republic of the Philippines, January 1956), p. 18.

Chart 7-2 (Continued)

b. Senior Trinidadian official.
c. National Tax Research Center, *Collection of Delinquent Taxes in the Philippines* mimeographed (Republic of the Philippines, August, 1973), p. 11.
d. Senior Jamaican official.
e. Ralph A. Pierre, "Public Attitudes to Property Taxation in Trinidad and Tobago," *Caribbean Tax Administrator.*
f. Priscila B. Pagarigan, *An Analysis of the Assessment Functions in the Bureau of Internal Revenue* (Unpublished Ph.D. Dissertation, Centro Escolar University, Manila 1973), p. 369.
g. B. Frank White, *Report of the White Mission on Tax Administration in Turkey* mimeographed (Ankara, December 1963), p. 18.

---

number of taxpayers to fulfill their obligations and the limited information and assistance available to make their task a bit easier. Chart 7-3 illustrates the problems posed by illiteracy.

Those who are able to read must invest a great deal of effort in finding out precisely what they must do and how. Getting answers to questions involves a special trip to the tax office, waiting in a long line only to be served by a junior official who himself may have only a general understanding of the tax code.

In most rich countries there are many publications about tax laws: the average individual would have to try hard in order not to know something about tax responsibilities. When he has a problem he cannot solve, an anonymous phone call to the tax office will provide him with the information he needs. None of these services are available to taxpayers in poor countries. Chart 7-4 contains illustrations of the problem.

The complicated tax structure that is undergoing major changes from one year to another does not make things easier. For, even when the information does reach the taxpayer, it is often too confusing to comprehend without expert help. In most rich countries a taxpayer can have his return prepared, for a relatively small fee, by a professional accountant. There even are large companies that specialize in medium and small returns. They provide inexpensive service for taxpayers whose returns would not tax a mediocre accountant's ability. The shortage in accountants puts this type of servicetoutside the reach of the average taxpayer in a poor country. There is no such thing as getting tax advice for a small fee since the number of people who are capable of providing it is much too small to keep up with the demands of big taxpayers.

In the words of a senior Trinidadian official: "Shortage of qualified accountants and tax practitioners makes it very difficult and expensive for the taxpayer to obtain good professional assistance and advice."

The environment of evasion is responsible for most of the difficulties of enforcement. Mass evasion provides shelter, as well as legitimation, to evaders and it amplifies administrative weaknesses in personnel, expertise

CHART 7-3
Illiteracy Is a Hindrance to Compliance

Iran:	How do you tax a merchant in the bazaar who is very intelligent as attested by his mere survival in a highly competitive situation, who keeps no financial records since he is illiterate, and who has no moral compunction about the payment of taxes so that voluntary compliance is unknown. (a)
Trinidad:	Poor tax conscience, inability to understand the intricacies of the tax laws and, . . . illiteracy pose many additional problems for the Board. Too many returns filed are incomplete, incorrect or otherwise imperfect. Few self-employed taxpayers keep, or are able to keep, adequate and complete accounts and records. Time consuming indirect methods must be used to compute their taxable income. (b)
Thailand:	Our main problem with the income tax is the low level of education in the kingdom. Not many people can fill out a tax return properly, let alone understand why they have to pay the tax in the first place. We don't have the manpower to go out . . . and explain to the people what is expected of them . . . (c)

Source:

a. David E. Shirley, "Income Taxes for Lesser Developed Nations?" *National Tax Journal,* XII, 3, p. 267.
b. S. M. Supersad, "Tax Administration Reforms in Trinidad and Tobago," paper presented to the Third Regional Conference on Income Tax Administration in the Commonwealth Caribbean, Antigua (Sept. 1972), p. 31.
c. Senior Thai official.

and information. The fact that there is so much evasion, for so many reasons, means that there is need for a good deal of enforcement and at the same time, that this level of enforcement is not attainable. The scale of the problems that require solutions is too large for existing resources.

The first element in the process of enforcement is follow up. Constant follow up that is not slackened until the desired results are obtained is a time-consuming activity. When the process is not computerized, and it rarely is in poor countries, repeated scanning of a great number of files must be carried out to discover deviations — when a deadline has passed

CHART 7-4
Information About Tax Laws and Regulations Is Limited and Difficult to Obtain

Thailand:	We have established an information service just recently; in the past if a businessman wanted to know something he had to buy the entire revenue code and look for it. Most people get information about what they should do from their neighbors. (a)
Laos:	Taxpayers complain more about the *uncertainty* surrounding the application of the laws to their business than about the weight of the taxes imposed. (b)
India:	Rates of tax were enhanced in January, 1966, but no one in the department even bothered to insert a small press notice or issue a pamphlet on it. (c)
Turkey:	Ignorance of income tax responsibilities or confusion about the income tax law, especially when the tax is new or when important changes have been made, create barriers to taxpayers' compliance. (d)

Source:

a. Senior Thai official.
b. Neil H. Jacoby, "Taxation in Laos: Policies for a New Country with an Undeveloped Economy," *National Tax Journal,* XIV, 2, p. 155.
c. R. V. Patel, "Sales Tax Administration," (Seminar on Tax Administration at the Indian Institute of Public Administration, Popular Prakashar, Bombay, 1969), p. 124.
d. Zeki Dosluoglu, "The Importance of the Development of Relations with the Public," *CENTO Symposium on Tax Administration,* p. 150.

and the taxpayer has not responded. The constraints that the Department is confronted with are described by a senior Jamaican official:

> Even in the few cases where we have made estimated assessments it didn't close the case. The taxpayer receives the assessment notice and writes back to us that he objects to our estimate and he will file a return in due course. What he means to say is: forget it! The minute he objects to our assessment we cannot collect. We wait a few months for his return and it doesn't come in so we send him a notice to remind him, he ignores it; in the meantime, the officer in charge of the file is taken away from his post to assist another

> section; when he comes back after a few months he must start the whole process from the beginning and the taxpayer is still holding his tax money.

A similar situation exists in Trinidad as portrayed by a senior official in the P.A.Y.E. section:

> There is no follow up, we send defaulters letters threatening to take action unless they pay immediately but we never carry out these threats. The result is that the employer gets one of these letters, he doesn't pay, waits to see what will happen, nothing happens, then he gets another letter with more threats, he simply takes it and throws it into the wastebasket. Now he knows that he need not take BIR very seriously.

Words cannot replace action. Threats cannot elicit reaction unless it is well known that they are immediately carried out. Says a Trinidadian official: "If, for example, we go out and tell people that they must keep records, very few will take us seriously. People don't believe even if we threaten; you must take action before they start paying attention." When threats are made and then are not carried out taxpayers learn to take the Department lightly. A Jamaican official describes his experience:

> Convince everyone that you mean business, that your threats are not empty but will be carried out. The forms that the taxpayer gets from the Department contain threats of prosecution that are then not followed through. So, people have become used to not paying attention.

Threats are made but rarely carried out. Taxpayers who do not pay or file on time receive a number of letters describing in detail the penalties prescribed by the tax code for their offenses. Only in a few exceptional cases are these threats carried out. A very small number of seizure warrants (in relation to the total number of outstanding accounts) are served and even fewer consummated. For example, in the Philippines out of 336 warrants served in 1964 only fifty were closed by year end, thirty-four of which because the taxes claimed were already paid. The status of the rest of the warrants was unknown. The Philippine Tax Commission concluded that

> the ineffective use of the summary remedies of distraint and levy is revealed by the fact that no sales of personal and real properties have been made. These remedies are the last resort of the government in tax collection. It seems they are used only as a threat and not intended to be consummated in accordance with their purpose to secure compliance.[6]

Shortage of staff and unreliable internal accounting are the two factors that appear most frequently in the explanations given to these difficulties in implementation. Enforcement activities are carried out by auditors and collectors each in his respective area; there is no separate organization whose sole task is follow up. Asked why the regulations requiring traders to keep books of account are not enforced, a Trinidadian senior auditor said, "To do what we are supposed to do we would have to assess each individual's needs and abilities, and then follow up on the implementation of our recommendations; that would be too much for the staff which we have." A similar explanation is given in an internal memorandum discussing enforcement problems in the Philippines:

> If we are going to interpret RA 5203 strictly, which is the collection of delinquent accounts past the ninety-day period, all the 177,039 cases listed as collectable accounts would all be subject to summary remedies. There are only some 132 Revenue seizure agents in our organization, some of whom are assigned to non-collection functions. The workload, therefore, would be too much.

Monetary penalties work best as a preventive device when they are imposed automatically. The taxpayer will be induced to pay on time if there is no doubt in his mind that late payment will cost him money. In many poor countries the application of monetary penalties is subject to the discretion of collection agents. When discretion is introduced, certainty of application is reduced. Discretionary power means that in some cases penalties will be reduced or not applied at all. Discretion is a simplifying device that is used when there are numerous acceptable exceptions to the rule that are not codified. Discretionary power is a must when the agency is not certain that all the deviations for which penalties are prescribed really warrant a penalty. Explains a Thai senior official: "Because of the backlog [in processing] we cannot put the full penalties on the delinquent taxpayers. The fault is with us, we didn't advise them on time." A similar explanation comes from a senior Trinidadian official:

> We can't push collections and enforcement too hard because our accounting is in a hopeless state. We can't really be sure that an account in arrears is indeed in arrears. It may have been settled years ago and no one bothered to record it and credit the account. We had quite a few cases in which we threatened taxpayers with court action and they told us "go ahead." How can we go ahead when we have reason to suspect that they have paid their debts and can produce receipts?

The problem with discretionary power is that once it is introduced, it is taken for granted that it will be used. The pressure on those who make the decisions is enormous, the higher the penalties the stronger the taxpayer will attempt to shake them off. No collection agent cares about penalties. It's the closing of the account that he is interested in. Waiving or reducing penalties is one of the few means available to the agent to make things easier for the taxpayer so that he will cooperate. The more frequently he uses his discretion the more powerful he feels he is, a feeling justified by the fact that he saves some people a lot of money. Since in addition the agent will rarely have the time to verify the taxpayers' explanation, the power of discretion will be used indiscriminately. Penalties will be waived and reduced across the board, and what may appear in the tax code as an awesome set of preventive measures will turn in practice to have no preventive effect at all.

Prosecutions in court are necessary even when routine enforcement is functioning smoothly but much more so when it is barely limping along. Prosecutions in court serve as a dramatic reminder that the law is enforced. In terms of deterrence, court cases, if well publicized, can be extremely effective. The exposure and the possibility of spending time in jail are frightening prospects for most people.

To obtain the deterrent effect from prosecutions, the Department need take only a small number[7] of exceptional cases — in terms of the amount involved and the seriousness of the offense — to court. All other evasion cases can be settled at an administrative level. For prosecutions to act as deterrents, to serve as evasion preventing mechanisms, they must be widely publicized and they must usually end with convictions and severe penalties. No one counts exactly how many cases there have been or measures the probability of his own possible conviction. What is ingrained in people's minds is that some tax offenders were brought to court and that quite a few of them had to serve time in jail. This effect can be produced by publicity; it is not necessary to lock up hundreds of people to obtain it.

If it is a question of preparing only a handful of cases each year, such arguments as lack of time and qualified personnel that are commonly used to account for poor implementation, can no longer hold. The problem of getting a few evasion cases to court certainly is not for lack of evaders. To obtain conviction in the criminal courts (where jail penalties can be imposed), the tax agency must prove willfulness beyond any reasonable doubt. In the words of Jamaican officials, "We must establish in the judge's mind that the man deliberately falsified accounts to evade taxes. This is extremely difficult to do . . . It would have to be a very obvious case for us to win in court." "The tax man is expected to present his case in such a way that it would be beyond any shadow of doubt; he cannot expect any sympathy from the judge."

The auditor's task, by comparison, is much simpler. He need only unveil suppressed income to obtain his goal of deficiency assessment. For the enforcement officer the knowledge that the taxpayer evaded is just the beginning and not the end of the road. To obtain a conviction he will have to prove in court that the evasion was purposely committed, that the taxpayer knowingly attempted to defraud the government of tax money. A Thai official, questioned on the paucity of prosecutions, explained the problem well: "You don't have to be an expert auditor to tell that they are lying, but you must be an expert auditor to prove that they are lying."

The first problem of prosecutions is that despite the fact that only a few cases need be prepared, each one requires a great deal of effort and expertise. A good investigator must have all the qualifications of an expert auditor plus a much better knowledge of the tax code, court procedures and methods of investigation. He must combine the talents of the accountant and the district attorney. These men are in extremely short supply. The second problem is availability of records. The auditor can manage without records since he can bring the taxpayer to a position where he will be willing to compromise. The investigator needs proof, evidence that will be accepted in court: "Investigation . . . is fruitless . . . unless there are records to inspect."[8]

Since the habit of maintaining books of account and written records of sales and purchases has not yet expanded far beyond the large open stock companies, the majority of evaders cannot be subjected to criminal investigation. They could be prosecuted in the civil courts for failure to keep proper records but the penalties that can be imposed for this type of offense usually do not warrant the effort. On the other hand, it is not desirable to systematically prosecute only those who do keep books. Those who do not keep books will be given a strong incentive not to start, while those who already comply will have poor reasons to continue. It is therefore those who do not keep books who should get the brunt of enforcement, but those are the hardest to prosecute.

Where records are available, the development of a successful criminal case requires that investigators start working as soon as evasion is suspected. A taxpayer who finds out that he is being audited will rush to cover his tracks. Therefore, the more the auditors advance in their work, the less likely it becomes that a criminal case could be developed. Since the auditors are interested in convincing the taxpayer to accept their findings, they destroy material evidence by using it to reach compromises. Explains a Jamaican senior official:

> Successful criminal investigations require early involvement of investigators and criminal lawyers. If you don't have this, material evidence will be destroyed . . . You must prepare a strong case before you take it to court because you don't want to have a compromise.

The investigator can get to a case at the early stage of inquiry only if he is called upon by the auditor working on it. Auditors can be instructed to call in the investigators as soon as evasion is suspected, but they cannot be forced to do so. Imagine an auditor who spent the entire year working on routine cases, hoping to get a real fat one where he could reach a big deficiency assessment and impress his supervisor. The last thing this auditor will do is to turn his prize case over to someone else. As he is the only one who has detailed knowledge of the file, his supervisor will never know that he suspected evasion and had not reported it. Cooperation between auditors and investigators is hard to achieve.

Wilkenfeld describes the Israeli experience:

> The assessment and collection programs had been stepped up considerably, and the professional staff were under heavy pressure to meet and exceed their prescribed quotas . . . recommending a case for criminal investigation; and the more "juicy" the fraud case, the more additional tax it was likely to produce. Thus there was a direct conflict between the collection program and the prosecution program.[9]

A study of a Philippine enforcement program describes a similar situation:

> Because the ultimate determination of criminal prosecution is not within the province of the Investigation Division, the examiners have the natural tendency to give more emphasis on assessment than on the criminal angle of the case . . . Adjustment of the tax due and the imposition of civil penalty seems to be the culminating point of satisfaction . . . There is a discernable lack of drive to proceed deeper into the other ramifications of the case and ultimately bring the offenders to court.[10]

The Director of the Thai Investigation Division said simply that he never gets cases from the examiners. He must develop his own investigations based on various other sources of information — informers, newspapers and reports from other government agencies (land and motor vehicle registration). The problem is unknown in Trinidad since it does not have fraud investigation at all. Jamaica recently hired two expatriate investigators to help establish fraud investigation, but so far their time has been devoted to various training activities. What investigations they have conducted were aimed more at reaching a compromise than obtaining convictions in court.

Auditors can ignore the criminal angle and get away with it because audit has a higher standing than investigation; unlike the latter, it produces revenue. This is the prosecutor's third problem. Everyone knows and agrees with the logic that more enforcement will produce more deterrence, will improve compliance, and, in turn, will increase revenues. But very few officials who are responsible for what the agency is doing will be willing to act on this basis. The Minister of Finance is not interested in long range goals but in this and perhaps next year's revenue. The quickest way to obtain revenue is to reach compromises at the lowest possible administrative level. The advantage is that the tax is paid as soon as the compromise is concluded. When the Department decides to prosecute, collection must be postponed till after the case is resolved in court. The court process takes far more time than administrative compromise, because investigators must collect evidence and prosecutors prepare the case that will then wait for its turn at the courts. A study of Jamaican enforcement policy concluded:

> Fraud is given some attention and activities are directed principally to civil (as opposed to criminal) actions. The reason for this seems to be (1) the length of time required to develop a supportable case . . . (3) the desire to assess and collect these large liabilities promptly.[11]

A Thai official stated that it is simply useless to send a case to prosecution because "unfortunately it takes too long to get a case through, sometimes it may take as long as six or seven years. The courts are crowded with other cases." Since only cases that involve large sums of money qualify for criminal prosecutions, the decision to send a dozen or so cases to the courts would cost the agency a substantial amount in terms of revenue that could have been collected.

Cost is meaningless unless weighed against benefits. The cost of prosecutions is postponement of collection; the benefit is the impact on compliance. The U.S. Internal Revenue Service, for example, brings its evasion cases to the courts shortly before filing period, because experience indicates that the publicity they receive has an immediate effect on compliance. Thus it may definitely pay to wait through the long process of prosecution if the end results are convictions and deterring penalties. Here is the fourth problem of prosecutions in poor countries: there is no certainty as to what the end result will be. The tax agency can find the evader, it can prepare an airtight case against him, but neither ensures that he will be convicted and penalized accordingly. Even in the face of excellent evidence the courts may refuse to recognize the seriousness of the offense. Tax evasion is a reversible offense; the taxpayer can pay back what he attempted to keep and with this (for all practical purposes) the case can be closed. The impact on compliance is indirect, nontangible, and can be, without much difficulty, discounted.

What limited experience tax agencies, in the countries studied, have had with prosecutions convinced them that there is very little to be gained from going to the courts. Here are a few descriptions of what this experience is:

> Prosecutions didn't prove effective. The judges used to treat evasion cases as if they were ordinary debt cases so that if the taxpayer agreed to pay the amount he owed there was no penalty. Investigators work for months to prepare a case for prosecution and then the taxpayer gets away with nothing. (Jamaica)

> The magistrates are lenient, too soft. Even in cases where the taxpayer admits that he owes the money they allow him to pay in small installments.

> When we bring a man to court for not filing his return the judge will find him $T10[five U.S. dollars] per return. This is ridiculous. (Trinidad)

> The income tax act allows us to demand imprisonment for fraud and for delinquent returns. I never heard of anybody being arrested for income tax offenses. (Trinidad)

Here lies the main problem of enforcement. There is a vicious circle in which voluntary compliance is low and therefore the effectiveness of preventive administrative measures, audit and collection, is limited. Since there are too many evaders, so that evasion cannot be regarded as deviant behavior, the courts refuse to treat severely the few that are discovered. That in turn fosters the low levels of voluntary compliance that already exist.

An explanation has been formulated based on cyclical logic. The agency's behavior is partly explained by the courts' reluctance to cooperate in fraud cases. The courts' behavior in turn hinges on the fact that the agency is not doing enough to prevent evasion. There must be a way out of this vicious circle or else it would not have been possible to develop an enforcement program such as exists, for example, in the United States.

The lag of time between administrative and legal enforcement is the link that closes the vicious circle of evasion. It takes time before changes at the administrative level begin to affect the legal machinery. When a new policy is implemented the courts will have to be convinced that it is here to stay, and that it is not a one-time shot that will be forgotten the next day even before they start adapting to it.

In a study on the development of enforcement in Israel, Wilkenfeld found that "in the earliest income tax criminal cases the courts indicated a tendency to impose relatively light penalties, taking into account the fact that for some years the income tax administration had itself been lax."[12]

It is the one shot campaigns rather than routine activity that characterize enforcement programs in poor countries. The magnitude of the problems of delinquent accounts and returns is so huge that with the resources available it cannot be routinely coped with. So every now and then, when things get out of control, or when the Ministry of Finance needs some additional revenue at the end of the year, or when the commissioner wants to prove that he is doing something about evasion, a collection drive is launched. These drives, as they are called in Jamaica, or campaigns, in the Philippines, are characterized by an intensive effort that dies out rapidly. The campaign is launched by assembling personnel from all branches of the Department. It is not long before their absence from their regular duties begins to adversely affect vital activities. Thus, even before the campaign picks up momentum, it has to be called off. If they only lasted long enough to leave a strong impression, it may have been possible to scratch the bottom of the barrel for resources to keep them going. Campaigns are quickly dropped because spectacular results are not immediately achieved. What justification there might have been to divert resources to the campaign is quickly overwhelmed by the mounting pressure of daily routine work.

The problem is one of a lack of redundancy. The agency does not have free floating resources that would enable it to engage in activities beyond the minimum necessary to keep the revenue flowing. There is not enough staff to carry out the daily activities of processing returns, audit and collection. The department cannot improve one activity without damaging the others.

An example that is a bit extreme but dramatizes the issue, is recent experience in Trinidad with fraud investigation. A few years back a decision was made to develop this activity. An experienced auditor with the proper qualifications was selected and sent abroad for training that lasted some two years. After successfully completing his studies the investigator returned home and shortly thereafter died. With him went the entire program. Experienced people do not come by every day, neither do training budgets. An accident that would have hardly left a mark on a rich organization determines the fate of a whole program in an organization that is strained for money and manpower. It will be years before another suitable person will be found, taken away from his post, trained and put back in the new function. The rule that in an organization no individual is indispensable, holds only when there is redundancy in men and money.

Things which cannot be obtained comprehensively may be achieved incrementally over a long period of time. Small investments in enforcement that would produce noticeable results in the long run are more feasible than the attempt to institute an entirely new function overnight. But there does not appear to be a marked difference in levels of enforcement between poor countries that have been independent for more than four decades and those that have gained independence only recently. Thailand and the Philippines do not boast a better enforcement program than, say, Jamaica and Trinidad. This suggests that factors other than administrative constraints are involved.

Take, for example, a situation where the government has the courts under its control and can more or less dictate their sentencing policy. In this case, the deployment of the courts in an enforcement program is independent of the administrative ability to carry out routine enforcement. Will the courts be deployed? Judged by the recent experience in the Philippines the answer is *not necessarily.* Here is a government that has been brought to the brink of bankruptcy by tax evasion. What does it do to collect back taxes, after declaring marital law? It institutes a series of tax amnesties. Instead of prosecuting a few evaders to deter the others into paying, the government makes a compromise deal with all of them. If you come out in the open and pay a small percentage of what you actually owe, all your past offenses will be pardoned. Why compromise when you have the power to enforce? Answers a senior official in the National Economic Development Authority:

> The government preferred amnesties over enforcement because it thought that that would be a better way of getting the necessary revenue and a much quicker way at that. Just before martial law the country was in a precarious financial position, it had to get more revenue and fast.

Filipino officials consider the operation a tremendous success, and judged by the immediate results it obtained, it definitely was one. Within a relatively short period of time (less than three years), the number of filers increased four-fold from slightly less than one million to more than four. Revenues (from income tax) went up from 946 million peso in 1970 to 1.9 billion peso in 1973.[13] No doubt a fair size increase. But the question is not what can be added to the revenue every now and then as a windfall but what can be added permanently. An amnesty in itself cannot guarantee improvements in compliance; it merely enables evaders to purchase, at low price, security against offenses. Deciding to go straight in the future is a completely separate decision from the decision to go clean in the past. Tax amnesties may work well once, but they cannot function as a routine.

The official justification for the amnesty program is the government's desire to permit citizens to start in the new regime with a clean slate. A serious attempt has been made to convince the citizenry that in the future there will be no leniency towards evaders. Whether or not the government will stand by its promise is, at the moment, an open question. Experience with amnesties in other countries as well as the Philippines itself shows two things: first, once the government declares an amnesty many taxpayers start to believe that it will continue with this policy. Hence the logic of don't pay, just wait for the next amnesty. Second, promises of tougher enforcement later on have rarely materialized and for the very same reasons that made the government prefer compromises to begin with. No country that has experimented with amnesties (Ceylon, India, Indonesia, Israel, Malaysia) can boast that, after the new page has been opened, enforcement is significantly different from what it was before. So again, why compromise and not enforcement? Because compromise is a faster and surer way of obtaining increases in the revenue yield with much less effort and at a lower political cost.

The political cost, in terms of the strong opposition of those who would be hardest hit by strict enforcement, is a prime consideration for weak governments. Policymakers may not want to prosecute and penalize tax evaders because in doing so they erode what support they have among the economically powerful groups. A Trinidadian official explains the problem his government is facing:

> Our present government was elected in 1971 by thirty-three percent of the registered voters. There was a no vote campaign and it was quite effective . . . The result is that we have only one party in Parliament and the government has a mandate to do nothing. To do something that the public does not like they will have to rule by force. If they want to stay in power without risking a civil war they must take things easy and not do anything that the public does not like.

A collection agent describes how this policy affects his work:

> We don't have the backing to press the taxpayers to pay; if a taxpayer gives me the run around or blatantly refuses to pay all I can do is report to my supervisor. Once I pass a case to him . . . I know that there it will be buried. You can't really blame them either, if something will blow up they will have to bear all the heat and their boss will ask them who told you to do this or that, how come you didn't consult with me before you took action. Who would want to risk this?

Another senior official summarized: "I don't think that the Department wants a confrontation with the taxpayers. We want to have a relationship of cooperation; there is enough hostility between us and the taxpayers as it is."

Jamaican officials, while strongly denying the existence of any political constraints, admitted that the Department is not sufficiently strong to withstand the pressure that strict enforcement produces. An example, given by one of them, is worth quoting here in full:

> Why aren't we rougher with taxpayers? I don't have a good answer but I can give you an example that would help you understand. A few years ago we had a case with a man who owed a few thousand dollars in back taxes. He made a part-payment agreement with the Collector General; the installments were to be paid by the first of each month. The first installment was paid in as agreed. The next month the money was not paid and on the second day the Collector General arrested the man. The money was paid on the following day. From our point of view this was the issue: the taxpayer had the means to pay by due date, the fact that he didn't indicates that he may have decided to try and see what will happen if he doesn't. That is why we believed it was important to react promptly and strictly.
>
> The public didn't share our view. A few days later there was an uproar because the man claimed he was arrested because the Collector General had a personal grudge against him. He argued that everyone knew he was able to pay and that he intended to, therefore it was not necessary to arrest him. The point of course is that he failed to specify precisely when he

> intended to pay. This set a sort of precedent and we are now reluctant to adopt tough policies because of what we think may happen.

Specific reasons for not initiating enforcement at the policy making level may be as numerous as the number of countries involved. In terms of the mechanics of the process, which are the same everywhere, there are two sets of constraints that work against enforcement: technical administrative and political — the cost of the policy, in terms of loss of support, to the policy makers.

Conclusion

Though it is not certain that enforcement without the aid of cultural factors can push and then maintain compliance to high levels, it is reasonably clear that lax enforcement encourages evasion and makes it harder to assess and collect taxes even from those taxpayers who are known to the tax department and who do comply, if only partially. The existing large number of evaders turns every effort at assessment and collection into a mere scratching of the ground. Both of these functions depend heavily on deterrence, and that goal cannot be achieved as long as there are so many evaders.

None of the officials spoken with had serious doubts as to what should be done to alleviate the problems of evasion. Though there were disagreements concerning the proper penalties and some thought that prison terms are in principle a much too coercive measure for even the most serious tax offense, on the whole no one questioned the need to prosecute and penalize evaders in a way that would deter others. The problem of enforcement is not finding out what to do but implementing what everyone already knows. The question of how to overcome difficulties of implementation cannot be answered as easily as the question: "What should be done to improve compliance?"

It has been observed that when governments of poor nations run short of money they tend to levy new taxes rather than improve the collection of those that already exist. In one of his recent comparative studies Due concluded that "many Governments have added more and more taxes instead of seeking to enforce effectively those they have."[14] This shows how difficult the problems of enforcement must be. Though little is known about the politics of taxation, we do know that politicians try to avoid policies which require new taxes or higher rates on existing ones. Opposition to higher taxation is usually strong. All that is needed to mobilize it is the announcement that taxes are about to be raised. Therefore raising taxes is normally the last resort after less painful alternatives for increasing the revenue have been exhausted.

The problem with enforcement is that it is inseparable from compliance. The ability to perform the enforcement tasks — follow up, investigation, prosecution — well depends, in addition to adequate expertise, personnel and information (all of which are in limited supply in most poor countries), on a high level of compliance. When the majority complies it is not difficult to operate effective enforcement against the few who don't. When the majority evades, the same administrative capability must be directed at a substantially larger population, which immediately reduces accomplishments.

At the high levels of evasion which prevail in poor countries, the technical difficulties encountered are insurmountable. Follow up procedures directed at detecting and correcting deviations break down as a result of the sheer volume of errors. There is never enough personnel, and considering the scale of the task, there can never be. Few evaders are caught, even fewer are prosecuted and almost no one is severely punished. The agency fails to obtain the support of the courts in penalizing evaders since it does not succeed in effectively preventing evasion. As long as mass deviations from the rules are tolerated or, worse, remain entirely undetected, the courts refuse to severely penalize the hapless few who were caught.

Enforcement is even weaker than audit and collection. Some countries do not even have a specialized enforcement organization within the tax agency. In all of the four countries studied, enforcement gets only second call on personnel and resources. Agencies worry first about satisfying urgent needs in audit and collection, turning to enforcement later when little is left to distribute. Nevertheless, it is hard to criticize policy-makers since enforcement poses more difficulties than any other task while promising fewer tangible results.

Enforcement is a slow process. It takes time to unveil evasion and gather sufficient evidence to prepare a convincing case, and it takes even longer for an enforcement program to penetrate public awareness and to begin to influence behavior. By contrast, investments in audit are capable of producing results immediately. If a handful of better trained auditors are added to the staff, their contribution will immediately show up on the record of increased assessments. Furthermore, the success of audit depends almost entirely on the auditor's skills, while even the most talented investigator still needs the courts to reach his goal. The merits of the case, the quality of the evidence, is only one and not necessarily the most decisive element shaping the court's decision. Enforcement is further weakened by bureaucratic politics, since investigators must rely on others for information. The auditors who know the files best have little interest in helping enforcement. Why should they relinquish a good case when what the investigator is likely to gain they definitely lose? As long as audit is in the process of development and "juicy" files are in limited supply, auditors who are under pressure to prove their ability will not give up a promising case.

The common denominator to these technical constraints is the nature of the enforcement process. This is a process that is dependent on others. It cannot function by itself. It is only when the entire tax agency is working smoothly that it becomes possible to set enforcement into full motion. There are no easy shortcuts to obtain successful prosecutions. While it is possible, for example, to conduct audits when written records are not available, it is not possible to take an evader to court without solid evidence that is legally acceptable. The shortcuts taken in audit work are based on the mutual interest of the taxpayer and examiner in reaching a compromise solution. The point in prosecutions is not to compromise but to prove guilt and impose penalties, hence the need for legal evidence.

So the conclusion seems to be that all available resources and energy are to be devoted to the development of audit, collection and processing. But a tax agency which will do just that will never get off the ground. Deterrent enforcement, it is recalled, is a necessary ingredient without which audit and collection will not be able to cope well with the problems of evasion. Therefore enforcement must be developed incrementally alongside the other functions. But since enforcement is not an expedient solution to the revenue problem, the pressure to raise revenue quickly may force the department to opt for solutions such as amnesties or administrative compromises — solutions which foster existing patterns of evasion and hence strengthen the links that keep the vicious cycle of evasion closed.

The problem of enforcement does not end with technical difficulties. The reason why enforcement is so overwhelmed by its environment is that it enjoys little, if any, political support. For it is not hard to imagine that a government determined to enforce its tax laws could pull together enough resources and effort to launch a strong program. Though cases such as this are rare they are not completely unheard of (there are no descriptive studies to support the claim, but the New York Times on a number of occasions reported about tightening enforcement in India and Brazil, in the late 1960s and early 1970s). The reason why this determination shows up so rarely is the cost of implementation. The task is immense; it requires no less than radically changing the behavior of thousands, or hundreds of thousands, as the case may be, of taxpayers. And it is not enough to change attitudes towards taxation, it is also necessary to change business practices, to make them more formal, to introduce bookkeeping as a means of managing economic enterprises and large scale organizations and not merely as gadgets to satisfy the tax auditor. The trouble is that these changes are unpleasant to the taxpayer; they require him to move from a state in which he paid little, or not at all, to a state where he routinely pays greater amounts than he was used to in the past. This is a major social and political reform that requires a varity of means as well as a fairly long period of time to mature.

Inability to operate at peak effectiveness, however, is no justification for complete passivity. Some enforcement is necessary to prevent the development of disincentives to compliance. More limited goals may produce better results than grand aspirations that do not match existing capabilities and opportunities to act. The question of how limited enforcement could work is taken up in Chapter Nine.

Notes

1. Avelino B. Lim, "Reshaping Tax Policy for Economic Development," *Congressional Economic Bulletin* (September 1970): 10.
2. Joint Legislative Executive Tax Commission (JLETC), *Tenth Annual Report,* (Manila, Republic of the Philippines, 1969), p. 34.
3. Joint Legislative Executive Tax Commission, "A Study on Tax Administration," mimeographed (Manila, Republic of the Philippines, 1965), p. 185.
4. Anan Lewchalermwong, *Taxation and Tax Reform in Thailand* (Bangkok: Kurusapha Press, 1972).
5. Accurate data on levels of tax compliance in different countries is not available nor are there many studies of compliance in individual countries. The problem of collecting data on compliance, particularly in a country that suffers from large-scale evasion, is that no one will be willing to give honest answers. Milton Taylor describes the problem well:

    > It is only to be expected that evidence of income tax evasion, since it is an illegal activity, is difficult to obtain in any country; it is not altogether different than trying to determine the consumption of Indian hemp or the degree of illegal gambling. Ministries of Finance . . . have more evidence of evasion than any other governmental office, are frequently restricted from divulging information by acts of official secrecy, or they are loath to be frank about the degree of evasion for fear that the information would encourage even more evasion. (Milton C. Taylor, "The Relationship between Income Tax Administration and Income Tax Policy in Nigeria," *Nigerian Journal of Economics and Social Studies* 9, 2 (1967), p. 204.)

    The information that is available is mostly descriptive. It consists of statements by experienced practitioners and tax experts who spent a good many years in advising governments on how to improve their ability to mobilize resources. But, since it is very consistent, it can, therefore, be taken as quite reliable.
6. JLETC, *A Study on Tax Administration,* pp. 119-20.
7. According to official annual reports of revenue agencies, in the U.S.A. there are 700 material convictions per year, in England 125 and in Israel 40; there are 2.5 convictions per million people in the U.S.A. and England and in Israel 13.

8. Public Administration Service, *Modernizing Government Revenue Administration* (Chicago, 1961), p. 75.
9. Harold C. Wilkenfeld, *Taxes and People in Israel* (Cambridge, Mass.: Harvard University Press, 1973).
10. JLETC, *A Study on Tax Administration,* p. 180.
11. K.J. Feifarek, *Project Termination Report, Tax Administration Improvement* (Kingston, Jamaica: USAID, 1974), p. 20.
12. Wilkenfeld, p. 219.
13. Bureau of Internal Revenue, *Annual Report* (Manila, Republic of the Philippines, 1973).
14. John F. Due, *Indirect Taxation in Developing Economies: The Role and Structure of Custom Duties, Excises and Sales Taxes* (Baltimore: The Johns Hopkins Press, 1970), p. 160.

Reforms

Chapter Eight

Normative Theories of Reform, and the World of Practice Where Few Things Work Well

The single most important aim of any tax reform in Colombia today should be to raise more revenue.

Richard M. Bird, *Taxation and Development*, p. 187.

. . . the formal existence of a sound tax law cannot be equated with an effective tax system. The difference lies in an inadequate administrative machine.

Raynard M. Sommerfeld, *Tax Reform and the Alliance for Progress*, p. 173.

Economic Theories and Tax Policy Reforms — Increasing Revenues by Strengthening Policy

Money touches on almost every problem poor countries have. Poor countries want to increase their wealth, but money is needed to make money. In poor countries the government, like the typical poor man, has just about enough to survive from one day to the next. While the government may want to make life easier for its citizens by providing more and better health services, schooling and communication, it typically fails to meaningfully expand its services because demands grow faster than revenues. The government will usually develop plans for moving from its present state of poverty to a desired state of wealth. Such plans, which may seem splendid on paper, are often disappointing in their implementation. There is simply not enough money to spend and invest. Things are made even worse by difficulties in estimating how much will be available, though it can usually be assumed that there would be less than originally estimated.

The ground is permanently shifting under the budgeters' feet and they must change priorities in spending to adapt to the new revenue conditions. Short range measures (such as printing money or borrowing it from abroad) help in dealing with immediate problems, but they are no solution for long range problems. Loans must be paid back with interest;

inflation may get out of control and lead to an overthrow of the government; and foreign aid is normally limited to specific projects, their number and size both small and unpredictable. No matter how ingenious such short term measures are, ultimately something will have to be done to raise the necessary resources internally. There is no such thing as a permanent free lunch.

The budgetary difficulties poor countries have are a result of three revenue problems: skimpiness, inflexibility and instability. Revenues are insufficient, do not grow quite as fast as demands for spending, and suffer from wild and uncontrollable fluctuations. The inability to raise more resources is a result of poverty. Economic theorists have been asserting that at low levels of economic development, the amount of wealth is low and its distribution in the society precludes effective mobilization by standard means such as income, property and sales taxes. A less developed economy has fewer taxable bases, each one smaller than its counterpart in industrial economies. The ability to raise revenue is determined by the availability of large concentrations of wealth and the existence of a relatively limited number of channels through which economic transactions are made and wealth flows. Thus when the economy develops, government revenues will go up because there will be more opportunities to effectively levy taxes.

What should politicians in need of money do besides wait for economic development to produce these results? The answer is simple: look for untapped potential and tap it. If the key to understanding the revenue performance of a country is the economic factors on which the taxing process rests, then the key to improving the revenue, short of waiting for economic development, is to add to the tax policy those ingredients that are necessary to capture existing taxable resources. James Cutt's proposal typifies this approach:

> The revenue productivity of a tax is dependent . . . on its income elasticity . . . [and] on the width of the tax base relative to national income. If the coverage of existing tax forms is incomplete — if, in effect, all those persons and/or things which should technically fall under a particular tax base are not so included — it should be possible to increase revenue mobilization by widening existing tax bases and curtailing exemptions.[1]

Where existing taxes do not cover the entire range of economic activity, the tax base should be broadened — new taxes imposed and the coverage of existing taxes expanded. Then the "exhaustiveness" of the taxes should be intensified by increasing each tax's yield through reduced exemptions, introducing itemized deductions for actual expenses instead of standard deductions that often include inflated expenses. Finally, improve progressivity by increasing marginal rates, replacing fixed with *ad valorem* rates, and supplanting indirect with more progressive and powerful direct taxes. This is the formula Bird uses to recommend changes in the Colombian income tax. According to him, "the income tax should be made more progressive by, for example, taxing capital gains more fully, by heavier use of net wealth taxation, and by more effective enforcement."[2]

Policy reforms are popular with practitioners because of the relative ease with which they can be achieved. Despite political constraints, few resources and little effort are required to formulate and enact changes in policy. With only a quick survey of the present situation and the tax potential of a number of economic activities, a basic economic analysis to give the proposal the semblance of rationality as well as to avoid coming out with something that would be economically disastrous, a dash of legal language, and you have it. In fact, this method works sometimes — for example, when a surcharge of ten percent is attached to a tax that is already reasonably well collected.

If the theory that ability to mobilize resources is a function of the size and structure of taxable bases is right, and if practitioners are prepared to follow it in practice, then we should expect to find that properly designed reforms will produce the desired results in terms of increased revenues, improved flexibility and stabilized inflow.

Reform is the test of theory. If attempts to institute certain changes systematically fail, there must be something wrong with theory and it would be foolish to put the blame on the practitioners' doorstep. Caiden and Wildavsky underscore this point:

> Social scientists must reject the assumption that repetitive patterns of behavior . . . are unmotivated. That would make a mockery of their vocation. . . . If we do not understand why citizens or bureaucrats act the way they do, the problem does not lie with them but with us. They see clearly, after a number of experiences, where their interest lies. They choose what experience reveals is best for them. They are wise; we are ignorant.[3]

One of the advantages to the researcher of tax reform is that its success or failure is measured in hard nickels and dimes. To the question "has the reform produced the desired goals?" we can provide an unambiguous yes or no. Experience with reforms covers a wide range of countries and issues. The literature, however, is remarkably consistent. Most observers report that changes in policy either do not last long or, worse, fail to produce projected results. Actual achievements are both rare and modest; records of truly successful reforms are scarce.[4]

After surveying experience with policy reforms in three Latin American countries (Venezuela, Chile, Colombia), McIntyre and Oldman[5] could not identify any outstanding successes in implementation. They found that years had gone by before any action was taken on recommendations submitted by study missons and that often by that time either the political will, the need to reform, had been dissipated or the original proposals were not longer useful. In Venezuela, for example, "the Shoup mission proposals, while detailed in economic sense, did not include draft legislation. Elected governments, one after the other, failed to implement any significant part of the Shoup mission proposal for almost ten years."[6] By the time some implementation started, the increase in income from oil eliminated the original motivation for tax reform — the need for more public revenues. There is good reason to expect that real achievements (if there were any) would have received wide publicity. Without such descriptions, it can be assumed that few, if any, systematic and lasting successes have been reached in policy reform aimed at increasing the revenue:GNP ratio in poor countries. Chart 8-1 exemplifies the typical assessments of reform experience.

Practitioners smile when they hear about suggestions for increasing their country's revenue by increasing the rates, cutting down exemptions or imposing taxes on hitherto untaxed bases. Asked to explain their reaction, they usually answer, "Ask why we haven't done it already?" Deductions are not, as some tax advisers think, unusually high for no good reason. In fact there is logic behind this seemingly irrational arrangement, and as long as it holds, no amount of theorizing will convince policy makers to introduce the recommended change. Deductions are unusually high because officials do not have great confidence in their ability to verify itemized deductions. By keeping deductions high, they manage to limit the scope of conflict with the taxpayer so that they may focus on the more important issues of getting taxpayers to file and of obtaining at least some relevant information about their businesses. In other words, there is no assurance that by reducing deductions the yield of the tax will be increased. Taxpayers will exploit other opportunities, perhaps less convenient to the tax department, for keeping their taxable income as low as it was in the past.

It is even harder to adopt proposals that impose a substantially higher tax burden on those who can afford it. In fact, the likelihood of enacting this type of tax reform equals the probability of a major political and social reform that would change the distribution of income and wealth.[7] Imposing a significant property tax on land holdings, for example, is dependent on land reform, a major political issue in those countries where the ownership of land is concentrated in a few hands. The reason why the tax burden is light and effective rates are low is that the economically powerful groups are usually sufficiently strong politically to prevent the passage as well as the implementation of legislation that might hurt them financially. Though aware of these difficulties, most tax experts tend to view them as external constraints blocking the implementation of otherwise good policies, rather than as part of the problem that must be

CHART 8-1
According to Assessments Made by Tax Experts, Results of Reform Efforts Have Been Modest

The considerable volume of tax research in Latin America since 1961 . . . has not as yet apparently resulted in much actual improvement of tax systems . . . . There have been a great many tax changes in recent years, but those that have lasted in most countries have mainly been broader and higher sales taxes and increased "incentives" to investment and saving. Personal income taxes have . . . been lowered about as many times as they have been raised. Similarly there has been a great deal of activity and inventive gadgetry in the property tax field but apparently few substantive improvements. (a)

Foreign tax experts . . . have tried to pour new wine into old goat-skins, and it has not worked well. They have trifled with the superstructure but have not really altered the substantive character of the Afghan tax laws and their administration. (b)

It is often discreetly admitted that results obtained from technical assistance rendered in the tax field have not measured up to the hopes and expectations of the organizations furnishing this assistance . . . There is a very human tendency to blame the foreign governments for these disappointments, and complaints are heard that measures recommended as most urgent have lain ignored in ministerial files. (c)

The limited success of financial programmes . . . suggested by western experts in underdeveloped and reconstructing countries since 1945 is a matter of . . . common knowledge. Results have fallen short of expectations, partly due to the unfamiliarity of the experts with the specific institutional background . . . The basic drawback of these reforms has been that fiscal policy and experience of advanced countries . . . have been drafted on to less-advanced economies. (d)

Source:

a. Richard M. Bird and Oliver Oldman, "Tax Research and Tax Reform in Latin America — A Survey and Commentary," *Latin American Research Review* 3 (Summer 1968).
b. Harley H. Hinrichs, "Certainty as Criterion: Taxation of Foreign Investments in Afghanistan," *National Tax Journal,* XV, 2, (June 1962), pp. 152-153.
c. Joseph P. Crockett, "Tax Policy for Underdeveloped Countries: A Political Approach," *National Tax Journal,* XIX, 4 (December 1966), p. 391.
d. M. H. Gopal, "Towards a Realistic Tax Policy for India," *The Indian Economic Journal,* VII, 3, (January 1959), p. 282.

incorporated in the policy itself. The Colombian Commission on Tax Reform, which submitted a massive report, wrote in the introduction that though the issue of implementation is of supreme importance, it decided not to take action on it, "although we have kept these needs in mind, our primary assignment is not to devise and recommend administrative improvements, but rather to develop a structural tax reform."[8]

Policy reforms fail not only because they so frequently do not take into account the factors that have been responsible for the situation they are trying to improve, but because they take implementation for granted. It may be an unfortunate situation, but implementation separates policy from outcomes. This statement is not quite as trite as it may seem at first glance. There is a widely accepted assumption that a good policy is always better than a bad policy. Though this rule is logically sound, it is empirically false. Good policy and bad policy may very well end up in the same place.[9] No policy can be better than implementation; poor implementation leads to poor policy outcomes. Regardless of how far-reaching policy changes are, unless something is done about implementation as well, the revenue will not be affected. To use Hinrichs' expression, you can't pour new wine into old goat skins and expect that it will taste good later on. Bird writes that "tax reform proposals that assume good administration exists are unlikely to be relevant in most poor countries."[10] Hinrichs elaborates:

> Tax reform that only alters the formal legal superstructure without touching the administrative-procedural foundation may be quite meaningless; it could even be detrimental by postponing real reform under the guise that something in fact had been changed or by instilling wishful thinking that reform indeed was underway. The efficacy of foreign advice is often overestimated, especially by foreign advisors.[11]

The treasury needs actual money and cannot settle for anything less. Plans, hopes and expectations, even laws, are not good substitutes when salaries and interest on loans must be paid.

Weaknesses in theory are reflected in the outcomes of reforms. A better understanding of the taxing process requires that more attention be given to the ways and means by which tax policies are implemented.

How Problems of Implementation Create Gaps Between Policy Goals and Outcomes

> [Our] tax laws are basically sound . . . their quality is debased by the way they are complied with by the taxpayers and enforced by the administra-
>
> Joint Legislative Executive Tax Commission,
> "Strengthening Tax Enforcement," p. 41.

> If you want an effective reform, it is not the taxing LAWS so much as the taxing PROCESS that requires attention.
>
> J. Lanning, Tax Revision Compendium, p. 19.

Revenues are unstable and inadequate in poor countries not only because of insufficient taxable bases and inadequate policies to tap them, but also because of partial implementation of existing tax laws. Most observers agree that even without any substantial change in policy, tax revenues could be increased significantly by strengthening implementation.[12] Implementation is also the key to better policy. With a stronger administration the possibilities for enacting more powerful and stable policies will be greater. Shoup emphasizes this point. According to him,

> the range of successful policy formulation depends largely on advances in administration. As tax administration becomes more and more efficient, policy makers can consider a wider range of possible tax patterns tax administration is the key to tax policy.[13]

Accurate calculations of the amounts that the government loses annually through nonfiling, underreporting and late payments are not now available, neither are these data readily obtainable. There are, however, informed estimates based on familiarity with the economy or extrapolations from indepth studies of selected sectors. In most poor countries, according to both observers and practitioners, the tax lost is often half or more of what is collected. This is what is meant when gaps between goals and outcomes are referred to. This is why no new policy that is enacted can hope to solve the revenue problem; it will always achieve less than anticipated.

Gaps between goals and outcomes are a result of two factors: the enormity of the task and the comparative weakness of the resources (information, personnel, expertise, and the instruments — audit, collection and enforcement) available for carrying it out. The volatility of policy compounds the weaknesses in implementation. To facilitate implementation, policy should be simple and stable. However, the conditions under which policies are made in poor countries do not permit policy makers to go by these two requirements. It is hard to predict financial needs since the information available on current spending and commitments is limited; nor is it updated or sufficiently accurate. This is why policy makers so often wake up one day in the middle of the year to find that there are certain needs that have not been provided for in the current budget. When there is no surplus to fall back on, there is no other choice but to change policy to obtain the additional revenues.

Policies made at the beginning of the year are rarely powerful enough to provide all the necessary resources for the budgeted commitments, since the political structure does not enable such policies to be implemented. The concentration of economic as well as political power in the hands of small elites forces policy makers to employ the "crisis" method. The only occasion for increasing the tax burden is a financial crisis, when the government faces the risk of not being able to pay salaries or comply with foreign loans agreements. Only under the threat of bankruptcy is it possible to overcome the strong objections to increase the tax burden on those who can afford to pay.

If policies are not made to last at least one year, but are changed whenever a crisis occurs, administrators cannot develop and stick to routines that simplify their work. They must then constantly adapt to new conditions, working harder and achieving less. A substantial portion of their resources and energy will be spent on learning and relearning procedures, regulations, and tax and exemption tables. Less will remain for implementing what they know. Finally, the more frequently the tax structure is changed, the more complex it becomes and the harder to implement.

The instruments of implementation — audit, collection, and enforcement — are shaped by the circumstances in the environment in which they are used. The taxing process, which consists of these instruments, works well only when most taxpayers comply voluntarily and little or no action is necessary to make them pay what and when they should. The process works on the basis of certainty and deterrence. Certainty means that there is no, or virtually no, escape from paying one's taxes. Deterrence means that the price paid for noncompliance is likely to be significantly higher than the benefit one stands to gain if one evades and is not caught. The desired forms of behavior are not obtained by influencing each taxpayer directly, but by triggering in each a rational choice calculation that would lead to the conclusion that complying is preferable to evading.

The three instruments with which the process is run are linked to each other in a system of mutually reinforcing relations. Each instrument must work well to permit the others to do so; each instrument reflects the strengths and weaknesses of the others. The goal of audit is to ensure that tax statements and related information submitted by the taxpayer will be reasonably accurate and true. Collection must assure that filing and paying deadlines are observed and that the number and amounts of delinquent returns and accounts are kept to a very small proportion of annual collections. The task of enforcement is to provide the ultimate thrust that the system needs to keep running well, by detecting any significant deviation and penalizing it to deter others from repeating it.

If audit does not unveil evasion or cannot produce the data that are needed for prosecution, enforcement will not be able to deliver the deterrence for which it is responsible. Similarly, if enforcement fails to prosecute fast enough or to obtain deterrent penalties once the case reaches the courts, it will be hard for collectors to carry out their task — there would be too many people who disregard deadlines and reminders to pay. So the performance of each of the instruments affects the performance of the others.

Let us now look at each one independently. The goal of audit can be achieved either by assessing every individual taxpayer prior to determining his tax bill, or by allowing the taxpayers themselves to calculate their tax and auditing selectively a sample of the returns to discover discrepancies between the statement and actual earnings. The first method works through the high level of certainty that every return is examined; the second achieves its goal through the rule of probabilities. Most taxpayers know that not all returns are audited (and therefore there is some chance for slipping through) but that there is a very high probability that those returns where evasion has been practiced will be selected for audit sooner or later. It therefore does not pay in the long run to evade, since those caught pay dearly for it. If the goal of audit is to ensure accuracy in reporting, the task of collection is to safeguard prompt payment and filing. Again no organization can go about collecting taxes directly from every single taxpayer. An incentive must be created that would make it worthwhile for the majority of taxpayers not to owe the government money. This incentive is achieved by demonstrating to the public that the tax administration detects delinquent payments immediately after they become overdue. In addition to the certainty of being found, there is the cost of the penalty that will be added to the tax bill.

Perhaps the most important contributions to the factor of deterrence are court prosecutions and administrative penalties. An organization that systematically and severely penalizes its delinquents can expect that the majority will hold the line. On the other hand, an organization that does not put a high price on delinquencies can expect them to become the common form of behavior rather than a deviation.

No organization, especially one that extracts rather than provides goods, can expect to function well without some measure of support from its task environment. Tough enforcement can keep a system based on voluntary compliance going, but it is quite doubtful that it alone can start and develop it. Remember the saying that you can rule with bayonets but you cannot sit on them for long. How voluntary compliance develops is a subject in its own right about which very little is known. Suffice it to say here that though enforcement alone cannot produce mass compliance where it does not exist, it is certainly an important ingredient, if not the key element, in the process. It can safely be said that some enforcement will produce some compliance, and that more enforcement will produce more compliance, though in order to push compliance beyond a certain point additional factors are needed. We certainly do not know of an example, contemporary or historical, where a high level of tax compliance has been maintained without tough enforcement. There is, on the other hand, overwhelming evidence that where enforcement is weak, compliance is low. This is the characteristic situation in poor countries.

Though there are no good answers to the question of how to develop a tax system based on a high level of voluntary compliance, it is possible to suggest how compliance can be marginally improved or how to improve the collection of taxes without it. This is what interests policy makers most. They have little use for evolutionary processes (and the development of a mass based voluntary compliance is definitely not something that can be quickly produced). What they need are solutions that can be implemented to solve problems that must be solved immediately and not twenty years hence.

If the taxing process had worked according to the deterrence formula, the difference between policy goals and policy outcomes would have been much smaller than it is. It would not have solved entirely the problem of compliance and evasion, but it would have reduced its proportions; revenues would have been proportionately higher and there would have been less need for frequent policy changes to raise additional revenues. However, the process does not work this way in practice. Instead of aiming at producing as much deterrence as possible with available means, the process is geared to accomplish quick settlements by means of compromise. Compromise is the magic word that looms behind almost every decision taken. Compromise among auditor, collector, investigator, prosecuter and the taxpayer has the double advantage of a relatively quick resolution and closing of the case plus some additional tax money — a hard, tangible and immediate result. The alternative poses insuperable demands. Compromise, however, destroys deterrence. Voluntary compliance will be eroded when taxpayers learn that one can cheat the tax collector and later, if and when caught, reach a compromise on the amount and form of payment and penalty. Since the enforcement ability is pretty much a constant, the gap between goals and outcomes will grow, the smaller portion of the tax legally due being realized. Yet, despite much talk to the contrary, classifiers, auditors, investigators and the courts prefer compromise over tough enforcement. Though it may not seem so, the behavior of each of these participants is, from his point of view, quite rational, irrational as it may be in toto. While the collective depends on deterrence to keep its work load within manageable proportions, each individual depends on compromise to solve his immediate problems.

The first problem an auditor in a poor country encounters is the lack of sufficient and reliable information, yet his work is to verify information and determine whether or not the taxpayer reported his actual earnings and spending. Formal auditing procedures are of little use with the majority of taxpayers since only a few keep books of account and even those are frequently incomplete. The only way to make some progress is to rely on surrogates to actual, hard data. Instead of making elaborate cross-checking examinations, the auditor tries to determine the extent to which the taxpayer himself can be trusted. He tries to identify odd figures, items that seem unusually large or excessively small, any sign that would indicate that the accounts have been manipulated to reduce taxable income. He tries to learn as much as he can through direct observation and face to face interviews about the taxpayer's business, his employees, internal procedures and routines, his customers and suppliers as well as his personal life style and property. He must win the taxpayer's cooperation by making things easier for him, while at the same time implying that they could be harder. He must create the impression that he knows a good deal while in practice there is little he can hope to find out that would qualify as hard proof.

There is some advantage to being on the government's side in this process but not an overwhelming one. There is no difficulty in laying hands on evaders; only a few taxpayers would come out clean from a tough examination. The real problem is to build a sufficiently strong case that would stand in court and would prove beyond reasonable doubt that the taxpayer has evaded. Only when the auditor is able to do that systematically would he be in a position to hold his ground and refuse to compromise. When he cannot hope to reach this level, except perhaps in a small number of unusual cases, he will be forced to deal with the taxpayer from an inferior position. The taxpayer will not be prepared to accept every reasonable demand because he knows that he may get a better deal from the courts, which as is well known do not accept suspicion as sufficient evidence for conviction. If the auditor wants results, as he must if he does not want to be in a position where all or most of his audits are challenged and then stuck in administrative or court proceedings for years, he cannot afford to meet the taxpayer midway. His problem is to insure that he does not retreat completely towards the taxpayer, that is, that he will get some additional tax from him.

The audit process is now geared to a goal other than compliance and that is tax money. The two are not necessarily mutually exclusive; in fact, even a process that is entirely geared to promote compliance will produce, as a side benefit, some tax money. But in practice the reverse does not work that way; a process aimed at primarily getting tax money is likely to weaken the ability to enhance compliance. One example will suffice. Investigators usually complain that there are not enough suspected evasion cases forwarded from the audit section. The auditors who are in the best position for discovering such cases early enough to permit the launching of an investigation have very little interest in letting a good case slip out of their hands to the investigators, and out of their credit log. A case that is promising for the investigator is equally appealing to the auditor. If the investigator can build a case that would obtain a conviction in court, the auditor can probably reach agreement on a large sum in additional taxes, and while the investigator may have to work months, sometimes years to develop the case, the auditor can produce results in a few weeks. Though it is not rational from the organization's point of view to settle the case at the audit stage, this is the most rational course of action for the individual auditor.

Auditors suffer not only from deplorably poor information, but also from limited expertise needed to obtain, analyze and interpret the information wisely. They are frequently poorly equipped to compete with the private accountants representing the taxpayers they audit, let alone to conduct the complex investigations necessary to substantiate suspected evasion in returns that are not supported by comprehensive documentation. The best they can hope for is that they will be able to unearth sufficient information to convince the taxpayer that it is better to reach a compromise and pay some additional taxes than take the risk, small as it may be, that the case will be forwarded to investigation.

The problems of collection are not significantly different. Lack of reliable and up-to-date information, insufficient personnel and limited expertise do not permit the collectors to prevent the accumulation of delinquent accounts. Collectors are forced to work with the past and not with the present; therefore, they cannot hope to have an impact on the future. The information system and the size of the work force do not enable early detection of delinquent payments. The lists of accounts paid and accounts outstanding are not accurate, nor are they produced immediately after filing dates have expired. In some countries the list is available only two years after filing; under those conditions it cannot be expected to be current. Even after the lists are available and the collectors know from whom they should collect, it takes time before the delinquent taxpayer is approached because it is necessary to verify whether the information, by now two years old, is still true. When the taxpayer is finally reached, he has already accumulated a significant amount of back taxes. It is going to be as hard for him to pay his entire debt in one shot as it is for the government to insist on prompt payment when it itself was rather slow in taking strong action to collect it. The result is almost always a part-payment agreement which enables the taxpayer to pay in installments. The government loses and the taxpayer invariably wins. Everyone would rather pay later than sooner especially under conditions of inflation when there is a general interest in postponing the payment of debts whose nominal amount is fixed. Thus, while collectors are sweating to clear away past debts new ones keep piling in, and the mountain of paper waiting to be processed never seems to shrink. They fail to influence most taxpayers to adhere to deadlines and pay on time because they cannot convince them that they have the ability to discover delinquencies, to make them pay promptly, and to add a substantial penalty as well.

Investigation and enforcement have the worst lot in the entire process. Their own weaknesses (caused again by insufficient staff and limited information and expertise) are amplified by the weaknesses of the earlier stages in the process. They deal with the hardest and most difficult cases, but the potential results of their work are perhaps the most dramatic, tangible and effective. Enforcement is the ultimate price-tag for noncompliance. But the price cannot be made high unless everything has been done in previous stages to prevent and limit the possibilities for evasion. Regardless of how hard the investigators work to bring cases to the courts, they cannot expect to obtain sufficiently severe penalties if evasion is the common rather than deviant form of behavior.

What an enforcement section can do, if it is well equipped, is to prepare a handful of good cases each year and push them through the courts. It can even ensure that a high percentage of the cases brought to court will result in convictions. What it cannot do is to ensure that the courts will impose the penalties that will have a deterrent effect. That is a function of social values and acceptable norms of conduct. What has not been achieved throughout the process of audit and collection cannot be hoped to be achieved at the last stage by sending a few luckless taxpayers to jail.

The system of mutually-reinforcing elements contributes to the further weakening of each individual instrument. Since there is not enough deterrence, there is too much evasion to enable the auditors to have an impact on the level of accuracy in reporting. Their natural tendency to compromise, and thereby the erosion of deterrence, is enhanced by the fact that any other goal besides higher revenue seems hopelessly remote. Since too many people flagrantly disregard deadlines, the problems of running an accurate and comprehensive system of internal accounting become enormous. Unless accurate information is available on time, the collectors cannot be expected to perform their task effectively.

Everyone involved in taxation is aware that implementation needs to be improved, but few have done much more than acknowledge the need to do something. Practitioners as well as academics have avoided issues of implementation. As Bird and Oldman write, "Few tax studies have been much concerned with the problems of implementing their recommendations."[14] Stanley Surrey describes the prevailing attitude among tax advisers in this way:

> Often the remarks devoted to administration are in the form of generalities, all of which notably come down to the repeated recommendation of "improvement" . . . usually tax administration is off the beaten mission paths. It is increasingly apparent, however, that the administration must receive far greater attention if the goals of the policy are to be attained.[15]

Sommerfeld describes how little attention is given to administrative issues when decisions on reform are made. According to him, "All too often tax reform discussions turn immediately to the need for a new and more progressive tax structure ignoring the administrative inadequacies of the existing system."[16] Milton Taylor describes how economic policy goals are set without incorporating any program for raising the required funds:

> The economic planners . . . have given little attention to the domestic financing of the public investment plans. After necessary levels of investment are determined to achieve target rates of growth, the planner then turns, in a disinterested way to the problem of financing. In other words, financial resources are expected to rise to expenditure needs, rather than vice versa . . . generous increases in tax revenues are extrapolated in a cavalier fashion.[17]

Improving administration is a much more complicated and difficult task than changing policy. Legislation is merely the first rather than the last step in the process. Implementation, as we shall shortly see, unlike policy, deals with the behavior of large numbers of people — revenue officials and taxpayers — and behavior is significantly more difficult to change than laws.

The next section tours a number of countries to review their experience with tax administration reforms.

Experience in Reforming Tax Administration

If the taxing process was sufficiently understood, there would be few problems in designing and implementing measures that would make it work better. Many questions to test the limits of our knowledge come to mind. For example, have plans to improve administration had better luck than attempts to increase revenues by changing policy? What happened to reform proposals when they reached the stage of implementation? What results have been achieved and in what areas? What were the constraints that prevented or seriously hampered the implementation of reforms? What opportunities for introducing reforms have been successfully used and which ones overlooked? Most have not been successful; failures in design and implementation can be exploited to further our understanding of the taxing process. They allow us to ask what went wrong and why, and what can be done to avoid similar pitfalls in the future. They help to focus efforts at reform on the parts of the tax process most likely to be successfully changed. The answers to these questions allow a position to design reform proposals that have a better chance of producing desired results. These answers can be sought in the experience of various poor countries in implementing administrative reforms.

The goal of reforming tax administration in poor countries is strengthening the ability to mobilize resources. The problem facing revenue departments is that resources — budgets, information, expertise, personnel, facilities — are so limited, and the instruments of implementation are so weak, compared to the enormity of the task that they must perform. Unless something is done to bridge the gap, simple improvements in organization and procedures will not have a noticeable impact on aggregate performance — i.e., the total revenue that is collected.

Taxing instruments work well only when they do not have to be applied to more than a minority of the taxpayers; therefore, proposed reforms must have the capacity to effectively reduce the number of taxpayers who do not comply voluntarily. It is not enough to improve the quality of the auditors alone. No matter how good they are, the number of audits they can make will be too small to make a difference. It is necessary to design a process that will reduce the scale and volume of evasion or enable revenue officials to cover a greater proportion of the returns filed. Then their work will be effective in terms of its deterrent impact on the rest of the population.

For reform to be successful, it must be comprehensive. It must improve not one but all phases of the taxing process. According to Hill:

> The key element to developing the design or objectives [of reform] is comprehensiveness. Tax administration is made up of a number of functions which must be integrated into a unified whole. Each impacts on the others, and concentration on some without considering this impact on the others will result in a lopsided administration which fails to meet the requirements set for it.[18]

The solution most frequently recommended for increasing the effectiveness of existing resources and instruments is the self-assessment system. The idea is powerfully simple — instead of calculating the tax liability for each individual taxpayer, let the taxpayer do it himself; instead of examining every return for accuracy and completeness, concentrate audit capacity on a small number of returns where potential evasion is deemed to be substantial.[19]

Having less routine work, the revenue department will have more time and energy to devote to finding and correcting deviations. Since taxpayers calculate their own tax liabilities and pay when filing, the great burden of assessment backlogs is once and for all eliminated. With the old method of office assessment, the government could not collect before an assessment had been made, and backlogs in assessment were a tremendous liability since they directly affected the tax yield. With self-assessment, in theory at least, the bulk of the annual tax payment is collected with very little direct action on the part of the government.

To do more with self-assessment than simply reduce routine work for the revenue department, it is necessary to institute the elements of a deterrent system — early and comprehensive detection of deviations, prompt action to correct them, and uncompromising and tough legal action against criminal offenses. To arrive at this goal the revenue department must be organized around four principal activities: classification; audit; collection; and enforcement. The old principle of dividing work according to type of taxes should be abolished in favor of a method that allows specialization in performing the vital functions of the taxing process. The staff should be reassigned according to abilities and qualifications. Machinery to improve listing, bookkeeping and billing operations should be installed. An annual audit plan based on indicators of potential evasion and manpower availability should be prepared. Enforcement should be emphasized, the legal staff increased and investigations expanded. The quality of personnel should be raised by instituting continuous formal training with tough entrance requirements and by paying higher salaries to attract and retain competent people. Finally, an information service should be instituted to disseminate the information the public needs so it may comply with tax regulations.

When an attempt was made to discover what had happened to these recommendations in the countries that were visited, the usual reaction received was that, though some progress has been made, it is questionable whether the old problems have been completely removed. What is certain is that the changes made or the attempts to introduce them created a new set of hitherto unknown problems. Since the same pattern of development was found in all four countries studied, it is enough to report the experience of two of them and then continue to describe the mechanisms that are responsible for the failure in implementation.

Jamaica and Trinidad were chosen to report on since their attempted reforms have been the most ambitious and took place most recently. The details were still fresh in the informants' minds and there was no need to dig into poorly documented history. The elements of the story are these: Following a period of indepth studies of the problems of revenue administration carried out by experts from the U.S.A. Foreign Tax Assistance Staff, the governments of Jamaica and Trinidad adopted the recommendations and changed their income tax law accordingly (Jamaica in 1971 and Trinidad in 1973), instituted a self-assessment method in place of the old British procedure of office assessment, and reorganized the Department of Income Tax (Jamaica) and the Board of Internal Revenue (Trinidad) along functional lines. The switchover was effected within a very short time and taxpayers started to file returns and calculate their own tax liability. It was an impressive operation; every single part of it was a major reform in its own right. There was a new organizational structure, and new procedures to be followed in classification, audit, collection and enforcement of a new law and regulations. The entire nation had to change ingrained tax-paying habits and acquire new routines and attitudes.

During a a visit to Jamaica and Trinidad in the summer of 1974, it was surprising to find tax departments that looked on paper remarkably like the U.S. Internal Revenue Service. Everything the book says should be there and the advisers recommended to install was in its proper place. There was an audit division complete with field and office audit sections. There was a collection section that actually did some field collections, and, in Jamaica, there was even a group of conferees that helped iron out disagreements between taxpayers and auditors and thus limit the number of cases that would be challenged in court. Both countries installed a computer to carry out return processing and internal accounting.

Things began to lose much of their glitter when officials were asked to describe how the new system actually works. Few seemed to be satisfied, nearly everyone complained that despite the semblance of rationality, orderliness and purpose, things were not really working the way they should. A senior official, who has been in the Jamaican Department of Income Tax for more than two decades, described his feeling in these words: "Something is wrong in the Department. I don't know what it is, but we don't seem to be moving . . . the Department is not doing what it is supposed to do . . . it is not enforcing the law."

The elements of a self-assessment system were there all right, but they did not function the way they should. The computer service which was introduced with the intention that it would help overcome the problems of processing information was a long way from producing what was expected. According to Trinidad's Commissioner of Internal Revenue, "Since 1969 we have not produced any meaningful statistical data. In that year we transferred our returns, processing and accounting work onto a computer." The problem is typical. In the Philippines a study carried out by the National Tax Research Center notes that

> the present collection machinery of the Bureau of Internal Revenue has not come up with the desired level of performance in the task of collecting delinquent accounts. The use of the EDP computer and the assignment of the Bureau's Assessment and Legal Departments to the job have not been too successful.[20]

Processing takes far longer than originally expected, information needed for audit and collection operations cannot be obtained when it is needed, and when it finally arrives no one can vouch for its reliability. Computer directors emphasize that the data are not complete, not fully updated (because substantial parts of the input were of poor quality), and could not be processed.

In the past, the director of a district office knew more or less what was happening in his own domain because he had the records at his fingertips. It was the head office that had difficulties in developing aggregate information. Once the computer took over from manual processing, things were reversed. Now it is the district officer who must wait, frequently for more than two years, before he can find out who has been delinquent in paying his tax bill. Though the head office has more information, it is doubtful whether it is more accurate than what was obtained previously. Many officials complained bitterly that they are not capable of obtaining policy relevant information when it is needed and that they never know when they do get it how reliable it is. This statement by a Jamaican informant is characteristic:

> They have tried to shift processing to the computer but their program doesn't seem to be working well. Even with the computer I can't get basic statistics to prepare revenue forecasts. I must go there and dig up the information myself.

Selective audit should have been based on an annual audit program which would ensure not only that the proper returns in terms of potential evasion are selected but that audit will leave a strong impact on the various professions, occupations, income levels and geographic areas. A selective audit program needs the support of classification to select the proper returns, of research to determine criteria for selection, of collection to implement audit findings, and of capable auditors to carry out the examinations. According to Trinidad's Commissioner of Internal Revenue

> a Balanced Audit Programme needs the effective support of a good collections programme; a capable and competent planning and research units; a well conducted taxpayer assistance, education and information programme; a legal ruling and interpretation service . . . A prerequisite of a Balanced Audit Programme is a corps of well-trained auditors who are capable of performing quality audits.[21]

Not one of these components functioned as expected. Let us start with classification.

In practice, as a senior Jamaican official testified, there are no formal rules for selection and the classifying officer goes by his experience and informed intuition. An audit plan and formal selection criteria do not exist because the expertise necessary for designing them is not available. Furthermore, even if such rules did exist, it is more than doubtful that they would have been used since Jamaica had only one classifier. Having to go over thousands of returns every year, he could not be expected to conduct complex cross-checkings. Informants had no doubts that for years to come, classification will continue to be done manually by applying simple rules of selection, since computer processing is now making only its first steps.

If classification has difficulties in producing a selection of files that would satisfy the requirements of a balanced audit program, the audit section lacks the ability to examine effectively all the cases that are assigned to it. The quantity is too small and the quality is not good enough. According to a senior Jamaican informant:

> The number of audits is not big enough. You want an increasing amount of audits relative to the number of returns filed each year, but we haven't been able to achieve that. We don't have enough auditors to make a strong impact. If there were many good vigorous audits we would have had quite a few disputed cases, but at the moment we are having almost none.

Aspirations aside, both Trinidad and Jamaica were still struggling in 1974 to recruit competent auditors to replace those that had recently left. More than half of the positions were not staffed and there were no prospective candidates. The handful of university graduates who were hired could not be counted upon to stay for long. Recent experience has shown that they leave as soon as they have learned the trade and acquired enough experience to obtain a better job in the private sector.

Even if auditors stumbled across a suspected evasion, there was no one they could refer the file to in order to conduct an investigation. An investigation section did not exist. In Jamaica there were two British expatriates who were hired specifically for this job, but their skills were needed elsewhere. With the great turnover the Department had, it was necessary to have a continuous training program that would prepare new recruits for their work in the departments. Investigation was considered a luxury, something that is done only after basic tasks have been provided for. Training auditors was much more important, since without them there was a real and immediate risk that the Department would not be able to continue doing its audit work.

The new collection section struggled with similar difficulties. The task it faced was enormous; the volume of delinquent accounts and returns and the difficulties in collecting them were huge. Compared to the enormity of the task, the means available to carry it out were, to say the least, modest. The shortage in competent personnel was felt here quite as badly as elsewhere in the Department. There was an added twist though;

the quality of the personnel was lower, since collection is considered inferior work to audit.

Added to the problem of personnel was the difficulty of obtaining reliable information. The collectors can collect only if they know from whom. Despite the promises made to the revenue officials, which raised their hopes, the system of internal accounting was not greatly improved with the introduction of the computer, and information about accounts paid and accounts outstanding is still too inaccurate to permit a vigorous collection campaign. As a result, most of the work the section did was in the area of withholding and very little effort was devoted to the central problem of collection — the self-employed.

This is what the disappointed informant meant when he said that something is wrong: we are not implementing the law. The department keeps hitting the taxpayers it knows about, which is not a very effective way for expanding the tax net and improving voluntary compliance. Yet the Department cannot do much more, since, though it managed to adopt the instruments of the process, it has failed so far in making them strong enough to function properly.

There is a great difference between setting up a new organization — equipping it with personnel, facilities, budgets and procedures — and actually getting it to perform its designed tasks. Structure should not mask performance, particularly in the poor countries where appearance is often quite as important as content. This phenomena may be illustrated by an example from the Philippines. The Marcos administration proceeded, on the basis of recommendations of U.S. A.I.D. advisors, to establish a prosecution division in the Bureau of Internal Revenue. Though the government succeeded in putting such a unit together, it was not quite as successful in making it work. According to a recent official assessment, the division failed to produce reasonable results:

> The record and accomplishments of this Division is not one to be proud of nor one to brag about . . . On the criminal aspect — convictions are few, dismissal of cases filed are as innumerable as those that are pending decisions in courts. It is noted that once a taxpayer is informed of a projected criminal charge . . . the tendency is to pay the tax due just to stop the filing of the case in court or to do away with the preliminary investigation.[22]

The trouble with self-assessment is that the first step in the reform — shifting the burden and responsibility for calculating tax liability to the taxpayer — is easily accomplished by a relatively simple change in regulations. The second and more important part — introducing the procedures for selective field audit, field collection, investigations and prosecutions — does not follow automatically from the first. Improving voluntary compliance in terms of more accurate and truthful reporting, filing and paying on time, is a task in its own right.

In fact, self-assessment increases the opportunities of evasion since the majority of taxpayers receive little or no examination. Therefore, unless the change in regulations is accompanied by some real change in the instruments of implementation, there is a serious risk that evasion will increase instead of decrease. Taxpayers who did not report their true income, or worse, did not report at all, are not going to do so now simply because the government announces that it has instituted a new procedure that is based on voluntary compliance. Those who never filed before can hardly be expected to run to the nearest tax office to do so now.

To obtain these desired changes in behavior the Revenue Department must bring about a serious improvement in recordkeeping and introduce bookkeeping practices in those sectors of the economy where they are not in use. It must increase the numbers of its audit personnel. A Balanced Audit Program must be designed that would cover all evasion-prone occupations and unveil most significant evasions, so that after a few years of operation taxpayers will have enough experience to convince them that it is both hopeless and dangerous to fool around with the Tax man. In addition, it must improve its own records and information system.

Unless these changes are put into effect, the introduction of self-assessment, while reducing the routine work load, will not help in increasing the tax intake. It may even weaken the department — as a senior Treasury official claims that it did in Jamaica:

> one of the problems of the department following the reform is that it tries to do too much with too little. The advisors created certain functions and convinced everybody here that a good Income Tax Department must do all these things. So the department tries to do it and the result is that it spreads itself thin over a broad range of activities and does nothing well . . . we [Ministry of Finance] have been telling the Commissioner that he does not run the show for the Department's sake but for revenue sake; since he has limited resources we must set priorities so that he will use them to the best of our interest, which is revenue.

Informants assured me that they do not suffer from lack of ideas as to what should be done to increase revenues. The problem is that there aren't many good ideas that they know how to implement.[23]

The proposals for reform require more information, better staff and more resources than are currently available or reasonably obtainable, and that, as Richard Bird so well describes, makes them useless:

> Advice to a Finance Minister which consists mainly in telling him all the things he should do — once he has all the things he does not have — is not likely to be very helpful. It is no wonder that so many technical assistance reports are considered useless by those advised, for they do not at all relate to the actual constraints within which the recipients must work.[24]

Everyone knows how to make good audits when reliable information and capable auditors are available or readily obtainable. The problem is that the necessary information is not available nor are the well-trained auditors. Moreover, no one knows how to generate the information or recruit the auditors with the means and resources which are at the Department's disposal. The question confronting practitioners is how does one carry out good audits with poor information and an insufficient number of auditors with limited training, and not what should or could have been done had these problems not existed.

According to practitioners, progress in the implementation of reforms in the taxing process, in the administrative mechanisms that produce revenues, is slowed down and halted by the constraints within which the taxing process is taking place. It is difficult to initiate reforms even with seemingly brilliant ideas because no one is willing to admit that things are so bad that they stand in need of such a far-reaching reform; because there are not enough capable and knowledgeable people between the policy designers and the line officers to translate ideas into the language of action and supervise the nuts and bolts of the process of implementation; because funds are scarce and no one is prepared to put up the fight necessary to obtain them.

The barrier is usually penetrated when a budgetary crisis occurs and the government finds itself in the dangerous position of not being able to stand by its commitments. Yet waiting for crises insures that the problems will always be big ones for which marginal improvements will not suffice. Carrying through major changes in procedures is almost a hopeless task. When the crisis is over, so will be the support that the reform needs in order to survive. Without support and prodding, it is hard to resist the temptation to give up and to retreat to the safety of old routines. The progress of reforms is excruciatingly slow because there isn't enough redundancy in funds, personnel, or means to sustain both the reform and the routine collection work. When everything is in very limited supply, it is difficult to do two things at the same time. One must wait until the other is completed and resources can be relieved for the other job. The trouble is that in the poor countries it is nearly impossible to pin resources and attention to one place for too long. Since revenues are limited and priorities are in a state of flux, reformers frequnetly lose their original allocation midway simply because something more important emerged and there was no surplus to fall back on.

The next section describes the constraints reformers encountered in the initiation and summation of reforms. In the light of this experience, principles for tax reform will be drawn and later they will be used to suggest specific improvements in the taxing process.

Difficulties of Initiation

Who is going to admit that things are that bad?

The more problems there are the greater will be the reluctance to admit them and the more difficult to do something about them. According to a Thai informant, "The department [of internal revenue] has been resisting attempts at reform adamantly. The state of affairs there is really so bad that if they would give their consent to the proposed reforms, they would be admitting their own incompetence. No one does that willingly." Thailand, according to this informant, instituted very few reforms in the last decade. Its weak administration was not under overwhelming pressure to strengthen its ability to mobilize resources since the revenue collected fell within range of the requests made by the Treasury. No major disasters occurred, the budget did not collapse, inflation was very limited and the economic goals that the government set for itself were generally attained.

No one should get the impression that the Treasury could not do with more revenue or was not under strong pressure to approve higher budgets for the spending departments. In the absence of a serious and concrete crisis, however, it had difficulties in putting sufficiently strong pressure on the Department of Revenue to convince it to introduce improvements that would lead to increases in the tax intake. A senior official offered this explanation:

> No one has paid serious attention to what is going on in the Revenue Department because so far it has been successful in delivering what it has been asked to. There is plenty of fat in their system that can be trimmed whenever they are asked to deliver more than they are used to. Therefore there is no incentive on their part either to improve things. They know and we know that affairs are very bad there, that the auditors are not as competent as they should be, that the collectors are not going after the delinquent taxpayers, that there is no real enforcement program, but no one has a strong motivation to fight.

Another informant added that in Thailand no one cries for reform because it will be a cry in the wilderness. As he put it:

> You see everything around you working relatively smoothly. Nobody is hungry, we don't have malnutrition, we don't have any major crisis, we are much better off than any of our neighbors, so what do you want? They will tell you why are you making such a big fuss. And, the Revenue Department gets to stick to its old ways.

Another reason the Treasury does not work harder to force reform on the Department of Revenue is the almost total lack of information on what the Department is doing. There are no annual reports and few reliable statistics about past and present operations. Yet before expensive reforms are undertaken or even seriously contemplated, there must be more than vague notions that things are not going well and that the Department could, if it wanted to, make them work better. Those who argue for reform must have something solid to counter the argument that even if not all is well, this is the best that can be expected under existing circumstances. A senior Treasury official describes his difficulties in this area in the following way:

> Due to lack of statistical data we really don't know exactly how well or poorly the revenue potential is tapped. My division is supposed to make fiscal policy, but each time we recommend something that the revenue people do not like they say it can't be done and what's more they can prove it by not doing anything. If I am to convince anyone that it can be done I must have some basic statistics, like how much is collected from whom during what period of the year. Since this information is not available the revenue people can tell us that they can collect so many billion Bahts and we really have no other choice except to accept their figure and haggle over an additional few percent.

Ideas, even brilliant ones, do not implement themselves

The ability to produce good policies is not the same as the ability to make them work. The design of policies requires the participation of only a small number of capable officials, while their implementation is dependent on the cooperation of the entire bureaucracy. An example that would illuminate this principle is the introduction of computer processing. All four countries studied have succeeded in installing a computer, but not one managed to use it properly. It was not too difficult to train the handful of people required to run the machine itself. That was not enough to ensure relevant and useful outputs, however, since this small group is not, and cannot be, responsible for the input. If the data input is poor, the processed output cannot be better. This first principle of computer processing has been too frequently ignored by those who advocated the use of computers and tried to sell them to poor countries. Computer processing can work well only when everyone handling information input, right down the line to the last collection and receiving clerk, is capable of meticulously complying with the required exacting regulations. When this capability is limited or altogether lacking, and many clerks have difficulties with even such a simple task as filling out a form legibly and consistently, the introduction of computer processing is not going to make things easier. Quite to the contrary, it is more likely to throw many officials off their bearings for long enough time to create a lasting confusion in accounting.

Equipping the entire bureaucracy with the required skills is no longer as simple a task as training or hiring a handful of computer technicians. This task does not only take longer to accomplish since it simply involves a substantially larger group of people, but it also requires a budget that would most likely leave all other training activities without adequate funding for a long time.

It is easier to plan than to implement the plans because, as the "Pearson Report" explains:

> The capacity to prepare . . . plans depends on a relatively small group of well-trained individuals. These can be trained quickly abroad and they can be supplemented readily by small numbers of foreign advisors. The implementation of such plans, however, involves the whole administrative structure of the government.[25]

The situation in many poor countries is that tax advisors make recommendations based on the assumption (valid in their own country but usually false in a poor one) that there are specialists who can translate the proposals into operative plans and specialized agencies who will later implement them. But this infrastructure does not exist. Therefore, when the Minister of Finance receives the recommendations for reform, he usually is not in the position to do anything concrete about them. He may suspect that the proposal cannot go as it is, that it must be modified, adapted and perfected. He does know for sure that before it is passed on to the line officers it must be translated into the language of action. Yet there is no one around with the knowledge, skill, and available time to do this work, or even to help the Minister make up his mind whether the effort is worthwhile. The typical result of these difficulties in initiation is the inordinate length of time that elapses between the moment a decision to do something has been made and actually enacting it.

When the Trinidadian Commissioner of Internal Revenue was asked why it takes so long to get anything done even after an agreement on what exactly should be done has been reached, he responded that there are only a handful of people capable of doing something beyond their routine work. They either refuse to work with reforms or one cannot take them off their regular duties. This is the answer in his own words:

> For many years, the Board of Internal Revenue [BIR] could not provide the counterpart support, which was almost a condition of the agreement for technical assistance. The BIR just did not have the personnel with the necessary experience and aptitudes . . . Many capable technical officers are unwilling to get too deeply involved in the development and implementation of administrative reforms. They prefer to continue in their specialized technical field because of the greater potential, marketability and, perhaps, glamor. The continuation of the reform after technical assistance has ceased appears to be in jeopardy.

Poorly trained and unskilled personnel are one of the main causes of weak administration. This very same constraint is also limiting the ability to introduce reforms. This was also the conclusion reached by the United Nations Expert Group on Tax Reform Planning.[26]

When multiple demands chase after limited resources, reformers must put up a serious fight to get a piece of the action

It is not enough to think up what to do, nor even to design programs for carrying these wishes into practice. Resources and support must be found and mobilized to maintain the reform effort until the new system starts to function and the old methods it was designed to replace are well out of the way. Many informants emphasized that even the simplest and least controversial proposal requires a great deal of administrative struggling before it gets approved by all parties concerned and can expect to receive the funding it requires. Here is an example coming from a Thai senior official:

> Take, for example, a noncontroversial issue such as a tax school. The universities do not train auditors and collectors. We must do it ourselves. The issue has been raised a number of times . . . We always get the same reply from the Civil Service Commission and the budgeting office. The program will cost too much and will take too long to bear fruits . . . The problem is that you must fight to get such a program through and no one is willing to put up a fight.

Trinidad's Commissioner of Internal Revenue voices a similar complaint:

> Many problems might be avoided and implementation speeded up if prior to their implementation governments allocate adequate sums to meet the cost of the improvements. At the same time governments must waive the cumbersome financial regulations to permit the expenditure of the funded sums. They must also be prepared to experiment and introduce new personnel policies.

Improvements come second when there is barely enough money to carry out essential routine functions. According to Caiden and Wildavsky, the conditions of extreme uncertainty under which budgetary decisions are made, force budgeters to shift at least part of the uncertainty to the spending departments. They do this by making it extremely hard to obtain funds for new projects, by cutting spending proposals drastically and by making it difficult to spend the money even after it has been allocated.[27] Under these circumstances, holding your own becomes a major task leaving little or no energy for initiating new ventures.

It Takes a Crisis to Put a Reform into Motion

With these constraints, only a crisis will enable reformers to make some progress. As Richard Bird explains:

> Decisions on painful and potentially dangerous matters like tax reform will generally be made only in times of crisis, particularly external crisis as reflected in the balance of payment, when they can be blamed on external forces and when it is obvious to all that some serious consequences will ensue if they are not made.[28]

A Trinidadian informant describes the circumstances that led to the initiation of a major reform in Trinidadian tax administration:

> The accounting system broke down when the Hollerith machines were introduced in 1958. There was no consolidated account for each taxpayer. Each year's account was kept separately and, generally, it took considerable time to ascertain the total outstanding taxes for an individual taxpayer. Also, to ascertain his accounting status, recourse to his file and relevant returns was necessary. Too often these files could not be located for long periods of time. In many cases duplicate returns were requested, but they met with a similar fate . . . The Revenue did not have the expertise to remedy these problems . . . Often when alleviating measures were introduced, rapid and major tax law changes made them obsolete . . . the more capable officers were overburdened with difficult tasks . . . Things were getting out of hand in the department, evasion was rampant, taxpayers paid whenever they liked and how much they liked . . . People at the Ministry [Treasury] were worried because they were making policies that never got off the ground because of difficulties in implementation at our level. This was quite frustrating to them because they could not reach the economic goals that the politicians have set. It was in this setting that in 1963 . . . reforms were started.

Small problems turn into big ones when left to take care of themselves long enough. A large number of big problems makes the task of reform a formidable one. The more complicated the task, the greater the tendency to postpone it. Let someone else take the risks involved in initiating improvements; let your successor fight the battles for resources and support and face the blame for continued failures later. These attitudes are characteristic of the difficulties involved in initiating reforms. This process increases the scale of the problems as well as the reluctance to do something about them. The cycle is usually broken by the occurrence of a crisis that no longer permits participants to persevere. Yet a crisis is a breakdown which is much harder to repair than a small routine malfunction, and its effects tend to linger even after the repair has been made.

Difficulties of Summation

Before you know it reformers have backed out — it is hard to persist and tempting to give up

The trouble with a process that is based on crisis is that when the crisis which sets the reform underway is over, so will be the reform. It is difficult to maintain the reform effort once the immediate circumstances that have led to its initiation are no longer in existence. Once the financial crisis is over, for example, the willingness of budgeters to allocate resources to reform efforts will not be quite as strong as before.

An organization needs a strong clientele to provide it with the support that is necessary for both obtaining resources and using them later to reach its goals. Who are the potential clients of projects to improve the implementation of tax laws? An improvement in tax administration means that some people will no longer be able to enjoy the shelter that a less efficient organization provided. When most people comply, it will not be hard to obtain their strong support for programs that would lead to better compliance among the few who don't carry their share of the tax burden. The opposite is true in societies where the majority benefits in one way or another from lax enforcement of the law. Some will lose more, others less, but everyone will lose something if implementation is tightened up. While plans for improvements in the spending departments can always find supporters, plans to improve the extraction of resources are usually strongly opposed by nearly everyone. Societies that have little need for reform because they already enjoy a high level of voluntary compliance are the ones that will have the fewest problems in further improving their systems. Where improvements are most needed they are the most difficult to introduce.

Without redundancy you can either introduce reforms or run the organization, but you can't do both at the same time

No matter how promising a reform appears, no department can afford to discontinue routine collection activities until it is successfully implemented. The first and foremost goal which can never be neglected for even the shortest spell of time is raising the revenue promised for the current year budget. Everything else the department may wish to do comes second. Here is how a senior Trinidadian official describes his experience in dealing with the conflict between getting things done and introducing improvements:

> I kept telling these advisors [U.S. Internal Revenue Service] that my objective is to get tax. Their objective was to create a new system, but while they were introducing new functions they were weakening the effectiveness of the department because the same staff has to collect tax and carry out the new functions. I told the advisors that whenever our objectives will be in conflict I want the money.

A redundant organization would have no trouble in doing both things at the same time. If there are staff and budgetary surplus, then some of the personnel and money that are not vital to current operations could be transferred to reform activities. What makes it easy for a redundant organization to keep improving itself, makes it difficult for a poor and simple one (simplicity here being the opposite of redundancy) to introduce any change at all. It is the lack of redundancy that creates the seesaw effect — moving personnel and resources around to assist sections that are under pressure, thereby perpetuating the state of crisis since while things get better in the assisted section, they are already getting worse elsewhere. It is the same lack of redundancy that limits the ability to introduce reforms. The Trinidadian Chairman of the Board of Internal Revenue describes the difficulties he has when he attempts to introduce reforms and to run the organization at the same time:

> One of our biggest problems is that we have no fat in our organization. If for any reason at all one section stops functioning, the entire operation of the department will be affected, for we don't have anything to fill the gap with. For this reason it is quite impossible for us to reform our organization and procedures and at the same time continue to collect money. We must therefore take a small step at a time, small enouh so that it would not disrupt the existing system before the new one is erected.

The important lesson the Trinidadians learned from experience is that if anything at all is to be achieved, it is necessary to aim low, to lower the sights, to try and hit one target at a time, and move to the next only after the first has been effectively taken care of. Only in this way can changes be introduced without completely disrupting the existing organization. How valid this lesson is can be gauged from the experience of another country that chose the opposite strategy and attempted to implement a radical, comprehensive reform. Jamaica overhauled its entire income tax administration, lock, stock and barrel within six months in 1971. A well placed Jamaican informant described the reform and its immediate consequences thus:

> In one year they changed the law faster than we could learn it and they also changed the structure of the department. We tried to do too much too fast. Even though we have a new system we carry a large backlog from the old one. So, while we are working to clear the backlog from the old system, we are developing backlogs in the new system. The new system didn't have a strong impact at its initiation because we were and still are busy with old problems . . . When the change was made we should have convinced the public that a change was really made and that we mean business, we didn't do that.

Another senior Jamaican official adds:

> Many of the problems we suffer from today [1974] are a result of the way in which the 1969 reform has been carried out. We had a crash reform, the whole thing was done in a few months, taxpayers had only three months to prepare 1969 returns. As a result we lost most of the revenue from 1968.

Speaking for many of his colleagues, he continued to outline what experience had taught them:

> The reform should have been gradual so that we would have time to educate taxpayers, and that way they would have had time to adjust to the new system. Today — three years after the reform — we still don't have enough enforcement power to impose the law on the taxpayers.

The worst part is that while the department was struggling to recover after introducing the reform, many taxpayers took advantage of the temporary lapse in enforcement and disappeared. The record shows that the number of individual income tax filers in the last year before the reform was 82,217. One year after the reform the number dropped to 37,825, and three years later (1974) went up only to 57,076. The department spread its meager resources thin by introducing a wholesale reform and thus lost what control it previously had on its taxpayers. The reform had a dramatic entrance but was not followed by an equally dramatic performance. Too much energy and too many resources were spent in setting up the new structures and procedures. Not enough was left over for actually running them and overcoming the problems of implementation.

An overall reform may overwhelm available resources, but incremental changes are overwhelmed by the rapidly increasing complexity of the environment

If pushing too many changes rapidly overwhelms the limited capability to absorb them, doing one thing at a time is likely to leave the department lagging far behind the rapid changes that are taking place in the economy and society. Even without introducing any meaningful improvements, the department must constantly adapt to changes that are literally forced upon it by such unavoidable developments as increases in the population, growing complexity of economic activities, and expansion in foreign trade.

The environment does not stay put. No department has time for doing things leisurely and carefully in great quantity. The pressure always gets worse; the atmosphere is rarely relaxed. There is always more rather than less to do. Informants from all four countries stressed that their problem is that the environment is changing faster than their ability to catch up. Chart 8-2 contains examples of the typical statements that were made.

If you thought you had enough resources to carry out the reform because a commitment has been made at the start, you are in for a big surprise

It is not only hard to obtain funding for a new program; it is often difficult to retain the funds till it is completed. Pinning down human energy, financial resources and expertise is an extremely demanding task because

CHART 8-2
Attempts to Introduce Improvements Are Overwhelmed by Efforts to Keep Up Existing Processes

Philippines:	The continuous rise in tax work load occasioned by the rising number of taxpayers and the growing complexity of taxable transactions imposes grave difficulties in effecting administrative efficiency. Despite augmentation of existing tax personnel complement, the increase does not rise proportionately with the magnitude of the work to be done and the growing number of taxpayers to be attended to.
Thailand:	. . . we don't seem to be catching up with the taxpayers. The implementation of changes is a very slow process and by the time we get approval to go ahead, the proposed change is already obsolete. On the other hand we can't change too much and too fast because people will get lost; neither taxpayers nor tax officials will know what to do. My goal is to have at least two small changes each year. Feed the changes very carefully once or twice a year and give them time to work out their problems.
Jamaica:	The problem with the Income Tax Department is that its structure and methods lag behind the developments that have taken place in the society and economy . . . . The structure of the ITD suits the conditions that obtained 15 years ago. In 1958 era we had fewer taxpayers (both individuals and companies); since that time, business grew rapidly, we are having a rash of small businesses. The ITD did not change fast enough to meet these changes . . . . They have tried to shift processing to the computer but their program doesn't seem to be working well. Even with the computer, I can't get basic statistics to prepare revenue forecasts.
Trinidad:	Now don't forget that while we are doing our job and reforming our procedures, the world around us is not sitting idle, it is changing constantly. Every now and then there are new policies and new tax rates. These changes put an additional strain on our limited manpower and resources.

these resources, while short in supply, are continuously attacked by scores of demands and problems that require immediate attention and quite frequently some sort of actual action. What seemed to be of utmost importance only yesterday, may lose much of its urgency tomorrow, simply because new problems have been added to the old stock, while the capacity to solve them has not been increased proportionately. Therefore, the longer it takes to implement a reform and the more complicated the task is, the more opportunities there are for losing the original allocation of funds and personnel. The temptation to cannibalize on tax reform to help other programs survive is especially strong when no tangible results, in terms of increases in revenue, are in sight. A senior Trinidadian official describes this problem well:

> The ground work for the tax administration improvement program took considerable time to complete. Not much progress was noticeable during that time. Also the revenue had shown little increase directly attributable to the reform efforts . . . those in positions of authority became concerned money was being expended but without any noticeable increase in revenues. This concern might at some stage reflect itself in a diminution of enthusiasm for the program, or pressure might be exerted to move the Board into activities without adequate preparation.

Surrey and Oldman describe a process that is excrutiatingly slow, and which, as it tugs along, frequently exhausts its energy, resources, and support before significant results are obtained:

> The most important point learned from this experience [in Chile and other unnamed Latin American countries, India, Korea, the Philippines, Turkey and Vietnam] so far, is that significant improvement in tax administration takes a great deal of time and patience. The original desire of a country to improve its administration often cools before sufficient change has been brought about. Governments which wish to rely on administrative improvement rather than changes in tax laws as a way to increase revenues cannot count on immediate results, . . . often the complete rebuilding of a tax administration as a human institution is required.[29]

What gets done under these conditions are mainly those things that are relatively simple, limited and well defined, where results are immediate and tangible.

Attempts to improve administration have not been significantly more effective than efforts to strengthen policy. There is again a large gap between plans and performance, between recommendations and actual action. Developments are laboriously slow and are dwarfed by the rapidly growing complexity in the environment. Programs for improvement are started with great enthusiasm and energy. They are often deserted, however, before they get a chance to leave an impact because resources and personnel are exhausted or must be transferred to other problem areas. Not one of the countries, whose experience has been reviewed, can boast an improvement in its revenue ratio that is a direct product of administrative reforms. Structural changes look nice and can be impressive but they are useless unless followed by similar changes in content. Units must function as well as exist. Yet experience shows that frequently structures have gone up while their contents have lagged far behind.

The experience with the implementation of tax reforms is a reflection of the constraints of the taxing process. The same forces that interfere with the taxing process are also impeding attempts to improve it. This is why it is vital that reform designs incorporate solutions for the constraints on implementation. Leaving the constraints out, to be tackled when encountered, is likely to lead to the choice of reforms that cannot be implemented because the constraints that they would encounter cannot be solved.

In the next chapter field experience will be used to suggest possible avenues for improvement. These include ways and means to either overcome or circumvent the constraints of poverty.

Notes

1. James Cutt, *Taxation and Economic Development in India,* Special Studies in International Economics and Development (New York: Praeger, 1969), p. 50.
2. Richard M. Bird, *Taxation and Development: Lessons From Colombian Experience* (Cambridge: Harvard University Press, 1970), p. 188.
3. Naomi Caiden and Aaron Wildavsky, *Planning and Budgeting in Poor Countries* (New York: John Wiley, 1974), p. 294.
4. A useful and quite unique study of the actual action taken on a proposed reform is E.F. Gittes, "Income Tax Reform: The Venezuelan Experience," *Harvard Journal of Legislation* 5 (1968): 125-73. Here is one of his typical findings:

   > The "essential first step" in administration recommended by the Report, the redesign of the declaration form has yet to be taken . . . Despite efforts at developing a comprehensive master list of taxpayers . . . there is still no sure means of ascertaining whether or not all taxpayers have in fact filed returns . . . no method yet exists whereby a taxpayer's complete record can be readily obtained; consequently bills are often issued for amounts already collected. (p. 159)

5. Michael J. McIntyre and Oliver Oldman, "Institutionalizing the Process of Tax Reform: A Comparative Analysis," Selected Monographs on Taxation, Vol. 2 (Amsterdam: International Bureau of Fiscal Documentation, 1975).
6. Ibid., ft. 2, p. 2.
7. Bird develops this point for Colombia.
8. Richard A. Musgrave and Malcolm Gillis (eds.), *Fiscal Reform for Colombia* (Cambridge: Harvard Law School, International Tax Program, 1971), p. 14.

9. This point is well emphasized by Bird in Chapter 6 of *Taxation and Development.*
10. Ibid., p. 200.
11. Harley H. Hinrichs, "Certainty as Criterion: Taxation of Foreign Investment in Afghanistan," *National Tax Journal* XV, 2 (1962): 149-50.
12. One of the leading authorities on tax reform in poor countries wrote that: "It is probably not an exaggeration to say that no Latin American country would have a revenue problem (in the limited sense of revenue adequacy) if levels of compliance and enforcement were comparable to those in advanced countries." Milton C. Taylor, "Tax Policy Goals and Economic Development under the Alliance for Progress," *National Tax Journal* XX (1967): 419. This view is held by other leading finance economists such as Walter Heller and Nicholas Kaldor; see: Walter W. Heller, "Fiscal Policies for Underdeveloped Countries," *Taxes and Fiscal Policy in Underdeveloped Countries* (New York: United Nations Technical Assistance Administration, 1954), pp. 1-22; and Nicholas Kaldor, "Will Underdeveloped Countries Learn to Tax?" *Foreign Affairs* 41, 2 (1963): 410-19.
13. Carl S. Shoup, "Tax Policy in Developing Economies" (Address delivered before the First General Assembly of the Inter-American Center of Tax Administrators, Panama City, Panama, 1967), quoted in Patrick L. Kelley and Oliver Oldman (eds.), *Readings on Income Tax Administration* (Mineola: The Foundation Press, 1973), pp. IX-X.
14. Richard M. Bird and Oliver Oldman, "Tax Research and Tax Reform in Latin America — A Survey and Commentary," *Latin American Research Review* 3 (1968): 9.
15. Stanley S. Surrey, "Tax Administration in Underdeveloped Countries," *University of Miami Law Review* XII (1958).
16. Raynard M. Sommerfeld, *Tax Reform and the Alliance for Progress* (Austin: University of Texas Press, 1966), p. 149. An example is the report of the Colombian Commission on Tax Reform. The bulk of the report is devoted to changes in policy and the tax structure and though the Commission acknowledged the great importance of implementation, it decided against taking up the issue.
17. Milton Taylor, p. 414. Musgrave and Gillis, p. 14.
18. Gordon C. Hill, "Implementing Reform in Tax Administration," mimeographed (Presentation before the Fourth Annual Conference of the Caribbean Organization of Tax Administrators, August 1976).
19. Reports of studies that preceded reforms as well as the actual recommendations made by the advisors to the governments concerned, contain politically sensitive material and are as a consequence confidential. I have been given access to this material on the basis of the understanding that it would not be used in such a way as would politically embarrass a government or disclose information that would be damaging to the revenue department. The study of reform would not have been possible unless I would have agreed to abide by these limitations on the use of information.
20. National Tax Research Center, "Collection of Delinquent Taxes in the Philippines," mimeographed (Manila, Republic of the Philippines, August 1973).
21. S.M. Supersad, "Present Problems in Organizing and Carrying out a Balanced Audit Program: Perspective for the Future," mimeographed (Port of Spain, Trinidad and Tobago, 1974).
22. Commission on Reorganization, "Report on Revenue System and

Administration," mimeographed (Manila, Republic of the philippines, 1970).

23. A similar conclusion is reached by Bird and Oldman in "Tax Research and Tax Reform . . . "
24. Richard M. Bird, *Taxation and Development.*
25. Report of the Commission on International Development, *Partners in Development* (New York: Praeger, 1969), pp. 42-43.
26. Department of Economic and Social Affairs, *Tax Reform Planning: Report of the Expert Group* (New York: United Nations, 1971).
27. Caiden and Wildavsky.
28. Bird, *Taxation and Development,* p. 190.
29. Oliver Oldman and Stanley S. Surrey, "Technical Assistance in Taxation in Developing Countries," in *Modern Fiscal Issues,* M. Bird and John G. Head (eds.) (Toronto: University of Toronto Press, 1972), p. 280.

Chapter Nine

Cycles of Ineffective Reform: Using Experience to Overcome Difficulties of Implementing Improvements

Where action is sought, what appears ideal must be tempered by considerations of what appears feasible.

Roscoe C. Martin, "Technical Assistance: The Problem of Implementation," p. 265.

Reform and Poverty

Reform means betterment. Its purpose is to make things work better than they already are. Poverty means inability to improve the future. There is a greater chance for tomorrow to be just like or worse than today, than to be better. How can the two be combined? This is the problem of reform in poor countries. There is an environment packed with conditions — weak political institutions, skimpy resources, acute shortage in everything organizations need to function effectively, primarily skills and information — which severely limit the opportunities for introducing improvements. The present is characterized by a constant struggle to keep the place together, to prevent it from falling apart. There is a constant pouring in of a multitude of enormous problems which demand immediate attention. This is what poverty is about — there are few areas of public activity that are stable. Crises are not unusual occurrences that disturb the tranquillity of existing routines, but rather the prevailing routine. Against this background incremental improvements are dwarfed, and even when small improvements are achieved they are hardly noticeable. Attempted reforms come up against the same constraints that limit the effectiveness of existing practices. Administration reflects the weaknesses of society, hence it cannot be expected to be much stronger than its environment.

The processes of incremental adaption to the changing environment are too slow to produce marked improvements. What reformers are trying to do is to engineer reform, to introduce change that would not have come about by itself. They aim at creating a process that will be better than the existing one. Whether their programs have intrinsic value is a secondary question. The important question is did the action taken follow recommendations and have the plans been converted into practice and the desired improvements obtained? Roscoe C. Martin wrote years before the big frustrations with technical aid had been experienced:

> The pages of the history of administrative reorganization . . . are heavy with accounts of notable reports that seemingly made small impact because nothing was done by way of following through. The same pages also tell of legislative enactments and executive promulgations of measures that had little tangible effect because they were ignored in practice.[1]

Instances of truly successful engineered reforms are rare. Technical aid missions have more frequently resulted in greater frustrations than in substantial improvements. Perhaps the social and political environment with which we deal is much too complex for engineered reforms. We certainly do not have adequate theories for social and political behavior and this is why there is such a heavy reliance on the intervening variables. The intervening variable is called upon to explain what the theory could not. This practice isn't harmful at the level of theorizing, but what happens when a number of these intervening variables emerge during the implementation of a reform? Here is the reason why follow-through is so riddled with problems. No theories are sufficiently comprehensive to allow reformers to ride, solely, on them till the desired goal is achieved. Problems are encountered for which there are no preconceived solutions — political support is feeble, taxpayers and bureaucrats do not respond quite as expected; developments elsewhere reduce available resources; the installation of a computer to handle information processing results (it nearly always does) in the creation of previously unknown problems. Who solves these problems? Who can solve them? What knowledge is required and what is available? The mighty theory, if there was one to begin with, must now be set aside and routine practices be called upon. The same staff using the same procedures, equipped with the same information and resources is asked to solve more complex problems than those which they are already incapable of dealing with effectively. This is the point where the reform becomes victim to the constraints which make gradual improvement so difficult. There isn't enough money; there are too many crises, few of which are not urgent or important; there isn't enough information, or skilled people, and those who are capable of providing solutions are overburdened with the routine problems of running the organization and perhaps with a handful of other reforms. Finally, there is the simple problem of limited knowledge and analytical capability — a good workable solution is hard to find.

The field of administrative reform in poor countries is full of partially completed structures. Usually, reforms succeed in creating a semblance of rationality. A new method, technology or organizational structure is introduced, sometimes even successfully, but after the initial applause and self-congratulations have died out and the dust has settled, bewildered officials discover that while old problems have been partially ameliorated, new ones have been added. It is not unusual that new sophisticated methods create more difficult problems than those associated with simpler means. We know this well from experience with advanced technologies in rich countries.[2] The difference between the poor and the rich is in the level of complexity which their organizations can effectively handle. The poor are capable of handling, reasonably well, simple problems with simple means but are overwhelmed when highly complex problems are created by newly adopted advanced techniques.

Perhaps this analysis does injustice to reforms and reformers by reckoning results before enough time has been allowed for overcoming initial problems. It is known, after all, that even in the best of circumstances new procedures rarely work immediately, and time is needed to iron out unexpected difficulties. This is tolerable when there is time to wait. The policy makers' problem in poor countries is that they must provide solutions that were already badly needed yesterday. Time is a scarce commodity. In an environment where new crises are constantly erupting, no one can take his time looking for a solution because things could get much worse while waiting. Politicians, always looking for results that can be achieved before their term in office has expired, are even more nearsighted in poor countries since they are up against a great deal of uncertainty. Their term in office is all too frequently abruptly terminated by others who feel that not enough has been done or that they could do better. Survival is often a function of the ability to work fast or at least faster than others. Under these conditions there is very little hope for retaining support for a reform which progresses slowly. The pressure to obtain immediate results will lead to compromises at the expense of reform. The steps taken to produce immediate results at the expense of long range goals leave basic problems unsolved. The crisis that has been treated today is most likely to show up again tomorrow.

Needed is a method, a strategy, a line of action, that would produce immediate results and go beyond simply introducing desirable changes to making them stay, reinforcing one another and encouraging further improvement. The problem is how to start and then catalyze a process of improvement that, while taking advantage of existing opportunities, will minimize or altogether avoid prevailing constraints. Here is the eternal question of how to avoid overly ambitious projects while at the same time not settle for too little.

It is appropriate to begin the search by looking again at the conditions holding back the mobilization of resources; next the uncontrollable constraints and the major opportunities for successful action will be separated; finally approaches to reform proposed in the literature will be examined and adapted to the problems at hand. Now to the problems of the taxing process.

Difficulties in mobilizing resources exist both in the revenue organization and in its task environment. The organization responsible for implementing tax laws is weakened by shortages in every resource and capability required for the fulfillment of its tasks. Skilled and knowledgeable officials are not only in acutely short supply, but are frequently leaving the agency faster than new ones can be properly recruited and trained. Vital information and statistics are not systematically generated and cannot be obtained when needed. Inability to handle the huge quantities of returns and related documents that pour in every year makes it hard to determine where the agency is at a particular moment, in respect to collecting due taxes, or exactly in what direction it should be heading. Problems of personnel and expertise are compounded by organizational structures which make it difficult to use effectively what limited resources are available. Decentralization is a must if anything is to be collected outside the capital city. While decentralization does spread thin scarce resources, it goes without the advantages of delegated authority. Though the best information is obtainable at the branch level, most decisions are made by a handful of officials at the head office. It does not help that the agency is entirely dependent on the courts for deterrence — the backbone of enforcement. It is virtually impossible to maintain an effective process of implementation unless evasion carries with it a reasonable probability of serious penalties for those who undertake it. The agency's lack of success in chasing the multitude of evaders creates a strong dependence on the courts for enforcing the laws. It is this very same weakness which makes the courts reluctant to assume a tough attitude towards evaders. This is the proper point to shift to the conditions prevailing in the environment. Here is found a culture of evasion, where the timely payment of true taxes is an irregularity rather than the dominant norm of conduct. The use of standardized bookkeeping practices is painfully limited; the number of tax professionals — lawyers, accountants and bookkeepers — is extremely small while most taxpayers lack the basic skills required for filling out a tax return. The structure of commerce, production and agriculture makes things harder for assessors and collectors. Fragmentation into small scale enterprises forces officials to deal with a large number of small taxpayers instead of concentrating their efforts on a smaller number of large companies.

While there is no shortage of problems, there are only a limited number of things that can be done. Even in the best of circumstances no organization can expect to be able to improve everything that is deficient.

The problem of poverty is that there are not sufficient resources for running routine operation let alone undertaking reforms. So, points of intervention must be carefully selected in order to get some, rather than no progress for the effort. The search for the most desirable or urgent projects is greatly simplified by the simple rule of elimination.

Opportunities for successful action are quite limited. There are problems which are beyond the capabilities of most governments to solve; they either cost too much, take too long to accomplish, or are dependent on information and knowledge that no one has. Can anyone reasonably hope to bring up, within a year or two, the level of education of the mass population to the point where every taxpayer could (if he only wanted to) prepare his own tax return? An equally distant goal is establishing a comprehensive and reliable system of national accounting. Or, can anyone suggest how to cut short the natural process of evolution and create a culture of compliance from one year to the next, or even within five years?

If these are some of the principal unobtainables, where are the major opportunities? One need not look hard to find them, they are familiar to every practitioner: the competence of revenue officials can be improved, and personnel policies, audit, collection and enforcement practices can be strengthened; and solutions can be found for the problems of organizational structure and the processing of information. The question is what specifically should be done, and how to combine improvements so that they will sustain the wear and tear of implementation under conditions of poverty. To this end the literature on administrative reform is examined.

The major reform effort thus far has been aimed at improving skills and introducing so-called modern, efficient and rational procedures. The approach called Technical Aid[3] is based on the assumption that once officials have acquired the necessary skills and have been shown the way to obtain progress, they will unhesitatingly follow it. What else is needed beyond will and skill? While attempts to introduce skills were generally successful (and more rather than less of this is required), efforts made to apply them to the solution of problems have often failed. Recommended procedures were either completely ignored, or on those rare occasions when they were adopted they underwent transformations which left little of their original efficiency.

As a single approach to progress, technical aid has been abandoned because it failed to meet its own standards.[4] The conditions that were necessary for the effective application of the new skills did not exist; they had to be created. This posed a problem for which technical aid had no handy solution. After the fact explanations state that reforms could not be implemented because their designers did not understand or take into consideration local conditions. As Jones put it:

> The history of technical assistance in public administration is replete with examples where well designed programs have been shelved . . . because projects were considered too political.[5]

Progress, according to Hirschman,[6] is held back by the inability to make decisions. There are many scarcities in skills, information and resources, but the scarcity in the ability to make decisions is the dominant one. There is need, in addition to skills, for devices which will enable participants to overcome difficulties in applying their knowledge. In the face of immense constraints, there is a strong reluctance to take action. Awareness of difficulties overpowers confidence in knowledge and ability to solve problems, thus leading to inaction. Hirschman suggests that in order to unleash man's creativity, we confront him with problems which he has no other choice but to solve. Problems lead to solutions, while a too strong awareness of possible difficulties prevents participants from entering dangerous ground. Hirschman proposes the principle of the Hiding Hand — underestimating difficulties and costs of introducing a new procedure — as a way for overcoming the reluctance and hesitation to undertake feasible and potentially productive projects. In his own words: "The Hiding Hand is essentially a way of inducing action through error, the error being an underestimate of the project's costs or difficulties."[7]

In case difficulties are too blatant to be hidden, prospective benefits should be exaggerated. The Hiding Hand is a useful strategy for those who wish to introduce and sustain reforms. It is helpful in overcoming difficulties of initiation — "look, it is really much easier (and cheaper) than it appears to be" — as well as for surviving attempts to remove resources and support when immediate results are not obtained — "improvements are going to be much greater than what we originally thought they would be." But Hirschman's solution could prove to be a recipe for frustration and disaster. He relies heavily on the assumption that in the face of problems man's creativity is unleashed and problems which no one believed could be solved find their answers. How true and yet how false. Brilliant solutions often need acute problems, but not every disaster that we inflict on ourselves is followed by an adequate solution. In fact, instances of brilliant solutions are rarer than lasting problems.

It may seem obvious, but experience shows that it is not, that the principle guiding reforms should be that they should not make things worse. In the rush to make things work better we tend to forget that while we are rarely guaranteed success there is always the danger that the new practices will not work quite as well as the old. An attempt to take one step forward may result in taking three steps backward. The precarious situation in which bureaucracies function in poor countries amplifies this risk.

Consider the situation a Revenue Commissioner will find himself in when an ambitious reform, whose corners he has helped to hide, encounters serious problems and cannot make headway. We told him that it is important that he attempt it and even provided strategies for introducing it; what help can be provided now that the underestimated difficulties have emerged in their full force? "Think," "Think," "Use your mind and be creative," as if he didn't know that this is what he should do; but thinking hard is not a good solution to his problem; this he has already done without too much success. The reformer is now confronted with constraints and problems that are far greater than the capacity of the organization to overcome.

It is not enough to find strategies for overcoming difficulties in introducing reforms, there is the problem of designing processes that would work. A number of organization theorists[8] are now asserting that even that would not suffice; progress would not be achieved unless organizations are created that would have the capacity to sustain and strengthen the new procedures. The values prevailing in traditional societies are incompatible with the values of rationality and secularity on which the bureaucratic form of organization is based. It is not possible to import ideas from a modern society and implement them in a traditional one. The only hope for improvement is a compromise solution in the form of an organizational structure that would introduce bureaucratic values and procedures but, at the same time, allow some room for traditional values and practices. This organizational form, developed by Martin Landau, is called the intermediary organization. Landau explains:

> It is by design (intention) nondeterministic in structure. The extent to which its internal processes are predictable and controllable is limited. . . . Its basic processes are not fully established, rules are neither comprehensive nor exact, lines of authority are less formal . . . jurisdictions overlap, its communications are diverse and multichannelled, its categories are not mutually-exclusive, and its codes are more natural.[9]

The intermediary organization is every reformer's dream. It functions well because it is an integral part of its environment, knowing and understanding what can be done, what should not be done and which practices would be effective. At the same time this organization will function as an agent of change leading to increased rationality and improved performance. This is how bureaucratic institutions can be built in a traditional environment.

The strategy of building institutions may very well be the best solution that we have for the persisting problems of bureaucracy in poor nations, but it is of limited use to the politician who, by force of circumstances, has one eye constantly trained on his watch. Changing organizational structures and forms of behavior is fine as a long range goal, but what do you do in the meantime with today's problems?

It has been shown how the three approaches to reform under conditions of poverty can help in introducing and sustaining improvements. Contributions are accompanied by limitations: technical aid is useful for improving skills but cannot by itself ensure that they will be applied effectively; the Hiding Hand helps to overcome difficulties in introducing reforms, but provides no guarantee against failure nor guidance as to what to do when it occurs; the intermediary organization is necessary to sustain reforms after they have been introduced but it cannot be made to work fast enough to solve immediate and pressing problems. Not one of the three helps determine what improvements are necessary, how to choose those which are more urgent than others, how to decide which alternatives have better chances of success, how reforms would be implemented and whether they work as expected, or how they would be sustained in the face of reactions from the environment (such as mass refusals to comply or organized efforts by taxpayers to devise methods of tax evasion which would be more sophisticated than the capacity of the new auditing procedures)?

Thus, prior to following Hirschman's strategy of hiding away difficulties as a means for overcoming opposition to reform, a trade-off analysis is suggested. In the process of designing reforms, the alternative courses of action considered should be confronted with the possibility of failure. What would failure look like under one alternative compared to another? Given the precarious situation in poor countries, the question often is not, can we continue without a major improvement, but, can we afford the possibility of a disaster? This should not be interpreted as advocating a principle of "do nothing and hope for the best, you have already succeeded in preventing the worst." It is vital to include possible costs of failure alongside expected benefits and estimated costs of inputs when alternatives are compared. It must be asked: What do we risk when undertaking a radical, and therefore highly uncertain, departure from existing practice and what could be gained by following an incremental practice and what would have to be given up to secure these benefits?

Suggested here is a policy analysis[10] approach to reform, where alternative courses of action are drawn from knowledge of what motivates the taxing process; where choices are made on the basis of comparisons between expected gains, prospects of success, costs and risks of failure; and where strategies are used to smooth the adoption of a reform project and to improve its chances of survival. The advantage of "policy analysis" over its separate components — technical aid, the principle of the Hiding Hand, the intermediary organization and knowledge of the taxing process — is that by combining them solutions are provided for each one's individual limitations. Furthermore, by emphasizing analysis and the weighing of promises against commitments, some protection is gained against a hasty adoption of overly ambitious projects.

The section that follows will present the principles for designing reforms and then use them to suggest concrete improvements in the taxing process.

Principles for Tax Reform in Poor Countries — How to Work with Rather than Against the Constraints of Poverty

> "Tax techniques and information systems need to be devised which can produce results without depending upon a generous supply of trained and skilled personnel in tax administration."
>
> Richard M. Bird and Oliver Oldman,
> "Tax Research and Tax Reform in
> Latin America, p. 14.

> One improvement would be to recognize explicitly the need for crude, arbitrary solutions . . . and to attempt to be consistent in applying them rather than assuming that a perfect law can be perfectly administered.
>
> Richard M. Bird,
> *Taxation and Development*, p. 201.

The field of tax reform is crowded; there are very few ideas that have not already been experimented with or explored. What can be added to existing knowledge are different ways for approaching old problems and new combinations of old solutions. The problem of tax reform in poor countries, stated again, is not so much in finding good ideas to implement but rather in discovering ways and means for carrying out what we already know.

We may start by saying that there is not too much hope for meaningfully alleviating the major constraints of poverty. In the foreseeable future, resources will continue to be mobilized under conditions of instability, lack of reliable, comprehensive and updated information. Insufficient redundancy in personnel, budgets and procedures and limited accounting and bookkeeping skills, both within the government and in the society at large, are conditions likely to continue. Therefore, suggestions that point to these problems not being in existence should be ignored. Something certainly should be done to speed up the process that would eliminate or mitigate these problems, but the immediate question that must be answered is: What do we do in the meantime? Richard Bird suggested wisely that "since the quality of tax administration is such an important constraint on the possibility of tax reform, it would appear logical to suggest reforms which can be handled by a poor administrator.[11]

So the first principle for administrative reform is: *Work with what you have.* When resources are poor, solutions cannot be grand. New methods should not be more sophisticated than the old staff. Plans to rationalize on administration seem fine until the question of who is going to make them work is raised. The principle that ought to guide the search for solutions is how can procedures and processes be improved within existing limitations.

The second principle is: *Do not disturb central and vital routines.* There are few procedures that work at all, and even if they are not working satisfactorily, they could even be worse. An organization that has limited or no redundancy takes a great risk when it begins to fiddle with its central mechanisms. Established routines have the advantage of almost working by themselves. When a problem is encountered, the procedure for dealing with it is automatically initiated. The officials at the lower levels of the hierarchy know what to do without having to seek the guidance of superiors, and managers are free to concentrate on their own duties knowing that everything else works by preestablished and predictable routines. Once these are set aside and replaced by new procedures that are yet to be learned, things stop functioning by themselves and require the permanent attention of everyone in the organization. Each time an unusual problem is encountered — and at first almost all problems are unusual because a routine has not yet been developed — it will be sent up the hierarchy to find out exactly which procedure should be applied. Since no one knows the complete implications of the new procedures and there is no relevant past experience to fall back on, there is a danger of making costly mistakes. A tax department that makes frequent errors in audit classification or collection, not to speak of enforcement, quickly erodes what little voluntary compliance still exists. The public learns that there is no need to take the government seriously. Thus routines that are central to the operation of the department should not be disturbed unless there is absolutely no other choice, or unless an extremely effective replacement is at hand.

The third principle is: *Be incremental and marginal.* Develop what you have, make old methods work better rather than attempt to introduce new ones which may not work at all. Resist the temptation to think big.

It is doubtful whether rich and powerful organizations are capable of introducing and implementing radical overall reforms in one single stroke. It is certain, however, that poor ones cannot. Therefore, small projects and minor limited improvements are to be preferred to more glamorous plans. There is a greater chance of success in working with small projects since there is a greater risk of failure in working with large ones. Small projects have the advantage of being simple and cheaper. They require less coordination before they are introduced. Since they are cheaper than large reforms, it is likely that it would be easier to obtain funding for them. If one small project fails, the energy and resources wasted are unlikely to have an adverse effect on the ability of the department to continue improvement efforts elsewhere. On the other hand, a failure in a major endeavor may cripple the organization for years to come. It would not be able to put together another allocation of funds for quite some time, nor will it be easy to find people willing to stake their professional careers on yet another attempt to improve an organization with a bad track record.

The director of the U.S. Internal Revenue Service Tax Administration Advisory Services cautions that "when goals of overly ambitious programs are not met, doubt may be cast on the whole improvement process."[12] Small projects help to facilitate the initiation of reform by overcoming the reluctance to admit that things are not going well and by underscoring the fact that there is an urgent need to improve. No one appears foolish by admitting that his operation could stand a small marginal improvement, but one does look awkward admitting that things are so bad that a small improvement would not make a difference.

Finally, a large number of successful small projects may bring the department the credit it needs to get broader projects into motion. Just as a failure can cripple the organization, success breeds more of the same. Nothing talks a more convincing language than action and actual achievements. A good track record may not always be enough, but it is certainly a great help in obtaining resources and support for future improvements.[13] Concentrating effort and resources in a process of continuous marginal and incremental improvements is more likely to enable the department to progress faster than the environment. The alternative approach — attempting to implement improvements by radical changes — will send the department flying sky high only to land it right back where it took off.

The fourth principle is: *Concentrate on areas where successes come easily and quickly* is intended to head off the danger of attrition. One of the major problems in implementing reforms is retaining attention, energy and resources long enough to get something done. The time available is short since other problems, often more acute, keep popping up all around, and there aren't enough resources to tend to all of them at the same time. Therefore, to increase the likelihood of success, the subjects for reform must be chosen from those areas where there is reasonable hope for achieving immediate impact on tangible outcomes, preferably on revenues. Though reforms must be simple and cheap to facilitate initiation, their results should not be trivial or else they will not reach summation. To retain the funds and support already available and to be able to obtain more in the future, reformers must be able to show that their work is aimed at the central problems of the organization. The rule is never to attack symptoms, but to go directly to the roots of the problem. If the roots cannot be treated effectively, go to other problem areas.

How can these general principles be used to devise reforms in the substantive areas of the taxing process that need to be improved — the expertise of the staff; the system of information: audit, collection, and enforcement procedures. Let us take each of these one by one, beginning with the issue of expertise.

The usual and not surprisingly the easiest recommendation is to raise salaries and to improve work conditions.[14] Though this may seem the most logical thing to do in order to attract competent people and retain those already in government service, it is frequently not feasible. Every senior official spoken to acknowledged that the main source of the government's failure to recruit and retain highly qualified people is the low pay scale. This is what the government pays across the entire public service, however, and so far efforts to convince the treasury and the civil service commission that the revenue department is a special case deserving preferential treatment has failed. Some departments, such as the one in Trinidad, are still struggling to convince the treasury and the civil service commission that their work is specialized and they cannot perform their tasks with a force of unskilled clerks. Be it as it may, the fact remains that the revenue department has little or no leverage on the pay scales of its staff. There are, however, other opportunities that can be used. Hill suggests to improve the working conditions:

> Recognizing the realities of the budgetary limitations the administrative reformer must try to implement other solutions to the problem of work incentives . . . Systematic recognition of employee efforts, better rationalization of job assignments to provide challenging and responsible work, improved system of career development, opportunities for improvement on the job and for preparation for promotion through training programs.

These methods may help retain personnel already in government service; they must be strengthened with others that would lure competent lawyers and accountants to join the Revenue Department.

Experience in taxation is a valuable asset for any lawyer or accountant who thinks of going into private practice or working for a commercial company.[16] At present the government imposes sanctions on employees who break contracts to join the private sector. This, of course, can never be an effective measure since private companies can always pay the fine for the employee they want. What the government can do to attract competent personnel is sell the asset it has for what it is worth. Practicing lawyers and accountants as well as young university graduates should be offered short, possibly three-year, contracts. Admittedly they receive a relatively low salary, but they are not charged for the expertise they acquire. Of course, to make this truly lucrative, the potential recruit must be promised a wide range of tasks in a variety of administrative levels. To protect the government, the contracts can be designed in such a way that a person breaking it would have to go through a long "cooling" period before he could work in the field of taxation.

Another factor that could make the idea attractive, especially to young graduates, is a well designed training program. The program should acquaint the trainee with the tax code, the structure and regulations of the Department, as well as with the procedures for performing the various functions in the taxing process. It is not hard to design a course that prepares university graduates for work in the U.S. I.R.S. The procedures by which that organization works are formal and predetermined. But what should a Trinidadian or Thai auditor know? Formal auditing procedures will be useful in only a handful of the cases he will encounter, while for the rest they will be quite useless. One thing that should be done is to improve the expertise of experience. The simple tricks of the trade should be upgraded rather than downgraded.

The future revenue official should be taught something practical — methods that would simplify his task, that would enable him to reach results rather than ideas that would leave him frustrated in front of seemingly insoluble problems. Sophisticated methods of accounting are absolutely vital in an economy where books of account are kept; they are almost useless when most of the auditor's prespective clients are not in the habit of keeping records for tax paying purposes.

If a training program is a valuable asset, many departments find it difficult to establish one. Despite the fact that the merits of such an activity are not difficult to see, resources for setting it up cannot easily be obtained. Senior tax officials constantly engaged in battles to get their pet programs approved and to obtain the resources they require, leave this particular battle to the end of their list of priorities since this is not something that has an immediate effect on daily operations. One way to get over this obstacle is to design a training program which is operated for some time with the department's own staff and resources. Teaching may not be quite as professional as it might have been had outside lecturers been used, but something is better than nothing. When the program proves itself a success, external help can be sought. It is now likely to be much easier to obtain the funding needed to expand and institutionalize the program since there are fewer doubts that it may be turned into an expensive recreation resort for senior staff, and it has shown itself to be a legitimate training program.

The program must be tough and highly selective. Tough programs attract serious people because they create competition and differentiation between those who have become accredited and those who have not.

Now that the function of these principles in improving expertise of staff has been considered, let us view their application to the improvement of the system of information. Every instrument of the taxing process depends in one way or another on the availability of reliable information. Not one of them can function well when the relevant information is incomplete, outdated or simply unreliable. Therefore administrative reforms should always start with the data base. Many existing procedures will work more effectively simply because the quality of the information they need has been improved.

Efforts to improve information should be first directed at efficiently utilizing the data that the government already possesses before further steps are taken to independently generate new data. Collecting data is an expensive process and an organization which lacks resources to carry it out, and has limited ability in using what is collected, should aim at using data that is already collected by others. There is more data lying around in various government departments than Revenue Departments are currently using. The problem is one of obtaining it regularly and organizing it in such a way that it would be useful to auditors, collectors and investigators.

An information system needs continuous and systematic maintenance and updating, otherwise it will become obsolete even before it is fully established. No reform should be started unless there are means and technical expertise to maintain it well. The problems of maintenance should be thoroughly studied before the improvement project is undertaken. It may be possible that the effort required to solve them may not be worth the potential benefits obtained. This is especially true with the department's internal records. The problems of processing returns and payments are enormous; speed and precision are of ultimate importance. If too many errors are made in recording payments or if reports cannot be made available when they are needed, the entire collection process may be brought to a halt. If the process of collecting delinquent accounts is to work well, accurate and updated information must be available within a very short time after deadlines have elapsed.

The most feasible solution for the problems of information is to decentralize its collection and processing. Decentralization simplifies problems by reducing their scale. The number of taxpayers in each administrative unit can be reduced to a manageable size that would not require computer processing which no one, so far, seems to be able to control. Decentralization also cuts down the stages of processing; paper flows through a smaller number of stations, thereby removing a major source of errors as well as shortening the length of time required to obtain final reports. Finally, it helps obtain more thorough and accurate data by placing the revenue official close to where the transactions he has to monitor are taking place.

The real problem is not in convincing practitioners that decentralization will solve some problems but in finding ways to make it work. As experience clearly shows, it is not enough to decide to decentralize to obtain an actual transfer of authority from the head office to the regions. In the absence of trust between participants, decentralization only amplifies its shortcomings. Mutual trust grows out of experience in which each participant learns to accept the decisions of his colleagues, even when he feels that they are not quite as good as they could have been had he himself made them. The official at the head office must be convinced that the decisions as they are made are good enough, and should be left in the hands of the regional officers. That can be achieved through perseverence. Even if things are not working quite as well as planned, authority should not be referred back to the head office. No one learns how to make good decisions unless given freedom to make a few bad ones and assume responsibility for the consequences. Easier said than done, particularly when the issues are as sensitive and the stakes as high as in tax matters. Again, a gradual approach rather than a radical change may help build up the capacity of local officials to make acceptable decisions and as a consequence stir up the experiences that would eventually lead to the development of relationships based on mutual trust.

From information we move on to the instruments of implementation, beginning with audit.

Simple procedures are the best procedures for an environment that is basically simple and for personnel lacking advanced education. It is hopeless to try to introduce formal sophisticated procedures since it will take many years of a slow evolutionary process before enough people acquire the basic technical skills that would enable them to master and follow complex procedures. What is to be done in the meantime?

How can audit and classification be improved, assuming no dramatic changes in the quality of personnel and information are forthcoming? What particular procedures can be used to squeeze a bit more from a greater number of taxpayers without being forced to engage in a complex search for information that may never be found? How can some selectivity be introduced where there is none? What procedures can classifiers use that would improve their ability to select files with high tax potential without having to carry out the elaborate research needed to establish formal criteria of selection? What can be done to put the government's auditors in a stronger position when they are assigned to audit large companies employing top-notch lawyers and accountants?

If the solution is to be of any value to practitioners, it must not require more funds or skills than what is presently available. It should not depart too far from existing practices and routines, and finally, the solution should be simple enough to implement so that it could produce immediate and tangible results.

One solution that satisfies all of these requirements is the presumptive method of assessment. In Israel, its country of origin, it is called *tahshivim,* which, if translated literally, would mean "calculator"; Wilkenfeld prefers to call it "standard assessment guide."[17] The Tahshive is actually both. It works as a preprogrammed calculator, which after being fed with basic information produces the desired answer. Its most important quality is that using it does not depend on understanding how it works. Yet despite its simplicity the Tahshive can be a high-powered tool of assessment, first because it allows the department to employ audit people who do not know much about accounting, and secondly because it enables the auditors to reach results with very little effort in gathering information.

The Tahshive is a model of a business showing average or "normal" income and expenditure. It works simply like this: "Tell me what your line of business is and I will tell you roughly what your taxable income is." The Tahshive for each type of economic activity may be subdivided into more refined calculators, accounting for differences in factors such as location, size, and quality relevant to the particular business.

The process of preparing a Tahshive is similar to the audit process except that it is done thoroughly, by professionals aiming at discovering the characteristic traits of various occupations. Wilkenfeld describes how this is done:

> One of the staff of economists . . . would be assigned to make a study of a number of files of taxpayers in the particular line of business. From these he would select a sampling of files which appeared characteristic and he would then visit the individual taxpayers to familiarize himself with the details of the business . . . The purpose of the analysis is to identify one or more objective factors which have a direct relation to the level of income which a particular operator might realize.[18]

After a draft Tahshive is prepared, it is sent around for testing and criticism to experienced auditors. Then the necessary corrections are made and the original design is perfected and submitted to the relevant trade organization for criticism. In this way the Tahshive gains legitimation. Once it is agreed upon by the trade union, there is no need to convince every single taxpayer to accept it. The process of negotiation and bargaining is carried out before the Tahshive is made public, and is carried out by experienced negotiators from both sides. Once it is accepted by the parties concerned, the government can count on smooth application.

There is the problem of keeping the Tahshive figures close to reality and resisting the pressure and temptation to settle for a low figure to obtain quick approval from the trade organizations. This is a universal problem. The tendency is probably stronger when no standard assessment guides exist and each auditor must tackle the pressure on his own. There are no simple solutions to this question except that with better research the government can hope to build stronger cases that would not crumble under attack.

The Tahshive can turn a major liability into an opportunity by enabling the department to use its abundant supply of unskilled clerks. This personnel, which is usually the majority in many departments, is presently a burden because there is little, if anything, useful that it can do. Selective audits or even regular assessments require fairly developed audit skills and cannot be carried out at a reasonable level of effectiveness by untrained people. The Tahshive, on the other hand, requires only a minimum amount of quite simple preparation. All the examiner needs to determine is under what category — type of business, size, location — the particular return falls. Then he just has to look for the Tahshive for that category, to determine what tax is due.

Unlike other assessment methods that can be used when books are not kept — net worth, bank deposits, or simple hunch — the Tahshive is not limited by the competence (or lack of it) of the auditors. It enables even those with minimum training to attain a high level of professionalism, a level they could not reach on their own. Since everyone uses the same "calculator," uniformity and objectivity (as opposed to arbitrariness) is assured.

The department would be able to make far better use of its capable auditors by assigning them to compiling the Tahshive. Thus, instead of working only on a few dozen cases each year, whose aggregate impact, by the auditor's own account, amounts to next to nothing, they would be used to prepare the ground for hundreds of audits that could be carried out by their less competent colleagues.

Once the basic research and calculations have been completed and the new system is operating, the Tahshive can be refined to incorporate differences in income and expenditures within the same business. Since the Tahshive is merely an averaged model of a line of business, it is important that the range of income it applies to will be kept as narrow as feasible to prevent serious biases towards nonaverage taxpayers.

Introducing the Tahshive should not pose too many difficulties since there is nothing truly novel about it. Presumptive methods of assessment are already used everywhere where information and auditing skills are limited.[19] So the issue is not so much a matter of convincing people that it is a good method, as a problem of improving, strengthening, and otherwise getting more mileage out of it by basing it on better information and analysis. It would help if the yardsticks used in the presumptive method

— "look for irregular expenses," "find out what is a reasonable profit in one business by comparing it with another" — would be based not only on hunch and informed guesswork but also on a good deal of indepth hard research and analysis leading to widely applicable generalizations. Available means rarely suffice for making a few hundred good audits each year as self-assessment and selective audit require. Even the poorest department, however, has enough to carry out a few dozen careful examinations that can later be used as models for conducting mass assessments.

The Tahshive is not going to improve compliance any more than selective audit is likely to. Its advantage over the latter, however, lies in its ability to cover a greater number of taxpayers. Coverage is vital. There is an assumption that most people will continue to evade no matter what the Department is doing. If this is even partially true, then a method like selective audit, which leaves most returns unexamined, is, as a Jamican informant called it, a gift to the taxpayer. It simply makes life easier for all those who wish to evade. The apparent rationality in audit methods is bought at a very heavy price in terms of revenue lost through all unexamined returns. When audit is not accompanied by a strong system of deterrence or an existing structure of mass compliance, a method is needed that would permit the government to examine, however roughly, most returns. What revenue is lost by using the Tahshive's averaging methods and lack of precision would be heavily regained through increased coverage.

Coverage is important not only for squeezing a bit more from some taxpayers, or doing part of the job that enforcement is not doing, but also as a longrange mechanism for bringing about an improvement in the public attitude towards the Department.

In poor countries where the government is a remote and vague entity for most citizens, it is important that the taxpayer meets his representatives face to face. This is especially true in a process such as taxing where positive action (as opposed to merely refraining from doing something) on the part of the taxpayer is required. The Revenue Department must make its strength known not only through advertising but also through some real action. Action has a much greater chance of penetrating the taxpayer's consciousness. Experience is helpful in fostering or changing attitudes. If experience tells the taxpayer that he has rarely, if ever, been challenged and his reports are accepted regardless of how far removed they are from reality, he will become even more obstinate. If, on the other hand, he begins to notice that almost every time he underreports his figures are challenged and he is requested to pay additional taxes, his attitude may slowly begin to change. He will at least begin to look for ways and means to limit the conflict. He will not necessarily start paying what he really ought to, but he may reduce the scale of his evasion so that he would not be bothered so much.

From audit we proceed to collection. The main question here is how to prevent the accumulation of delinquent accounts. No department has the ability to run after thousands of taxpayers each year to collect their taxes owed. The system of collection must be made to work by itself so that all that the collection officials have to do is keep a watchful eye to detect deviations as they begin to form and immediately initiate corrective action before the deviations have had enough time to take root. A field collection procedure, where collection officers work from the list of delinquent taxpayers proceeding to collect directly from the taxpayer at his doorstep, requires, if it is to be effective, more accurate and timely information and manpower than is currently available or can reasonably be expected to be obtained.

The alternative that will be compatible with both needs and available means seems to be withholding. In withholding, at least part of the tax is collected at the source, thereby reducing the number of taxpayers with whom collectors must deal directly. The mechanisms of withholding should be extended to as many sources of income as possible.

Points in the channels in which money flows, where money could be easily funnelled into the treasury coffers, should be sought and later used. Tax can be withheld, for example, from payments of interest and dividends and from contracts the government signs with private contractors for the supply of goods or services.

The rule "be modest and aim low" is helpful here. The main constraint on the introduction of withholding to new areas of economic activity is complexity. A method such as Pay As You Earn (PAYE), which aims at collecting the exact amount of tax liability for each period of withholding, requires complicated calculations as well as detailed and quite often sophisticated recordkeeping. In poor countries as the complexity of the requirements goes up, the number of business establishments capable of complying with them goes down sharply. The desire to attain a high level of precision and perfection, valuable as it may be, is quite likely to overwhelm the ability to implement.

Though fixed percentage withholding taps only a portion of the tax liability, it has the advantage of greater coverage and simplicity in application. Coverage is important not only from the point of view of the amount of intake, but also from the longer range goal of enhancing voluntary compliance. Once a person is brought into the tax net, the opportunity for making him pay what he ought to is opened up even though at present he would be paying a fraction of his true tax liability. Simplicity is important because neither the revenue officials nor the private businessman have the necessary skills and the means required to work successfully with a complicated method.

No method will work effectively for too long unless there is an improvement in enforcement. When enforcement is lax or altogether nonexistent, every method of audit or collection is liable to deteriorate quickly. The trickiest problem of the taxing process is the vicious cycle of enforcement. There is so little enforcement because there is so much evasion. There is so much evasion because the other instruments of the taxing process are not strong enough and they cannot be sufficiently strengthened so that they will have an impact on evasion without strengthening enforcement. It is not possible to start reform with enforcement, as desperately as it is needed, because it comes at the end of a chain process and is dependent on the successful completion of preceding functions.

The world is full of good (or if you wish bad) intentions that are voiced but rarely carried out. Threatening the public with tough enforcement is not going to achieve anything, only real action might do the job — induce people to start complying voluntarily — and there is no need to announce it until after it has been carried out, whereupon it will announce itself.

The decision to tighten up enforcement is partly a political one; it concerns values — should everyone pay his due share — in addition to means. As things stand now, it is difficult to say with confidence whether the reason for the politicians' reluctance to support enforcement is a result of their lack of trust in the ability of their bureaucrats to overcome the enormous constraints standing in their way or whether they simply prefer a system with lax enforcement. Such a system would enable them to say one thing and do another; they could say to the national audience: "We are for a progressive system of taxation, where everyone pays proportionately to his income and wealth, where the rich pick up a greater portion of the tab for running the government than the poor," pacifying the business concerns and the moneyed elites immediately afterwards by saying that there will be plenty of slack at the level of implementation for them to escape from the tax collectors.

In practice there is a little of each of these considerations in the politicians' decisions. It is not all technical problems. I am not prepared to admit that it is all opportunistic, corrupt politics either. There is definitely no reason to believe that all or even most governments, with their different structures, personalities and heritages, are equally corrupt. Therefore, it can be expected that greater political support will be forthcoming if the politicians could be convinced that the administrative difficulties are being gradually overcome. Once there is evidence that the administration is capable of implementing the law, it would be easier to get the courts to cooperate in handing out penalties that would deter potential evaders, or to convince budgeters to allocate more and better resources to enforcement activities.

A collection and audit program that would drastically reduce the lists of delinquents and would meaningfully increase the tax intake (through tougher audits and prompter collection) is likely to start the revenue department on the right way towards gaining the political support necessary for setting in motion a system based on voluntary compliance.

The worst thing that happens to the taxing process is that it is not taken seriously either by those responsible for enforcing it, or by those who have to comply with it. When officials lose belief in their ability to stand behind what the regulations require them to say, taxpayers learn that announced intentions and even overt threats have little if anything to do with action actually taken, that deadlines need not be observed, that seemingly automatic penalties can, and are, being waived, and that contrary to official statements criminal offenses do not necessarily lead to the courtroom and eventually to the jail house. Once this happens, even what limited amount of compliance that exists will be quickly eroded.

Asking for a lot and later doing far less is a dangerous strategy especially when the effectiveness of the means of implementation is so heavily dependent on their image among the organization's clients as it is in the taxing process. The desirable situation is one in which the taxpayer believes that the revenue official can do more, perhaps much more, than he is prepared to say. That can be obtained only by lowering demands to meet existing capabilities so that rules could be implemented as well as enacted.

Notes

1. Roscoe C. Martin, "Technical Assistance: The Problem of Implementation," *Public Administration Review* 12, 4 (1952): 260.
2. Martin Landau, "On the Self-Correcting Organization," *Public Administration Review* 33 (1973): 533-47.
3. The most comprehensive description is by Edward W. Weidner, *Technical Assistance in Public Administration Overseas: The Case for Development Administration* (Chicago: Public Administration Service, 1964).
4. See Albert O. Hirschman, *A Bias for Hope* (New Haven: Yale University Press, 1971), pp. 255-56.
5. Garth N. Jones, "Failure of Technical Assistance in Public Administration Abroad," *Journal of Comparative Administration* 2, 1 (1970): 29.
6. Albert O. Hirschman, *Development Projects Observed* (Washington, D.C.: Brookings Institution, 1967). See also the notion of "Possibilism" in his introduction to *A Bias for Hope*, pp. 26-37.
7. Hirschman, *Development Projects Observed*, p. 29.
8. See Milton J. Esman, *Administration and Development in Malaysia* (Ithaca: Cornell University Press, 1972), Chapter 9.
9. Martin Landau, "Linkage Coding and Intermediacy: A Strategy for Institution Building," *Journal of Comparative Administration* 2, 4 (1971): 413.
10. Yehezkel Dror invented this term. See his influential study *Public Policy Making Reexamined* (San Francisco: Chandler, 1968) and "Policy Analy-

sis: A Theoretic Framework and Some Basic Concepts," (Santa Monica, California: The Rand Corporation, 1969).

11. Richard M. Bird, *Taxation and Development: Lessons from Colombian Experience* (Cambridge: Harvard University Press, 1970), p. 201.
12. Gordon C. Hill, "Implementing Reform in Tax Administration," mimeographed (Presentation before the Fourth Annual Conference of the Caribbean Organization of Tax Administrators, August 1976).
13. For an insight into the analysis of the advantages and disadvantages of large and small development projects, see Caiden and Wildavsky, *Planning and Budgeting in Poor Countries* (New York: John Wiley, 1974), pp. 308-09.
14. One of the best studies in this field is Stanley S. Surrey's "Tax Administration in Underdeveloped Countries," *University of Miami Law Review XII* (1958).
15. Hill.
16. How this works in the U.S.A. is well described by Pendeton E. Herring in "Internal Revenue and the Taxpayer," in *Public Administration and the Public Interest* (New York: McGraw-Hill, 1936).
17. Harold C. Wilkenfeld, *Taxes and People in Israel* (Cambridge: Harvard University Press, 1973), p. 144.
18. Ibid., pp. 148-49.
19. On the use of presumptive methods in Latin American countries see Sommerfeld, *Tax Reform and the Alliance for Progress* (Austin: University of Texas Press, 1966), pp. 156-57.

Appendix

Questionnaire

1. What is the function of this office?
2. Can you tell me a little bit about the way your agency is organized? Is there a chart of your organization? May I see it?
3. I am interested in the day by day operation of your office; would you describe it to me? Is there anything else I should know?
4. Would you describe your job to me? What do you do in your work? How do you do it? Is there anything else?
5. What are the principal constraints limiting the effectiveness of your work? What else?
6. What, in your opinion, are the principal constraints preventing the increase of the revenue? What else?
7. What do you do when you encounter these constraints? What else?
8. Why do you employ these methods? Are you satisfied with the results? Why not?
9. What other methods could, in your opinion, be used? What else? Have they ever been tried? How successful were they? Why did they fail? Why haven't they been tried? Were you satisfied with the results? If not, why not?
10. Which of your taxes poses the most difficult problems in implementation? What are the problems that you have? What is the source of these problems? What else? What do you do when these problems are encountered? What else? Do you think that more could, or should, be done? What would you recommend? Why do you think it would help? Why isn't this done? Are there any other reasons for not doing it?
11. Is there any particular group of taxpayers that is especially hard to deal with? What are the problems? What else? How do you approach these difficulties? How do you solve them? Why do you prefer this approach and this solution? Do you think there is a better way? Has it been tried? Why not?
12. I am interested in how you deal with the small businessman, the farmer and the urban self-employed. How do you reach these taxpayers? What other ways do you have? Do you think that this is effective? Are you satisfied with the results?
13. How do you explain the high level of tax evasion in your country?

Why is it that so many people do not pay anything at all and others only a fraction of what they really ought to? What other reasons are there? In your opinion, would harsher penalties induce more people to comply voluntarily? If not, could you explain why. What measures would you recommend for increasing voluntary compliance?

Questions for Auditors-Assessors

1. Do you have a taxpayer roll? What information does it contain? How is it updated? What sources of data are used to update it? Do you feel that it is sufficiently accurate and comprehensive? Why is it not comprehensive? What is being done (if anything) to expand it?
2. Do you actually rely on the roll in your work? If not, why not? What other sources of information do you use? What else? Why these? In your opinion, are there other sources of information that could be used, but are not? Why aren't these used?
3. How do you select returns for audit? What criteria do you use? Why these? How do you know that these are good criteria?
4. Is there an annual audit plan? Do you set goals that you will later try to reach in the course of your work? How is the plan prepared and the goals determined? How do you know what would be reasonable? What sources of information do you use to determine that? What are the procedures you follow when you make your decision?
5. Is the plan followed in practice? Are the departures from it reasonable? Why not? What is being done about the uncompleted portions of the plan? What else?
6. What do you do with the returns selected for audit when they reach your office? Would you describe the process and procedures to me?
7. When you start examining a return what is the first thing you do? Why that? How is it going to help you? What, precisely, are you aiming at? What are you trying to achieve?
8. How do you know that the information on the return and accompanying documents is correct? How do you know that the return contains all the relevant information? What other methods do you have for finding that out? Are you satisfied with the results they allow you to reach? Why not?
9. Suppose the taxpayer has no books or reliable records, what then? What other methods do you use in this case? Which ones do you prefer? Which ones are used more often than others? Can you explain these preferences to me?

10. Are there officials assigned specifically for auditing businesses and taxpayers who do not keep proper records? Is there someone who specializes in this type of audit? Could you suggest names of officials with whom I could discuss these issues?
11. Are you expected to complete an audit within a certain time limit? Do you feel that the time constraints are reasonable, too much or just about right? If the time is too short, what is being gained and at what cost? What else? Do you think you should have more time? Why? Why is the time constraint kept so tight?
12. What shortcuts do you have to carry out the job when the time available is so short? What else?
13. Do you have field audits where the auditor interviews the taxpayer and surveys his business? How do you determine which cases will be field audited?
14. Could you describe the field audit procedures? What does the auditor do, step by step? Will he write a report about his findings? To whom will it be submitted? How will it be used?
15. What do you do when you suspect that the information the taxpayer furnished is not accurate? What else? What, precisely, would these methods help you achieve?
16. If there are absolutely no reliable accounts available and you must make a decision, what do you do? If you are forced to guess, would you go high or low? Why? Are you instructed, or just expected (encouraged) to follow one way rather than the other? Why is that alternative preferable? What would you do if it were left entirely to your discretion?
17. I am interested in learning how you audit-assess the small businessman, the traders and the self-employed? Could you describe the procedures you follow, the typical problems that are encountered and the methods used to overcome them?
18. Are you trying to reach an agreement with the taxpayer before the audit is made official? Why? Are you expected (encouraged) to do so? What procedures do you use to reach an agreement? Where do you draw the line behind which you will not retreat to obtain a compromise? What else? Why these?
19. What happens when you fail to reach an agreement? What are the procedures that are followed in this case? Is the taxpayer entitled to defer payment until the case is officially resolved? How long does it take to settle the average contested case? Why does it take so long? Do you think that there are ways for reaching quicker and simpler solutions? Why aren't they followed?

Questions for Collectors

1. Are you supplied periodically with information on taxpayers who do not pay on time? How frequently do you get this information? How long does it take from the time a deadline has elapsed until the moment you receive the data? Is this, from your point of view as a collector, reasonable or too long? What kinds of problems in collection are encountered as a result of this timing? What else?
2. Is the information with which you are furnished reliable? Do you plan and carry out your collection programs on the basis of this information solely? Why not? If the information is not reliable what do you do? What other sources do you have?
3. Can you describe the procedure for collecting a delinquent account?
4. Can you describe the problems you most frequently encounter when applying these procedures. What else? How do you overcome them? What other methods do you use? Do you feel that you have sufficient authority-power to effectively deal with these problems? Why are you not using all the powers that you have? What other reasons do you have? If you need more power why can't you get it?
5. Do you make field collections from delinquent taxpayers? Could you describe the procedure to me? What methods are the most effective in making the taxpayer pay? What else? If field collections are not normally made, why not? What other reasons are there? What else?
6. Do you have routine follow-up procedures on action that you take against delinquent taxpayers? Could you describe it to me? Does experience indicate that this suffices to ensure the implementation of your decisions? What additional methods are needed? Why are they not being used? If there are no follow-up procedures, why are they lacking?
7. Suppose you encounter a taxpayer who refuses to pay, what steps are you authorized to take and what do you normally do? What else? Are these methods sufficiently effective? Why not? What, in your opinion, should be done in these cases? Why is it not done?
8. What do you do when the taxpayer agrees to pay but offers a smaller amount than he owes? What do the official procedures prescribe for such a case? What do you actually do? Why do you prefer these methods?
9. If you reach a compromise on a part-payment agreement, what does it depend on? How do you determine the size of the installments? What else? Does your experience show that a part-payment agreement is an effective method for dealing with delin-

quent taxpayers? Why not? What method would you use if it were left up to you?

10. Are the penalties for late payment/late filing automatically imposed? Why not? What other reasons are there? What do you have to do to add the penalties to the tax bill? When are the penalties waived? Who has the authority to waive them? Do you feel that it is justified to waive penalties? Why not?
11. Does your experience indicate that the penalties are adequate? Do they actually deter? Why aren't they harsher?
12. Could you describe the procedures you follow to discover taxpayers who have never filed a return? How are these procedures initiated? Is the search a routine one? Why not? Are you satisfied with your accomplishments in this area? Do you think that more ought to be done to bring people into the tax net? What, specifically, would you recommend? Why is this not done?
13. In your opinion, why is it that so many people become delinquent in their payments? What else?

Questions for Policy-Makers

1. I have noticed that there is more emphasis and attention given to audit than to collection and enforcement. Could you explain to me why this is so? What other reasons are there?
2. Many theorists think that strict enforcement and harsh penalties for evaders are the key to voluntary compliance. What does your own personal experience indicate? What else? What, in your opinion, should be done to improve voluntary compliance? What else? What would be feasible in the conditions of the situation in which you operate? What else? Have these ideas been tried? (Why not?) With what success?
3. When the minister of finance demands that more money be raised from existing taxes, what do you do? Do you have a routinized procedure for dealing with such a situation? (Why not?) What other procedures are there? Why do you use these procedures, have others been tried? What were they? Why have you stopped using them?
4. Do you think that decentralization will help in making better decisions by making it easier to obtain useful information? (If not, why not?) In what other ways might it help? What kinds of problems does it raise? What else? What can be done about them?
5. How do you ensure uniformity in enforcement when the organization is decentralized? What other methods do you employ? Are you satisfied with the results? Why not? What should be done to improve the situation? Why isn't this done?

6. Do you think that you ought to have annual plans for audit, collection, enforcement? Why are such plans necessary? How are the plans made? Could you describe the process to me? What are your sources of information? How do you know whether they are reliable? How do you set your goals? How do you know that a certain target would be too easy or impossible to achieve?
7. Are plans usually carried out? Are you satisfied with the results? Why not? What else?
8. People in your organization repeatedly complain that salaries are low, that they are, in fact, too low to hire and retain competent staff. Do you agree? If the personnel problem is so acute why aren't the salaries raised? Have you tried to increase salaries to the level where it would become possible for you to compete successfully with private firms? What strategies did you use? What were the results? Were you satisfied? Why not? What prevented you from achieving more than you did?
9. Could you describe to me the major attempts to introduce administrative reforms? Who normally initiates reforms? Why him (them)? I have noticed that it takes an extremely long time to implement a reform. Why is that? What kinds of difficulties do you usually run up against? What else? How do you cope with them?
10. You have recently introduced a major reform in filing and audit procedures. Are you satisfied with the results? Why not? What else? What do you think went wrong? What should have, but hasn't been done? Why? What course of action would you have taken if it were completely up to you? Why hasn't this course of action been followed?
11. Some people say that things are now substantially better than they were before the reform was introduced. Do you agree? Why not? What else? What hasn't changed?
12. Are you under pressure from outside to introduce reforms and strengthen your ability to implement? Does the fact that such pressures exist help in obtaining the resources needed to carry out the reform?
13. Line officers repeatedly stress that it would be easier for them to implement policies if they were more simple, if, for example, there were fewer rates, fewer exemptions and exceptions to the rule. If you agree, why are your policies complicated? What prevents you from simplifying them? What else?
14. Despite the obvious cost involved, whenever politicians are in need of more revenues they look first at increasing tax rates or levying altogether new taxes; getting more out of existing taxes by tightening up the administration is a measure rarely counted on. Could you try and explain this paradox to me?

Index